GCSE
Food Preparation & Nutrition

Struggling with sauces? Confused between calcium and carbs?
Fear not, with this brilliant CGP book you'll be able to serve up a top grade!

It's packed with easy-to-follow study notes and realistic exam-style
questions for every topic to check it's all been digested correctly.

With well-seasoned sections of advice for the assessments, a practice paper and
step-by-step answers at the back, it might just be the best thing since sliced bread...

Complete
Revision & Practice
Everything you need to pass the exams!

Contents

Contents

Published by CGP

Editors:
Liam Dyer, Rob Harrison, Simon Little, Sean Walsh.

Contributors:
Anne Hilton, Angela Nugent, Lesley Woods.

With thanks to Ana Pungartnik for the copyright research.

Photo on p 4 Science Photo Library and p 33 Mark Sykes/Science Photo Library

Photo on p 2 KMI Images / Alamy Stock Photo, p 34 Food and Drink Photos / Alamy Stock Photo,
p 35 funkyfood London - Paul Williams / Alamy Stock Photo, p 41 Dale O'Dell / Alamy Stock Photo,
p 42 Westend61 GmbH / Alamy Stock Photo.

Definition of food security on page 88: © FAO 2006 Food Security Page 1.
Available: http://www.fao.org/forestry/13128-0e6f36f27e0091055bec28ebe830f46b3.pdf [14/12/2016]

ISBN: 978 1 78294 655 7

Printed by Elanders Ltd, Newcastle upon Tyne.
Clipart from Corel®

Proteins

Proteins, fats and carbohydrates are macronutrients. 'Macro' means large, and funnily enough our bodies need these macronutrients in large amounts. First up we have proteins — don't say we never treat you...

Protein is Needed for Growth, Repair and Maintenance

1) We get protein from a wide range of foods, including: meat, fish, dairy products, nuts, seeds and beans.
2) Our bodies need proteins for a variety of reasons:

- Growth — e.g. from childhood to adulthood, and for the growth of nails, hair and muscle mass.
- Repair — e.g. repairing our muscles, tissues and organs after illness or injury.
- Maintenance — e.g. to make enzymes for digestion and antibodies to stop us getting ill.

3) Proteins are made up of amino acids — these can be thought of as the building blocks of the body.
4) Our bodies can make some amino acids (these are called non-essential amino acids). There are 11 non-essential amino acids, including: alanine, asparagine, aspartic acid and glutamic acid.
5) We have to eat the amino acids that our bodies can't make (these are called essential amino acids). There are 9 essential amino acids: histidine, isoleucine, leucine, lysine, methionine, phenylalanine, threonine, tryptophan and valine.

Proteins Have Different Biological Values

- High biological value (HBV) proteins contain all of the essential amino acids we need.
- They're mainly found in animal sources — e.g. meat, fish, poultry, eggs, cheese and milk.
- Soya beans and quinoa are plant-based HBV protein foods (see next page).

- Low biological value (LBV) proteins are missing one or more of the essential amino acids we need.
- They're only found in plant sources — e.g. peas, lentils, nuts, seeds and most beans, and in smaller amounts in vegetables like spinach and broccoli.

Protein Complementation Combines LBV Protein Foods

1) If we don't get enough HBV protein, we have to combine different LBV proteins to get all the essential amino acids in our diet — this is called protein complementation.
2) For example, hummus and pitta are LBV protein foods (they're missing some essential amino acids), but when we combine the two, the meal as a whole provides all the essential amino acids we need.
3) If you're eating a balanced diet, you probably combine proteins without realising it — e.g. a vegetable lasagne with six different veggies in the recipe is good protein complementation.

Different People Need Different Amounts of Protein

1) Dietary reference values are estimates of the amount of nutrients people should have in their diet.
2) An average male should consume 55 g and an average female should consume 45 g of protein each day.
3) In reality, the amount of protein different people need varies:

- Growing children need a greater amount of protein relative to their size and body mass.
- Physically active people need more protein for muscle growth and repair.
- Pregnant women need about 6 g more protein than normal to help the baby grow. During breastfeeding, women require even more.

Proteins

I won't pretend this stuff is particularly exciting, but <u>proteins</u> are <u>very important</u> to our <u>health</u>.

Too Much or Too Little Protein Causes Problems

An <u>excess</u> (too much) or <u>deficiency</u> (too little) of protein in the diet can have <u>serious consequences</u>:

Excess

- The <u>liver</u> and the <u>kidneys</u> help <u>process proteins</u>. Too much protein in the diet puts a lot of <u>pressure</u> and <u>strain</u> on these organs, which can be dangerous.

Deficiency

- Without protein, <u>growth</u> is <u>slowed down</u>, especially in children who are still growing.
- Because <u>hair</u>, <u>skin</u> and <u>nails</u> don't grow as fast, they can get into a <u>poor condition</u>.
- The <u>immune system</u> can't work properly without protein — this means <u>wounds don't heal</u> as <u>quickly</u> and people have a higher risk of catching <u>infections</u>.
- People struggle to <u>digest</u> food <u>properly</u>, which means some <u>nutrients</u> aren't taken in by the body.
- Protein deficiency can also lead to <u>oedema</u> — a <u>build up of fluid</u> in the body that causes <u>swelling</u> (often around the feet).
- In <u>severe cases</u>, a disease called <u>kwashiorkor</u> can develop. A symptom of the disease is oedema around the stomach, which is why some severely malnourished children have <u>swollen abdomens</u>.

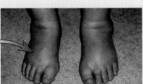

There are Now Loads of Alternative Proteins

1) <u>Vegetarians</u> don't eat meat, so they need to get their protein from elsewhere.
2) <u>Beans</u>, <u>lentils</u> and <u>nuts</u> are all good sources of protein, as are <u>eggs</u>. There are also <u>alternative proteins</u>:

Soya
- Soya beans are one of the few plant-based <u>HBV protein</u> sources.
- They can be eaten <u>whole</u> (but must be cooked to remove toxicity) in <u>salads</u>, used to make <u>soya milk</u> and processed to make other protein alternatives like <u>tofu</u> and <u>TVP</u>...

Mycoprotein
- Traditionally made from a <u>mushroom-like fungus</u> and <u>egg white</u> (although there are now vegan alternatives that use potato starch instead).
- It's often used where you'd normally use chicken, and is available as <u>chunks</u> (e.g. for stir-fries), <u>mince</u> (e.g. for chilli con carne) or <u>fillets</u> (e.g. to serve in sauces).

TVP
- TVP (Textured Vegetable Protein) is also made from <u>soya beans</u> — specifically <u>soya flour</u> (made by grinding soya beans).
- The soya flour is used to make a <u>dough</u> which when baked has a <u>meat-like texture</u> and can be made into <u>sausages</u>, <u>burgers</u> and <u>ready meals</u>.

Tofu
- Tofu is made by <u>curdling soya milk</u>.
- It can have different textures depending on how much water it contains: it can be <u>soft</u> (for use in desserts and dips), <u>firm</u> (for use in stir-fries) and <u>extra firm</u> (this is sometimes called <u>dry tofu</u> because it has the least amount of water).

3) Alternative proteins usually <u>don't taste of much</u> on their own. Luckily, they're great at <u>absorbing</u> the <u>flavours</u> of the foods they're cooked in, e.g. <u>sauces</u> and <u>marinades</u>. There's also a massive range of <u>pre-prepared</u> flavoured alternatives, e.g. <u>bacon-style slices</u>, <u>meat-free chicken fillets</u>, etc.

Proteins are needed for <u>repair</u>, growth and <u>maintenance</u>...

Use a mnemonic like '<u>R</u>eally good <u>m</u>acronutrient' (RGM) to help you remember these functions.

Fats

While it's easy to assume fats are really unhealthy, they're actually an essential part of our daily diet.

Fats Provide Energy, Nutrients and Insulation

Our bodies need fats and oils (sometimes referred to as lipids) for a variety of reasons:

- They provide a concentrated source of energy (twice as much energy per gram as proteins and carbs).
- They are a source of fat-soluble vitamins A, D, E and K (p.10) and help the body absorb these vitamins.
- They're a source of essential fatty acids (omega-3 and omega-6 fatty acids — see next page).
- Fat forms an insulating layer under our skin which helps to keep us warm.
- These layers of fat also protect our bones and organs (e.g. our heart and kidneys).
- Our bodies use fat to make cholesterol, a fatty substance that is an essential part of all cell membranes. However, too much cholesterol can be bad for us (see next page).

Fats Contain Saturated and Unsaturated Fatty Acids

1) Fats are made up of fatty acids and glycerol in the form of triglycerides.
2) Fatty acid chains are made of carbon and hydrogen. They can be saturated or unsaturated — the difference is in how carbon atoms bond with hydrogen atoms:

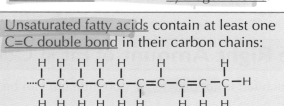

A triglyceride

Glycerol	Fatty Acid
	Fatty Acid
	Fatty Acid

Saturated fatty acids only have single C-C bonds:

Unsaturated fatty acids contain at least one C=C double bond in their carbon chains:

3) Our body breaks fat down into fatty acids during digestion — the ratio of saturated to unsaturated fatty acids decides whether it's a saturated or unsaturated fat.

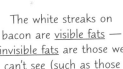

The white streaks on bacon are visible fats — invisible fats are those we can't see (such as those in cakes or biscuits).

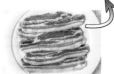

Saturated Fats are Bad for Your Health...

1) Saturated fats are classed as unhealthy fats, especially if eaten in large amounts.
2) They're generally solid at room temperature and tend to come from animal sources such as meats (including processed meats like sausages and burgers), butter, lard, suet and cheese, but they can also come from plant sources like coconut butter.
3) Too much saturated fat in the diet can increase cholesterol levels in the blood, which can increase the risk of cardiovascular disease (see next page).

... Unsaturated Fats are Generally Healthier

1) Unsaturated fats are usually healthier than saturated fats.
2) They're generally soft or liquid at room temperature and come from vegetable sources that are high in fat (e.g. flax seeds and peanuts) and vegetable oils (e.g. sunflower, rapeseed and olive oils).
3) Unsaturated fats can be monounsaturated and polyunsaturated:

- Monounsaturated fats contain one C=C double bond in their carbon chains.
- They are found in foods such as olive oil, almonds, peanut butter and avocados.

- Polyunsaturated fats contain more than one C=C double bond.
- They are found in foods such as sesame oil, soybean oil, seeds and oily fish.

4) Replacing the saturated fats in your diet with unsaturated fats has been shown to lower blood cholesterol — this is why unsaturated fats are often referred to as 'good' fats.

Section One — Food, Nutrition and Health

Fats

If we <u>didn't get enough fat</u> in our diet, our bodies <u>wouldn't</u> be able to <u>function properly</u>.
However, if we get <u>too much</u> fat in our diet, it can lead to some very serious <u>health problems</u>.

Omega-3 and Omega-6 Fatty Acids are Essential Fatty Acids

Our body can't produce omega-3 and omega-6 <u>essential fatty acids</u>,
so we have to consume them as part of our diet.

- <u>Omega-3</u> fatty acids are found in foods such as <u>oily fish</u> and <u>seeds</u>
  — they help our <u>brain function</u> and may <u>reduce</u> the <u>risk</u> of <u>heart disease</u>.
- <u>Omega-6</u> fatty acids are found in foods such as <u>chicken</u>, <u>nuts</u> and <u>vegetable oils</u>
  — they help to <u>lower blood cholesterol</u> and <u>reduce inflammation</u>.

Some people take fish-oil capsules to get their dose of omega-3 fatty acids.

Fats Should Make Up Less Than 35% of Our Daily Food Energy

- According to government guidelines, <u>fat</u> should make up <u>no more than 35%</u> of our food energy per day (see p.23), with <u>no more than 11%</u> coming from <u>saturated fat</u>.
- It's recommended that an average adult consume <u>70 g</u> of fat every day, with a <u>maximum of 20 g</u> of this being <u>saturated fat</u>.

As with protein, the amount of fat a person needs may change depending on <u>age</u> and <u>physical activity</u>.

We Need the Right Amount of Fat in Our Diet

A <u>fat excess</u> (too much fat) or <u>fat deficiency</u> (too little fat) can be <u>unhealthy</u> and <u>dangerous</u>:

Excess

- Too much fat can lead to <u>weight gain</u>, where excess fat is stored under the skin (and around organs in some cases).
- Excessive levels of fat in the body can lead to <u>obesity</u> (see p.19). Obesity can lead to diet-related health issues like <u>type-2 diabetes</u> (see p.20), where the body struggles to control blood sugar levels.
- Too much <u>saturated fat</u> in the diet can <u>increase blood cholesterol</u> levels, restricting blood flow and increasing the risk of <u>high blood pressure</u> and <u>cardiovascular disease</u>, e.g. <u>CHD</u>, a <u>stroke</u> or <u>heart attack</u> (see p.19).

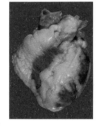

Excess fat in the diet can lead to the build-up of fat around vital organs like the heart (yellow fat can be seen around the red heart muscle).

Deficiency

- A lack of fat in the diet means that less <u>fat-soluble vitamins</u> A, D, E and K are absorbed by the body. This causes <u>vitamin deficiency</u>, which leads to various health issues (see p.10).
- If there's also a lack of carbohydrate in the diet, the body will start to use its <u>fat store</u> for <u>energy</u>. Therefore, not eating enough fat can lead to <u>weight loss</u> if there's also a lack of carbohydrate in the diet.
- Less body fat means there's <u>less insulation</u> to keep the body warm, and so a person with a fat deficiency may become <u>colder</u> faster.
- It also means there will be a <u>thinner layer</u> of fat under the skin to protect the body from knocks.

REVISION TASK

Fat is essential, but make sure you don't have too much...

It's really important that you know the differences between saturated and unsaturated fats.
Draw out a table of all the differences between them to make sure it sticks in your head.

Carbohydrates

Carbohydrates are the final macronutrient we have to look at. Time to get your teeth into this stuff...

Carbohydrates are Needed for **Energy**

Carbohydrates can be split into two main types, sugar and starch:

- Sugar, e.g. glucose and fructose, can be found in food naturally (e.g. sugars in fruits and vegetables), or can be added to food during the manufacturing process (e.g. sugars in cakes, sweets and fizzy pop).
- Added sugars are often referred to as 'empty calories' because they have no nutritional benefit other than energy.

- Starch can be found in foods such as potatoes, bread, pasta, rice and cereals, as well as vegetables and fruit (in smaller amounts).
- Starchy foods contain lots of nutrients including B vitamins, iron and calcium.
- Wholegrain starch foods also have really high fibre content (see p.13).

When we eat carbohydrate-based foods, our body breaks down the sugar and starch into glucose, which is absorbed into our blood and used by our body for energy.

Simple Carbohydrates are Digested Quickly...

Simple carbohydrates such as sugar can be divided into monosaccharides and disaccharides:

Monosaccharides are the most basic sugar molecules, e.g. glucose and fructose.

Disaccharides are made up of two monosaccharides, e.g. sucrose is made up of glucose and fructose.

The body rapidly digests simple carbohydrates, making blood sugar levels rise quickly and providing a short burst of energy.

'Sugary' foods like cakes, jams and sweets are mainly made up of simple carbohydrates.

...While Complex Ones Take Longer to Digest

Complex carbohydrates such as starch are polysaccharides:

Polysaccharides are made up of lots of monosaccharides joined together, e.g. starches are made up of lots of glucose molecules.

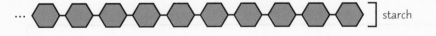

Complex carbohydrates take a lot longer to digest than simple ones, so they gradually increase blood sugar levels and provide a slow, steady release of energy.

Complex carbohydrates include 'starchy' foods like wholewheat bread and potatoes.

The **Glycaemic Index** Shows How Carbs Affect **Blood Sugar Levels**

The glycaemic index (GI) rates carbohydrates on how quickly they affect blood sugar levels:

- High GI foods are digested quickly and cause a rapid rise in blood sugar levels — high GI foods include white bread/pasta/rice, cornflakes and watermelon.
- Low GI foods are digested slowly and cause a gradual rise in blood sugar levels — low GI foods include wholewheat bread/pasta, brown rice, peaches and porridge.

The glycaemic index is especially helpful to people with diabetes because it allows them to choose low GI carbohydrates so they can avoid surges in blood sugar levels.

Carbohydrates

I don't know about you, but I'm in the mood for another page all about <u>carbohydrates</u> — no, just me?...

50% of Our Energy Should Come from Carbs

According to government guidelines, <u>carbohydrates</u> should make up approximately <u>half</u> of our <u>food energy</u> per day (see p.23).

- Ideally, <u>most of this energy</u> should come from <u>starchy foods</u> and <u>natural sugars</u> such as those found in bread, pasta, fruit and veg.
- <u>Free sugars</u>, such as those added to food and drinks during manufacturing and those found in sweet foods like syrups and fruit juice, should take up <u>no more than 5%</u>.

On average, people in the UK consume <u>too much sugar</u>. To help with this, food labelling not only has a section for <u>total carbohydrates</u>, but it also has an extra section called <u>'of which sugars'</u> — this helps people separate their sugar intake from their total carb intake (see p.70).

Eating Too Many or Too Few Carbohydrates Is Unhealthy

Like with fat and protein, <u>too much</u> (excess) or <u>too little</u> (deficiency) carbohydrate in our diet is <u>unhealthy</u> and can have <u>serious effects</u> on how our body functions:

Excess

- If we take in more energy from carbohydrates than our body uses, the extra <u>carbohydrate</u> is <u>converted</u> into <u>fat</u>. Too much fat causes <u>obesity</u> and other diet-related health issues (see p.19-20).
- <u>Sugars</u> are the worst for this because they're digested quickly, meaning the <u>energy</u> they provide is ready to use <u>almost immediately</u> — if it's not used quickly, we store it as <u>fat</u>.
- Eating <u>too many sugary foods</u> can lead to <u>tooth decay</u>, sometimes called <u>dental caries</u> (see p.20). <u>Free sugars</u> are the worst type of sugar for tooth decay — e.g. mango juice is more likely to cause tooth decay than if you ate chunks of mango because the sugars are already released and ready to attack your teeth.
- Because <u>simple carbohydrates</u> (e.g. sugar) are <u>quickly digested</u>, they cause <u>rapid surges in blood sugar levels</u> (see previous page). If our blood sugar levels <u>fluctuate</u> (move up and down) too <u>wildly</u> it can lead to the development of <u>type 2 diabetes</u> (see p.20).

The <u>natural sugars</u> in whole fruits are much better for our teeth than the <u>free sugars</u> found in fruit juices.

Deficiency

- A lack of carbohydrate in our diet causes our <u>blood sugar level</u> to <u>drop</u>. This drop can cause <u>hunger</u>, <u>dizziness</u> and <u>tiredness</u> because our body has <u>less energy</u> than it needs.
- If our bodies don't have enough carbohydrate for energy, they need to find another source of energy and will start to use up <u>fat</u> in the diet or body.
- If we also have a fat deficiency then our bodies start to use up <u>protein</u> — this causes us to <u>lose muscle</u>, which makes us <u>weaker</u>.

Make sure you know the differences between sugar and starch...

That's it for macronutrients. As the name suggests, they're a large part of our nutrition and you need to know the role each of them plays in our diet. They'll show up again later, so it's best to learn them now.

Warm-Up and Worked Exam Questions

Your body needs macronutrients in large amounts, and hopefully your mind will have absorbed a large amount of information about them too. Check you've taken everything in by having a go at these questions.

Warm-Up Questions

1) Give two groups of people that may need more protein in their diet.
2) Name two alternative proteins that are suitable for vegetarians.
3) Name two foods that are high in saturated fat and two foods that are high in unsaturated fat.
4) Describe three problems that are associated with a fat deficiency in the diet.
5) Why do we need starchy foods in our diet?
6) How can GI ratings help a person with diabetes to make dietary choices?

Worked Exam Questions

1 Although fats are often seen as unhealthy, they form an essential part of the diet.

Give **two** reasons why fats are important for a healthy, balanced diet.

1. <u>They're a source of fat-soluble vitamins.</u>

You could have given different answers here — flick back to p.3 for more functions of fat.

2. <u>They provide the body with a concentrated source of energy.</u>

[2 marks]

2 Meat and fish are both good sources of **protein**.

a) What is the best source of protein in the meal shown on the right?

<u>The egg</u>

[1 mark]

Baked beans and egg on wholemeal toast

b) Explain why protein is essential in a person's diet.

<u>Protein is essential for growth, repairing body cells and tissues, and also for maintenance, such as the production of enzymes and antibodies.</u>

[3 marks]

3 Hugo says that the pie chart below shows how our daily food energy should be divided up. Mathis disagrees, saying that the ratio in the pie chart is incorrect.

Who is correct, Hugo or Mathis? Explain your answer.

<u>Mathis is correct, as no more than 5% of our daily food energy should come from free sugars and the pie chart shows them as being 25%.</u>

[2 marks]

Key
A: Proteins
B: Fats
C: Starchy carbohydrates and natural sugars
D: Free and added sugars

Exam Questions

1 Protein molecules are made up of small 'building blocks' joined together.

   a) Give the name of these 'building blocks'.

   ....

   [1 mark]

   b) Give the name of the building blocks that can't be made by the body.

   ....

   [1 mark]

   c) An average adult should consume around 50 g of protein a day.
   Give one health risk that can be caused by excessive protein intake.

   ....

   ....

   [1 mark]

2 Most fish and chip shops use vegetable oils to fry chips, but some still use lard.
   Explain why chips cooked in lard would not be suitable for vegetarians.

   ....

   ....

   [2 marks]

3 Proteins can be either 'High Biological Value' or 'Low Biological Value'.

   a) What is meant by a 'Low Biological Value' protein?

   ....

   [1 mark]

   b) i) Other than soya products, how can a vegan ensure they get
         the equivalent of 'High Biological Value' protein in their diet?

   ....

   ....

   ....

   ....

   [3 marks]

      ii) Give **one** example meal to illustrate your answer to part i).

   ....

   [1 mark]

Exam Questions

4   Too much or too little sugar in the diet can have health implications.

   a)   Outline **one** health issue that can be caused by having too much sugar in the diet.

   ....

   ....

   [2 marks]

   b)   Outline **one** health issue that can be caused by having too little sugar in the diet.

   ....

   ....

   [2 marks]

5   Marathon runners might be advised to eat wholegrain pasta the night before their race.
   100 metre sprinters might be advised to take a glucose tablet 30 minutes before their race.

   Discuss the reasons behind these two different pieces of advice.

   ....

   ....

   ....

   ....

   ....

   ....

   ....

   [6 marks]

6   John's doctor has warned him that he has too much fat in his diet and
   he will need to make lifestyle changes in order to become healthier.

   Discuss the health risks of John's diet and the changes
   he could make to reduce the level of fat in his diet.

   [10 marks]

   *Answer these extended questions on a separate piece
   of paper so that you have all the room you need.*

Vitamins — Fat-Soluble

<u>Vitamins</u>, <u>minerals</u> and <u>trace elements</u> are all <u>micronutrients</u> — we need them in small amounts. Vitamins are <u>organic compounds</u> (they come from plants and animals) and are used in processes that keep us <u>alive</u> and <u>well</u>.

Vitamins A, D, E and K are Fat-Soluble

If you're doing the <u>Eduqas</u> course, you can skip the boxes on vitamins E and K below.

1) <u>Fat-soluble vitamins</u> are found in <u>fatty foods</u> (e.g. meat, fish, animal-based products and vegetable oils).

2) There are <u>four</u> fat-soluble vitamins you need to know about — meet vitamins <u>A</u>, <u>D</u>, <u>E</u> and <u>K</u>:

Vitamin A

- Vitamin A is needed for <u>good eyesight</u> (especially night vision), <u>growth</u>, a healthy <u>immune system</u> and <u>skin</u> — it's also an <u>antioxidant</u> (see next page).
- The main <u>source</u> is <u>retinol</u>, which is found in <u>liver</u>, <u>butter</u>, <u>oily fish</u> and <u>eggs</u>, but it can also be made from <u>carotene</u> (found in <u>margarine</u> and <u>orange or yellow fruit and veg</u>).
+ <u>Too much</u> over time can <u>weaken bones</u>, and foods containing very <u>high levels</u> (e.g. liver) should be avoided during pregnancy.
- <u>Too little</u> can lead to <u>night blindness</u>, a <u>weaker immune system</u> and <u>stunted growth</u>.
- The NHS recommends <u>0.7 mg</u> of vitamin A for <u>men</u> and <u>0.6 mg</u> for <u>women</u> each day.

Vitamin D

- Vitamin D helps the body absorb various <u>minerals</u>, including <u>calcium</u>, which is important for the development of healthy <u>bones</u> and <u>teeth</u>.
- It's found in <u>oily fish</u> and <u>egg yolks</u> and is also produced when <u>skin</u> is exposed to <u>sunlight</u>.
+ <u>Too much</u> vitamin D makes you <u>absorb too much calcium</u> — this can lead to <u>kidney damage</u>.
- <u>Too little</u> can lead to <u>bone diseases</u> like osteomalacia (where bones become soft), rickets and osteoporosis (where bones become brittle, see p.20).
- The NHS recommends <u>0.01 mg</u> of vitamin D a day, although in summer most of us should be able to get enough through <u>natural exposure</u> to the <u>sun</u>.

Vitamin E

- Vitamin E is important because it keeps <u>skin</u> and <u>eyes healthy</u> as well as improving our <u>immune system</u> — as an <u>antioxidant</u> it may protect us from <u>free radicals</u> (see next page).
- It's found in <u>leafy greens</u> (e.g. <u>spinach</u> and <u>kale</u>), <u>broccoli</u>, <u>nuts</u>, <u>vegetable oils</u> and <u>wheat germ</u>.
+ <u>Too much</u> can interfere with <u>blood clotting</u>, cause <u>nausea</u> and <u>blurred vision</u>.
- <u>Too little</u> is <u>rare</u> but leads to <u>weak muscles</u> and <u>problems with sight</u>.
- The NHS recommends <u>4 mg</u> of vitamin E for men and <u>3 mg</u> for women each day.

Vitamin K

- Vitamin K helps <u>clot blood</u>, <u>heal wounds</u> and maintain our <u>immune system</u> and <u>bones</u>.
- It's found in <u>leafy greens</u>, <u>cereals</u> and <u>vegetable oils</u>, plus some <u>meats</u> and <u>dairy foods</u>.
+ There is no 'excessive' level of vitamin K.
- Having too little is <u>extremely rare</u> in adults, but it can cause <u>uncontrolled bleeding</u> in newborns.
- The NHS recommends a daily intake of <u>0.001 mg</u> of vitamin K <u>for every kg of body weight</u>.

3) Any fat-soluble vitamins that aren't used up by the body are <u>stored</u> in <u>fat tissue</u> for future use. This means that we don't necessarily need to take in the same amount of each vitamin every day.

4) However, we need to be careful that we don't build up an <u>excess</u> of these vitamins. This is unlikely to occur through a balanced diet — the main risk comes through <u>multivitamin supplements</u> (see p.95).

I'm afraid this isn't a licence to eat cake every day...

Way before we knew about vitamins, the ancient Egyptians would use liver as a treatment for night blindness. These days we know why this remedy was so successful — because of the high level of fat-soluble vitamin A.

Vitamins — Water-Soluble

Water-soluble vitamins <u>aren't generally stored in the body</u> like fat-soluble ones, so we should take them in <u>daily</u>.

B Vitamins and Vitamin C are Water-Soluble

'<u>Water-soluble</u>' vitamins <u>dissolve in water</u> — there are lots of them, but you need to know these for the exam:

Vitamin	Function	Sources include	Problems caused by having too little
B1 Thiamin	Helps the <u>nervous system</u> and with <u>energy release</u> from foods.	Bread, pasta, rice, peas, eggs and liver.	<u>Tiredness</u>, <u>weak muscles</u> and <u>beriberi</u> (in severe cases) — a disease that affects the heart, blood vessels and nervous system.
B2 Riboflavin	Helps with <u>energy release</u> from foods and <u>repair of tissues</u>.	Milk, eggs, cheese, and leafy greens.	<u>Dry skin</u>, a <u>sore throat</u> and <u>sores</u> around the <u>mouth</u>.
B3 Niacin	Helps with <u>energy release</u> from foods and maintaining a healthy <u>nervous system</u> and <u>skin</u>.	Wheat, nuts, meat and fish.	<u>Pellagra</u> (a disease causing fatigue, depression and loss of memory).
B9 Folic Acid (or folate)	Crucial for <u>growth</u>, <u>healthy babies</u> and works with vitamin B12 to make <u>red blood cells</u>.	Liver, peas and leafy greens.	<u>Anaemia</u>, <u>tiredness</u>, <u>weak muscles</u> and <u>mouth sores</u>. Folic acid is especially important for women planning <u>pregnancy</u> as low levels at conception can cause <u>spina bifida</u> in babies (see p.18).
B12 Cobalamin	Helps the <u>nervous system</u> and works with vitamin B9 to make <u>red blood cells</u>.	Milk, eggs, meat and fish.	<u>Tiredness</u> and <u>nerve damage</u> in extreme cases. <u>Vegans</u> (who don't eat any animal produce) are <u>most likely</u> to have <u>too little</u>.
C Ascorbic acid	<u>Protects</u> the body from infection and allergies, keeps <u>blood vessels</u> healthy and <u>heals wounds</u>.	Citrus fruits, tomatoes, strawberries, green veg and potatoes.	<u>Anaemia</u> (see p.19) and <u>scurvy</u> (tiredness and bleeding gums). As vitamin C is an <u>antioxidant</u>, too little may increase the risk of <u>cancer</u> (see below).

<u>Water-soluble vitamins</u> are <u>lost in urine</u>, so in most cases it's unlikely they'll build up to levels where there are serious side effects. However, <u>excessive amounts</u> of <u>vitamin C</u> can cause <u>stomach pain</u> and <u>diarrhoea</u>.

Prepare Fruit and Veg Carefully to Keep Vitamins

1) Once exposed to air, fruits and veg start losing <u>vitamin C</u>, so prepare them <u>just before</u> you need them.
2) Don't leave your fruits and veg to <u>stand in water</u> because vitamins B and C <u>dissolve</u> into the water. <u>Steaming</u> or <u>microwaving</u> are the best ways to keep these water-soluble vitamins.
3) Don't chop fruit and veg into <u>small pieces</u> as it <u>exposes</u> more of the surface to <u>air</u> and <u>water</u>.
4) There are more nutrients <u>in or just below the skin</u>, so <u>peel</u> them <u>thinly</u> or use them <u>unpeeled</u> if possible.

Antioxidants Protect Us from Free Radicals

1) <u>Free radicals</u> are <u>chemicals</u> that we encounter every day of our lives.
2) They're able to <u>damage</u> our body's <u>cells</u>, leading to diseases like <u>cancer</u> and <u>heart disease</u>.
3) <u>Antioxidants</u> (e.g. <u>vitamins A</u>, <u>C</u> and <u>E</u>) are found in foods such as <u>fruit</u> and <u>vegetables</u> — many people believe they help <u>protect</u> our bodies from these damaging free radicals.

Blueberries contain lots of antioxidants.

The way you prepare food can affect its vitamin content...

There are lots of vitamins to remember here, and you need to know all the information above. To test your knowledge, write out each cell of the table on a piece of card and jumble them up — then see if you can put everything back together correctly.

Minerals and Trace Elements

We also need small amounts of <u>minerals</u> and <u>trace elements</u> in our diet — nutrition is just full of surprises...

We Need **Minerals** in Small Amounts

In addition to food, minerals and trace elements can be taken in through multivitamin supplements (p.95).

<u>Minerals</u> are chemical elements that our bodies need in small amounts. They help in various <u>chemical reactions</u> in our body and are needed for a variety of reasons:

	Function	Sources include	Problems caused by having too much	Problems caused by having too little
Calcium	Needed for <u>strong bones</u> and <u>teeth</u>, <u>healthy nerves</u> and <u>muscles</u> and <u>blood clotting</u>. *Growing children need calcium every day to help build strong bones and teeth (see p.17).*	Milk, cheese, tofu, green leafy vegetables, hard water and sesame seeds.	Too much is rare, but any excess is stored in organs like the kidneys — this can increase the risk of <u>kidney stones</u> and could even <u>stop the kidneys working</u>.	Too little during childhood can lead to problems such as <u>rickets</u> and <u>osteoporosis</u> (see p.20) because bones become weaker. It can also <u>slow down blood clotting</u>.
Iron	Forms part of the <u>haemoglobin</u> which gives <u>blood cells</u> their red colour.	Dark green vegetables (e.g. spinach) and meat (especially liver and kidney).	<u>Stomach pains</u>, <u>nausea</u>, <u>constipation</u> and even <u>death</u> in extreme cases (too much is toxic / poisonous).	A deficiency disease called <u>anaemia</u> (see p.19).

For the <u>OCR</u> and <u>AQA</u> course, you'll also need to learn these two minerals:

	Function	Sources include	Problems caused by having too much	Problems caused by having too little
Sodium	Sodium chloride (salt) controls the body's <u>water content</u> and helps our <u>nerves</u> and <u>muscles</u> to function.	Most foods — many people add it to food as well.	<u>High blood pressure</u> and <u>heart disease</u> — most people in the UK eat too much salt in their diet.	<u>Nausea</u> and <u>muscle cramps</u>.
Phosphorus	Needed for <u>healthy bones</u> and <u>teeth</u>.	Protein-rich foods like meat, fish, dairy products, nuts, beans and cereals.	Makes it <u>harder to absorb calcium</u>.	<u>Weak muscles</u> and <u>painful bones</u>.

For the <u>Eduqas</u> course, you'll also need to learn these two minerals:

	Function	Sources include	Problems caused by having too much	Problems caused by having too little
Potassium	Needed for good <u>cardiovascular health</u> and to control the <u>balance of fluids</u> in the body — it even works with sodium (salt) to control our <u>muscles</u> and <u>nerves</u>.	Lots of food, including fruit and veg (especially bananas), pulses, nuts and seeds.	<u>Nausea</u>, <u>stomach pain</u>, <u>weak muscles</u> and an <u>irregular heartbeat</u>.	An <u>irregular heartbeat</u>, and <u>paralysis</u> or <u>heart failure</u> in severe cases.
Magnesium	Helps to <u>release energy</u> from our food and keep our <u>bones healthy</u>.	Green leafy vegetables (e.g. spinach), nuts, seeds and dark chocolate.	<u>Nausea</u> and <u>diarrhoea</u>.	Problems are rare, but include <u>nausea</u>, <u>lack of appetite</u> and <u>weak muscles</u>.

<u>Fluoride</u> and <u>iodine</u> are trace elements — <u>trace elements</u> are minerals, but are needed in even <u>smaller amounts</u>:

	Function	Sources include	Problems caused by having too much	Problems caused by having too little
Fluoride	<u>Strengthens teeth</u> and <u>tooth enamel</u>, and helps to <u>prevent tooth decay</u>.	Fish, tea, fluoridated water and dental products (toothpaste and mouthwash).	<u>Brown-coloured teeth</u>, <u>bone problems</u> and <u>cancer</u>.	<u>Weak teeth and enamel</u>, which leads to <u>tooth decay</u>.
Iodine	Needed to make some <u>hormones</u> used by the body.	Seafood, dairy foods and vegetables.	Rare, but can affect the function of the <u>thyroid gland</u>.	<u>Goitre</u> (neck swelling) and <u>complications in unborn babies</u>.

We need a balance of different micronutrients in our diet...

Remember — v<u>i</u>tamins and m<u>i</u>nerals are m<u>i</u>cronutrients. The second letter is the same in each word.

Fibre and Water

As well as proteins, carbs, fats, vitamins, minerals and trace elements we also need <u>fibre</u> and <u>water</u>.

Fibre Isn't **Digested** by the Body

1) <u>Fibre</u>, sometimes called <u>NSP</u> (non-starch polysaccharide) or '<u>roughage</u>', is a type of <u>carbohydrate</u> that helps to keep your digestive system <u>working properly</u> and keeps food <u>moving</u> through it. Fibre is found in things like:

Fibre also makes us feel fuller for longer.

- <u>Vegetables</u> — e.g. peas, beans, broccoli, carrots and potatoes (especially the skin).
- <u>Fruit</u> and <u>fruit juice</u> — raspberries, prunes, bananas, apples.
- <u>Brown bread</u> and <u>wholemeal</u> or <u>whole grain</u> foods — e.g. wholemeal bread/rice/pasta/flour.
- <u>Lentils</u>, <u>beans</u>, <u>seeds</u> and <u>nuts</u>.

2) You need to eat lots of fibre to stay <u>healthy</u>. If you don't, it can lead to <u>health problems</u> such as: <u>constipation</u>, <u>bowel</u> and <u>colon cancer</u>, <u>heart disease</u>, <u>high blood pressure</u>.

3) The NHS states that the average adult should take in <u>30 g</u> of fibre every day. <u>Young children</u> need <u>less fibre</u> because the 'fullness' fibre gives people can stop them from eating foods that contain other important nutrients.

Most people in the UK don't eat enough fibre — some of the health problems mentioned are very common in people over 40.

You Can't Live Without **Water**

1) Around <u>60%</u> of your body is <u>water</u> — it's found in every cell of your body, as well as fluids like blood, sweat and saliva.

2) Our bodies need water to:
- <u>Eliminate waste</u> from the body (e.g. excretion)
- <u>Control body temperature</u> (e.g. sweating)
- Aid the process of <u>digestion</u>

3) You get water from <u>drinks</u> like water (obviously), fruit juice, tea, lemonade, etc. It's also found in <u>food</u> — vegetables and fruit contain quite a lot, and even things like meat and bread contain water.

4) Our body loses water in a variety of ways including our sweat, breath, urine and faeces. If you don't drink enough to replace the water you've used or lost, you become <u>dehydrated</u> and your body can't <u>work properly</u>. Dehydration also causes:

- <u>Slower reactions</u> and <u>poor decision-making</u>, as your <u>brain</u> needs water to function well.
- <u>Blood to thicken</u>, making it <u>harder</u> for the <u>heart</u> to pump the blood around the body.
- An <u>increase</u> in <u>body temperature</u> (the body can't sweat effectively).

5) You should have about <u>2 litres</u> of water a day — but if you're <u>hot</u> or <u>exercising</u> you need to drink <u>more</u> to get enough water into your system.

6) <u>Overhydration</u> can also be very <u>serious</u>. It's caused by drinking <u>huge amounts of water</u> in a <u>short period of time</u>, leading to headaches, nausea and confusion. It also <u>dilutes</u> the concentration of <u>nutrients</u> in our blood — this can affect the function of organs like the <u>kidneys</u>, which in some cases can be fatal.

Diet isn't just what you eat — staying hydrated is important too...

Make sure you know why we need water, how our bodies lose it and the times we need more of it than usual.

Warm-Up and Worked Exam Questions

There's a lot of information squeezed onto those four pages, so have another flick through and make sure you know it all like the back of your hand. When you're happy with it all, give these questions a go.

Warm-Up Questions

1) What roles do vitamin A and vitamin K play in the body?
2) Give one type of food you would recommend to someone suffering from scurvy.
3) Why is it unlikely that an excess of water-soluble vitamins will cause problems?
4) Give two ways you can preserve water-soluble vitamins when cooking.
5) Give two reasons why good sources of fibre should be included in the diet.
6) State two ways in which water can be lost from the body.
7) Give two examples of when a person needs to drink more water than normal.

Worked Exam Questions

1 Good sources of **iron** include beef liver and dark chocolate. *Try and learn a few examples of how different dietary groups can source certain minerals — e.g. tofu can be a good source of calcium for vegans.*

a) Outline why iron is needed as part of a healthy diet.

<u>Iron is needed to form red blood cells.</u>

[1 mark]

b) Name **one** condition that can be caused by an iron deficiency.

<u>Anaemia</u>

[1 mark]

2 A lack of vitamin B12 can cause tiredness and nerve damage.

Explain why a vegan may not get enough vitamin B12 in their diet.

<u>Vitamin B12 is found in meat, fish and animal products such as eggs. As they don't</u>
<u>eat any animal products, vegans won't get vitamin B12 from these sources.</u>

[2 marks]

3 **Fluoride** is a trace element that our body needs in small amounts.

a) Outline the function of fluoride in the body.

<u>The function of fluoride is to strengthen our teeth and harden tooth enamel.</u>
You could have also said that fluoride helps to prevent tooth decay.

[2 marks]

b) Identify **one** food source that is high in fluoride.

Other answers include fluoridated water and tea.

<u>Fish</u>

[1 mark]

Section One — Food, Nutrition and Health

Exam Questions

1   Our bodies need water-soluble vitamins for lots of different processes.
Identify which water-soluble vitamins are being described below.

   a)   A deficiency in this vitamin can cause a disease called beriberi.

   ....

[1 mark]

   b)   These vitamins are important for the production of red blood cells.

   .... and ....

[2 marks]

2   Our health is at risk if we don't get enough of each vitamin in our diet.
Describe the health risks associated with the following vitamin deficiencies.

Deficiency	Health risks associated with this deficiency
Vitamin D	
Vitamin E	

[4 marks]

3   **a)**   Tanya states that children should take in a greater proportion of fibre than adults.
Is she correct? Circle the correct answer.

YES / NO

[1 mark]

   b)   Give a reason for your answer to part a).

   ....

   ....

[1 mark]

4   It's vital that our bodies remain **hydrated** throughout the day.
Discuss the importance of hydration for our health and well-being.

....

....

....

....

....

[4 marks]

Healthy Eating Guidelines

The <u>government</u> issues <u>guidelines</u> on healthy eating. Crunch some lettuce while you read all about it.

The **Eatwell Guide** Gives **Recommendations** for a **Healthy Diet**

The <u>Eatwell Guide</u> is an easy way of showing <u>how much</u> or little of each <u>food group</u> is recommended.

Fruit and vegetables:
- About <u>1/3</u> of your daily food intake.
- Aim to eat at least <u>5 portions</u> of <u>fruit and veg</u> every day.

One portion is:
- <u>One piece</u> of <u>medium-sized</u> fruit, e.g. apple, banana or orange.
- <u>One heaped tablespoon</u> of <u>dried fruit</u>, e.g. raisins, sultanas.
- <u>Three heaped tablespoons</u> of <u>cooked vegetables</u>, e.g. carrots, sweetcorn.
- 150 ml of <u>fruit juices</u> or <u>smoothies</u> (only <u>one glass</u> per day).

<u>Total calories per day</u>
Women: 2000 kcal
Men: 2500 kcal

Starchy carbohydrates:
- About <u>1/3</u> of your daily food intake*.
- Choose <u>higher fibre</u>, <u>wholegrain</u> options with less <u>fat</u>, <u>sugar</u> and <u>salt</u>.
- Try to include a <u>starchy</u> food in <u>every meal</u>, e.g. <u>potatoes</u>, and <u>wholegrain</u> <u>bread</u>, <u>pasta</u> and <u>cereals</u>.

*Careful here — we're talking about the <u>amount of carbs</u> you eat, not how much <u>energy</u> you get from them (p.23).

Oils and spreads:
- Use <u>unsaturated</u> <u>oils</u> and <u>spreads</u>, and not very often. E.g. <u>sunflower</u> and <u>olive</u> oil.

Beans, pulses, fish, meat and other protein:
- Aim to eat <u>two portions</u> of <u>fish</u> a week (one <u>oily</u>, e.g. <u>salmon</u>, <u>sardines</u>).
- <u>Pulses</u> are a <u>good alternative</u> to meat.
- Choose <u>lean cuts</u> of meat and eat less <u>processed meat</u> (e.g. <u>bacon</u>, <u>sausages</u>).

Dairy products and alternatives:
- Have <u>some dairy</u> and try <u>lower fat</u> options, e.g. <u>1% fat milk</u>, or <u>reduced-fat cheese</u>.
- You can also try dairy alternatives, such as <u>soya</u> or <u>rice-based milks</u>.

 Drink <u>6-8 glasses</u> of <u>fluids</u> a day — hydration is part of a healthy diet.

 Eat less <u>sugary</u>, <u>salty</u> and <u>fatty</u> foods, e.g. <u>muffins</u>, <u>cakes</u>, <u>biscuits</u>.

Food Labels Show **Guidelines** for an **Average Adult**

<u>Reference Intakes</u> (RIs) are <u>guidelines</u> that are often shown on food <u>labels</u>.

1) RIs are based on an <u>average adult</u>, so they are only an <u>indication</u> of the amount of <u>energy</u> and <u>nutrients</u> an adult requires each day.

2) Adults will have <u>different requirements</u> depending on their <u>age</u>, <u>gender</u>, how <u>active</u> they are, and if they have any diet-related <u>health conditions</u>.

3) Food labels also list each <u>nutrient</u> in the food as a <u>percentage</u> of the RI (this can be for <u>100 g</u> of the food, per <u>portion</u>, or <u>both</u>).
E.g. If 100 g of cake contains 9 g of sugar, it would be labelled as 10% of your RI for sugars.

Energy / Nutrient	Reference Intake (RI)
Energy	2000 kcal
Fat	70 g
Saturates	20 g
Carbohydrate	260 g
Sugars	90 g
Protein	50 g
Salt	6 g

 If only custard creams were 1 of your 5 a day...

This stuff is really important, so give this task a go. Cover up the Eatwell Guide and sketch a copy from memory — label each section and give some example foods.

Nutritional Needs of Different Age Groups

Everyone should roughly aim to follow the healthy eating guidelines, but our nutritional needs change throughout each stage of our lives. These pages will give you the low-down.

Children Grow Quickly and Need Lots of Energy

Babies and Toddlers

1) Babies are born with a store of iron. They get other nutrients from breast milk or bottled milk formulas.
2) Babies should then be introduced to soft, easy-to-eat food between the ages of four to six months.
3) Toddlers do not have large stomachs, so they should have small and frequent meals to get the energy they need.
4) Milk is an important source of nutrients — 300 ml each day gives toddlers the daily calcium they need and it's also a good source of vitamin A.

...although it's better to get calcium from a range of foods.

5) Toddlers should be frequently encouraged to try a variety of foods. Kids can be dead fussy though, so experiment mixing new foods with things they like and offer them different choices.
6) They should gradually start moving towards a diet based on the Eatwell Guide.

Children

1) Children grow quickly and are very active, so there is an extra demand for energy and nutrients — they need more than adults (in proportion to their body size).
2) Good amounts of these nutrients are important for children:

Nutrient	Reason	Example Foods
Protein	To help them grow and repair the body.	Fish fingers, boiled eggs
Carbohydrate	Starchy carbohydrates and some fats provide energy for growth and physical activity. Saturated fats should be eaten in moderation.	Mashed potato, pasta
Fat		Peanuts, avocados
Calcium	For healthy teeth and bone development.	Milk, yoghurt tubes, cheese
Vitamin D		Tuna, salmon

3) Foods high in sugar should be eaten infrequently, and only ever at mealtimes. Too many of these foods can cause tooth decay and weight gain.
4) Eating habits of children may be adopted from their parents, so families should eat healthily together.

Teenagers

1) Teenagers should aim for a balanced diet, according to the Eatwell Guide.
2) Rapid growth spurts happen around the early teens — girls usually start these earlier than boys.
3) Good amounts of these nutrients are important for teenagers:

Nutrient	Reason	Example Foods
Protein	To cope with growth spurts. Boys tend to need more protein than girls as muscular tissue develops.	Omelettes, chicken
Iron	Teenage girls lose iron when they have their period so it needs to be replaced or they could become anaemic (p.19). Vitamin C helps the body absorb the iron.	Spinach, beef
Vitamin C		Peppers, strawberries
Calcium	The skeleton grows quickly during this time. These nutrients are necessary as they help the skeleton reach peak size and bone density.	Milk, yoghurt, kale, tofu
Vitamin D		Tuna, salmon, mackerel

4) During the teen years there can be lots of stress (e.g. exams, media pressure) which affect eating habits — stress can lead to conditions like anorexia, but also overeating which can cause obesity.

Nutritional Needs of Different Age Groups

Here are some more life stages that you have to look forward to. You may as well start planning now...

Adults Stop Growing and Nutritional Needs Don't Vary Much

Early / Middle Adulthood

1) Growth and development stops, so adults should focus on maintaining a healthy lifestyle — they are encouraged to follow the Eatwell Guide to keep the body disease-free.

2) Men usually require more calories than women because they have more lean muscle (muscles require lots of energy to function properly) and are generally taller and larger.

3) Iron is especially important for adult women as they continue to lose it through periods.

4) Calcium and vitamin D are important for all adults to reduce the chance of bone diseases in later life — women can quickly lose bone strength after the menopause in their 40s or 50s too, so these nutrients are needed to keep the skeleton strong.

5) During pregnancy, women should adapt their diet to help the baby. Pregnant women should:

   • eat about 200 more calories per day towards the end of the pregnancy to support the baby's growth. They should be careful not to overeat as it can cause excessive weight gain.

   • consume more folic acid — it helps to reduce the risk of birth defects such as spina bifida.

Late Adulthood

1) As we age, our muscle is replaced with fat, and so our body needs less energy for maintenance.

2) Elderly adults need to take great care with their energy intake — cutting down on excess saturated fats will help avoid health risks like coronary heart disease (see next page).

3) The senses of taste and smell change, which can affect the enjoyment of food. Recipes and meals need to be adapted to make them appealing and interesting.

4) Elderly adults have similar nutritional requirements to younger adults, but they must make sure they get enough:

Nutrient	Reason	Example Foods
Calcium	To help stop bones becoming weak and brittle and reduce the risk of developing bone diseases.	Milk, yoghurt, kale, sardines
Vitamin D		Tuna, salmon, mackerel
Vitamin B12	To keep the brain healthy and prevent memory loss.	Milk, fish, beef
Fibre	To help prevent constipation as the digestive system begins to weaken.	Lentils, wholemeal bread
Vitamin A	To help maintain good eyesight.	Liver, scrambled eggs

5) Vitamin supplements are useful if your diet doesn't contain enough, e.g. less active elderly adults may not get enough vitamin D from sunlight, so may benefit from vitamin D tablets.

You'll need lots of practice planning meals for different ages...

In the non-exam assessment you might have to plan a meal for a certain age group. You should get plenty of practice doing this, so have a go at one or more of the planning tasks below.

Research and plan a dish which is a good source of...
1. protein and would appeal to a teenager.
2. calcium and is suitable for a toddler.
3. vitamin B12 and would appeal to an elderly adult.

Diet-Related Health Problems

A bad diet will affect your health, and certain diseases affect your nutritional needs.

Obesity is When the Body Has Too Much Fat

Working out BMI
Divide your weight (kg) by your height (m) and divide the answer by your height again.

1) Obesity is very common — it affects roughly one in every four adults in the UK.
2) Body Mass Index (BMI) is often used to check if someone is overweight or obese.
3) For adults, a BMI between 18.5 and 25 is classed as a healthy weight, between 25 and 30 as overweight, between 30 and 35 as obese and above 35 as extremely obese.

BMI is not always a reliable indicator of someone's body fat — a person could weigh a lot (and have a high BMI) due to a large amount of muscle mass rather than body fat.

Causes
- An incorrect balance of energy — a person consumes more calories than they burn off.
- Eating lots of food high in fat and sugar.
- Having a sedentary lifestyle.

A sedentary lifestyle is one with little or no physical activity.

Health Problems
- High blood pressure and high cholesterol increase the chance of cardiovascular disease (see below).
- There's a greater risk of other serious health conditions such as type 2 diabetes, liver disease and cancer.
- Breathing difficulties, tiredness and low self-esteem are also common.

Cardiovascular Disease is Often Caused by Clogged Arteries

1) Cardiovascular disease (CVD) refers to any disease related to the heart or blood vessels.
2) The most common type is coronary heart disease (CHD) — arteries (which supply the heart with blood full of oxygen) are narrowed, because they are filled with fatty deposits.
3) CHD can lead to angina, heart attacks and strokes:

Causes
- Eating lots of saturated fats.
- Being physically inactive — because exercise keeps the heart and the cardiovascular system healthy.
- Smoking — damages the lining of arteries and reduces the oxygen in the blood.
- High blood pressure.

Health Problems
- Blood cannot pass through your blood vessels efficiently, which can cause a squeezing pain in your chest (angina).
- Blood clots can form and block blood flow.
- Strokes occur when blood flow to the brain is blocked, and heart attacks occur when blood flow to the heart is blocked (both can be fatal).

Blood pressure is how much pressure the blood puts against the walls of your arteries.
High blood pressure puts strain on blood vessels and organs and can increase the risk of CHD / strokes.

Anaemia can be Caused by Iron Deficiency

1) Iron is needed to make red blood cells — these cells carry oxygen from the lungs and travel in your blood around the body to where it is needed.
2) People with anaemia have a reduced amount of red blood cells.

Causes
- Not eating enough iron-rich foods, e.g. red meat and dark green leafy vegetables.
- Women lose iron during their periods.
- Pregnant women lose iron to their baby during pregnancy.

Health Problems
- Tiredness
- Pale complexion
- Heart palpitations
- Headaches
- Abnormal fingernails

Diet-Related Health Problems

Oh, there's another page on this? Sorry, you just can't get away with having a <u>poor diet</u> scot-free.

Diabetes Lets Your Blood Glucose Levels Run Out of Control

1) <u>Insulin</u> is a <u>hormone</u> that allows <u>glucose</u> to be <u>absorbed</u> by cells in the body.

2) Insulin is created in the <u>pancreas</u> — if there is <u>too much glucose</u> in the blood, the pancreas <u>produces</u> insulin to <u>reduce</u> the <u>blood glucose level</u>.

3) <u>Type 2 diabetes</u> is a disorder where blood glucose levels stay too high because the pancreas either can't <u>produce enough insulin</u> or the <u>body resists it</u>.

There are two types of diabetes — <u>type 1</u> and <u>type 2</u>. You'll only need to learn about type 2.

Causes
- Being <u>overweight</u> or <u>obese</u>.
- <u>Excessive sugar</u> in the diet can lead to obesity (increasing the risk of type 2 diabetes) — this is affecting more <u>young people</u>.

Health Problems
- Diabetes can cause <u>long-term health problems</u> such as <u>poor eyesight</u> (or even <u>blindness</u>), <u>limb numbness</u>, <u>kidney failure</u> and <u>cardiovascular diseases</u> such as CHD.
- People with diabetes can feel <u>tired</u> and <u>thirsty</u>.
- The body <u>flushes</u> out glucose by <u>passing urine</u> more often.

Poor Diet Can Affect the Skeleton Too

Your <u>bones</u> and <u>teeth</u> can become <u>diseased</u> if you don't get the <u>right amount</u> of nutrients.

Rickets
- <u>Rickets</u> is a condition that means that the <u>bones</u> are <u>soft</u> and <u>weak</u>.
- This occurs in <u>children</u> if they don't have enough <u>vitamin D</u> or <u>calcium</u> — e.g. little exposure to <u>sunlight</u> or not eating enough <u>foods</u> rich in these nutrients.
- Rickets causes <u>pain</u> in the bones, increases the chances of <u>fracturing bones</u> and can cause physical <u>deformities</u>, e.g. <u>bowed legs</u>.

Both of these are linked to a lack of vitamin D or calcium — think of some example foods for different age groups that would help prevent these conditions.

Osteoporosis
- Osteoporosis is a <u>bone disease</u> which <u>weakens</u> bones and makes them <u>brittle</u>, increasing the chance of breaking bones from <u>simple falls</u> (called fragility fractures).
- It is <u>common</u> in older people because <u>bone density</u> is lost <u>naturally</u> as we age.
- Women tend to lose bone density <u>more rapidly</u> after the <u>menopause</u>.
- Eating foods rich in <u>vitamin D</u> or <u>calcium</u> can help prevent osteoporosis.

Tooth Decay
- <u>Plaque</u> is a <u>sticky substance</u> that contains lots of <u>bacteria</u> — it <u>builds up</u> on your teeth over time from <u>leftover food</u>.
- Bacteria <u>feed</u> on <u>sugars</u> and create <u>acids</u> that can <u>destroy tooth enamel</u> and cause <u>tooth decay</u> (also called <u>dental caries</u>).
- <u>Brushing</u> your <u>teeth</u> with <u>fluoride toothpaste</u> twice a day and eating <u>fewer</u> foods <u>high in sugar</u> can help <u>prevent</u> tooth decay.

<u>Genetics</u> have an effect on health too — people with a <u>family history</u> of high <u>blood pressure</u>, <u>type 2 diabetes</u> etc. may have a <u>higher risk</u> of developing these health problems themselves, regardless of a poor diet.

EXAM TIP

People with health problems have certain nutritional needs...

In the exam, you might have to plan a meal for someone with a health problem — think about what causes the condition to help you understand which nutrients to include (or avoid).

Warm-Up and Worked Exam Questions

Try these warm-up questions on nutritional needs and diet-related health problems — if there is anything you're unsure about, take a look back through the section before trying the exam questions on the next page.

Warm-Up Questions

1) List the five sections of the Eatwell Guide.
2) What is a Reference Intake?
3) Name one nutrient that is important for each of the groups listed below:
   a) Toddlers   b) Teenagers   c) Pregnant women   d) Elderly adults
4) What does BMI stand for?
5) Explain one way someone could reduce their risk of developing: a) anaemia   b) diabetes

Worked Exam Questions

1 **Obesity** can have a real impact on everyday health and well-being.

Tick the **five** conditions below which are associated with obesity.

- Tooth decay ☐
- High blood pressure ☑
- Increased risk of a stroke ☑
- Type 2 diabetes ☑
- Osteoporosis ☐

- Hyperactivity ☐
- Breathing difficulties ☑
- Liver disease ☑
- Anaemia ☐
- Lactose intolerance ☐

[2 marks]

2 Jade wants her **three-year-old son** to have a healthy, balanced diet.

Describe how Jade can set a good example of healthy eating habits to her son.

Jade should set regular mealtimes and gradually introduce her son to meals that are based on the Eatwell Guide. Jade should also limit the snacks she gives her son between meals, and any snacks should be low in free sugars, such as breadsticks or carrot sticks.

You could have mentioned serving smaller portions for her son as he should eat less than an adult.   [4 marks]

3 Plaque can build up on teeth over time and cause **tooth decay**.

Describe how parents can reduce the risk of tooth decay developing in their children.

Parents can encourage their children to drink water, milk or diluted fruit juices instead of fizzy drinks, and encourage them to brush their teeth twice a day with a fluoride toothpaste. Parents can also adapt their own recipes or make their own stocks and sauces to include less sugar.

[3 marks]

Exam Questions

1 High levels of cholesterol in the blood increase
the risk of **cardiovascular diseases**, such as **CHD**.

Healthy artery

a) What does CHD stand for?

....

Artery showing signs of CHD

[1 mark]

b) Give **two** other risk factors for CHD.

1. ....

2. ....

[2 marks]

c) Describe the effects of CHD on the body.

....

....

....

[3 marks]

2 **Teenagers** with poor eating habits can develop vitamin deficiencies and health conditions.

Explain how the following pairs of nutrients are important in the diet of a teenager:

a) Iron and vitamin C (especially for girls)

....

....

....

[2 marks]

b) Calcium and vitamin D

....

....

....

[2 marks]

3 A Year 10 pupil is preparing a packed lunch to take on a school trip.

Suggest **one** food item from each section of the Eatwell Guide they could include in their
lunch and explain why each of your choices is important in the diet of a teenager.

[10 marks]

Energy Needs

BMR, PAL and LOL are all energy key terms that you'll need to know (alright, I lied about one of them).

BMR is the Minimum Energy Needed to Function

1) Basal Metabolic Rate (BMR) is the smallest amount of energy needed for you to stay alive — this is stuff you don't think about, like breathing and keeping your heart beating.

   The average BMR for an adult is about 1500 — 2000 calories.

2) These basic life processes can use up to about 75% of the energy we use each day — other things like digestion and physical activity make up the rest.

3) There are many factors that affect a person's BMR.

   - Age — BMR decreases as we get older due to reduction of muscle mass.
   - Gender — Women, in general, have a lower BMR than men as they're generally smaller and tend to have less muscle.
   - Weight and height — Heavier or larger bodies need more calories, so have a higher BMR.
   - Exercise — Again, it's all about the muscle — regular exercise (especially strength training) increases muscle, which raises your BMR.
   - Genetics — Other genetic factors may also have some effect on metabolism and BMR.

PAL is a Way to Express Your Physical Activity

Competitive gymnast PAL = about 2.0

1) Your Physical Activity Level (PAL) is a measure of how active you are/how much exercise you get.

2) If you are more active, e.g. a competitive gymnast, you will have a higher PAL than someone with a sedentary lifestyle.

3) BMR and PAL multiplied together give your daily energy requirement:

   Daily energy requirement (kcal) = BMR × PAL

Office worker (with little daily exercise) PAL = about 1.6

4) You have to balance your energy intake to maintain a healthy weight:
   - If you consume more energy than you use you will gain weight.
   - If you consume less energy than you use you will start to lose weight.

5) This energy balance changes throughout life — for example:
   - As you get older your BMR decreases, so you'll need fewer calories to maintain a healthy weight.
   - As you exercise more your PAL increases, so you'll need more calories to maintain a healthy weight.

Have the Right Balance of Energy Sources

Carbohydrates, fats and proteins are our main sources of energy.

According to government guidelines, they should be consumed in a certain ratio:

- Try to get a good variety, if eating low biological value proteins (p.1).

Carbohydrates 50%

Protein 15%

Fat 35% "or less"

- The majority should come as starches and as sugars present in milk (lactose) and fruit (fructose).
- No more than 5% should come from sugar added to processed foods.

- Getting less than 35% is fine.
- Try to eat less saturated fat.

Alcohol also provides energy — however, the calories from alcohol are empty calories (see p.5) because they have no other nutritional value and are not required for a normal diet.

Put your time and energy into remembering these important terms...

Know your BMR from your PAL and learn how to calculate how much energy we should consume each day.

Nutritional Analysis

...lysis is about working out the nutritional content of foods... yup, this first bit is a little mathsy.

Macronutrients Have Different Energy Values

1) Energy can be expressed in kilojoules (kJ) or, more commonly, kilocalories (kcal) — when people talk about calories in food, they're usually referring to kilocalories.

2) 1 gram of each major macronutrient (fat, protein and carbohydrate) gives us the approximate energy values shown in the table.

3) If you know how many grams of each macronutrient are in a food, you can calculate its energy value.

4) You can do this for an ingredient, a recipe and even a diet to work out the total energy value. For example:

Macronutrient	Energy value (kcal)
Fat (1 g)	9
Protein (1 g)	4
Carbohydrate (1 g)	4

To calculate the total energy value for a boiled egg with toast soldiers, look at the table to find the energy value for 1 g of each ingredient and multiply it by how many grams of each macronutrient there are.

Ingredient	Macronutrient content		Energy value		
1 egg	Fat	7 g	7 × 9 = 63 kcal	63 + 36 + 2.4 = 101.4 kcal	Total energy = 101.4 + 69 = 170.4 kcal
	Protein	9 g	9 × 4 = 36 kcal		
	Carbohydrate	0.6 g	0.6 × 4 = 2.4 kcal		
1 wholemeal bread slice	Fat	1 g	1 × 9 = 9 kcal	9 + 12 + 48 = 69 kcal	
	Protein	3 g	3 × 4 = 12 kcal		
	Carbohydrate	12 g	12 × 4 = 48 kcal		

Use Reference Tables and Software to Find Nutritional Data

Fortunately, you won't have to calculate the energy value of each ingredient — there's loads of nutritional data available out there for both energy and nutritional values, you just need to know where to find it.

1) Packaged foods have to include nutritional labels on their packaging by law (p.70).

2) Reference tables of nutrients for different foods can be found in books or online:

   • Foods are listed alphabetically or by food group.

   • The nutritional values are usually given per 100 g or per portion of the food...

   • ...which means you can't just use these figures as they are. E.g. if you use 10 g of garlic in a recipe, you'll need to divide the values in its row by 10 to give the nutritional value for just 10 g.

Value per 100g	Energy (kcal)	Protein (g)	Carbohydrates (g)	Sugars (g)	Fat (g)	of which saturates	Fibre (g)
Garlic, raw	150	6	30	1	0.5	0.1	2
Gooseberries	45	1	10	8	0.5	0.1	4
Gouda, cheese	350	25	2	2	28	18	0

3) You can also use nutritional analysis software on a computer:

   • It lets you input the ingredients of a recipe, and the weight of each.

   • It calculates the energy and the amount of nutrients present in the entire meal, and if the recipe serves multiple people, you can find the nutritional content per portion.

   • It can have additional features such as comparing nutritional values to the recommended amounts for different ages.

   "Explore food" is a free nutritional analysis tool you can try online — visit http://explorefood.foodafactoflife.org.uk/ for more info.

Nutritional Analysis

You can <u>look up</u> and <u>work out</u> the energy and nutritional information of foods... so what?
Well, armed with this data you can <u>suggest</u> and <u>change</u> ingredients to make meals more <u>healthy</u> and <u>balanced</u>.

Modify Meals to Follow Healthy Eating Guidelines

Nutritional analysis helps you <u>identify</u> and <u>adapt recipes</u>, <u>menus</u> or <u>diets</u> to follow <u>healthy eating guidelines</u>.

EXAMPLE:

Look at the ingredients in the recipe on the right. Find the nutritional content of the recipe and modify the ingredients to meet healthy eating guidelines.

The nutritional values of foods are often given in grams, so estimate the weight of the lemon juice — 60 ml ≈ 60 g.

Use reference tables or nutritional analysis software to find the nutritional values for each ingredient, for the whole recipe and per portion:

E.g.

Rhubarb Crumble	Energy (kcal)	Protein (g)	Carbohydrates (g)	Sugars (g)	Fat (g)	of which saturates	Fibre (g)
per recipe (~800 g)	1708	16	258	106	68	42	10
per portion (~200 g)	427	4	64.5	26.5	17	10.5	2.5

The recipe serves <u>four</u>, so divide by four to get the nutritional values per portion.

Rhubarb Crumble
(*Serves four*)

Ingredients:
400 g rhubarb
100 g demerara sugar   80 g salted butter
150 g white flour   60 ml lemon juice

<u>Modifying the recipe:</u>

- Switch to a wholemeal flour to give the crumble more <u>fibre</u> and substitute <u>25 g</u> of the flour for <u>oats</u> to give a <u>better texture</u>.

- The sugar content is <u>really</u> high — reduce the amount of <u>sugar</u> used to 50 g or use a <u>natural</u> alternative sweetener such as <u>stevia</u> or <u>xylitol</u>.

- Add a handful of <u>walnuts</u> to provide extra nutrients (<u>unsaturated fats</u>, <u>fibre</u> and <u>vitamins</u>).

Here are some ways you can <u>modify</u> recipes to reduce <u>sugar</u>, <u>salt</u> and <u>saturated fat</u>, and to increase <u>fibre</u>:

Reducing Sugar

- Sugar can be 'disguised' as other names (e.g. sucrose, corn syrup) on packaging, so study labels carefully.
- Use fewer sugary condiments (e.g. ketchup, barbecue sauce).
- Use less sugar when baking.

Reducing Salt

- Use less foods that have salt added to preserve or flavour them, e.g. cured meat.
- Create your own sauces and stocks — ready-made ones are often very high in salt.
- Use seasonings other than salt to add flavour, e.g. ginger or chilli.

Increasing Fibre

- Go for wholemeal bread, flour and pasta.
- Include more beans, lentils (and other pulses) and vegetables in meals.
- Keep skins on potatoes.

Reducing Saturated Fat

- Use low-fat spreads and vegetable oils.
- Eat lean cuts of meat, and grill, bake or steam foods instead of frying or roasting.
- Allow fat to drain away when cooking.

You also have to consider whether your meal is <u>appropriate</u>. A person:

- with a <u>high PAL</u> / about to take part in <u>physical activity</u> will require <u>more energy</u> in a meal.
- with a <u>dietary requirement</u> will require <u>substitutions</u> of certain <u>ingredients</u> (see p.27-28).

REVISION TASK

Adapt your recipe to meet healthy eating guidelines...

Use a reference table or nutritional analysis software to investigate the nutritional value of your favourite recipe. Does it meet healthy eating guidelines? If not, which ingredients could you adapt?

Planning Meals for Different Groups

There are many <u>factors</u> to consider when planning meals, e.g. <u>costing</u>, <u>portion size</u> and <u>dietary requirements</u>. You need to cater for different <u>ages</u> too — children might not rave about your <u>healthy cabbage soup</u>.

Research the **Cost** of **Ingredients**

1) <u>Healthier</u> and more <u>nutritional</u> ingredients are often <u>more expensive</u> — e.g. <u>lean meat</u> (p.79).

2) Buying <u>individual</u> ingredients for a recipe is often <u>cheaper per portion</u> than buying <u>ready-made</u> food, e.g. a <u>pizza</u>. However, you'll usually have to buy <u>more</u> ingredients than you need for the recipe.

3) You can <u>compare</u> the prices of <u>ingredients</u> at <u>different shops</u> (or use <u>comparison websites</u>) and <u>reduce</u> the <u>quantity</u> of <u>expensive ingredients</u> (e.g. <u>cheese</u>, <u>meat</u>) to make your meals <u>cheaper</u>.

4) You can <u>work out</u> the <u>total cost</u> of a meal by working out the cost of each <u>individual ingredient</u> — <u>write down</u> each ingredient and <u>calculate</u> its <u>cost</u> from its <u>weight</u>:

	Ingredient	Weight	Cost (per 100 g)	Cost (per ingredient)
Spanish omelette (serves 4)	Potatoes (500 g)	500 g	£0.10	£0.10 x 5 = £0.50
	Butter (20 g)	20 g	£0.40	£0.40 ÷ 5 = £0.08
	2 Onions	200 g	£0.06	£0.06 x 2 = £0.12
	1 Red Pepper	150 g	£0.50	£0.50 x 1.5 = £0.75
	9 Eggs	500 g	£0.30	£0.30 x 5 = £1.50

<u>Total cost</u>
£0.50 + £0.08 + £0.12
+ £0.75 + £1.50 = £2.95

<u>Cost per portion</u>
£2.95 ÷ 4 = about £0.74

Control Your **Portion Size**

<u>Portion size</u> is <u>important</u> — good portion <u>control</u> means you can avoid <u>overfeeding</u> or <u>underfeeding</u> people. For ingredients and meals you may want to use <u>guidelines</u> and <u>equipment</u> to get the portion size correct:

<u>One portion</u> of <u>meat</u> should be roughly the size of your <u>palm</u>.

<u>One portion</u> of <u>cooked vegetables</u> should be roughly the size of your <u>fist</u>.

Use <u>scoops</u> to measure out the <u>same</u> portion size <u>each time</u>.

Use <u>cutters</u> and <u>dividers</u> to <u>divide</u> pizzas, pies, cakes etc.

Meal Ideas for Different **Age Groups**

Make sure you plan your meals to be <u>nutritionally balanced</u>, <u>appropriate</u> for the <u>age group</u> (p.17-18) and that any <u>dietary requirements</u> (next page) are catered for. Take a look at these <u>examples</u>:

	Ingredients	Nutritional importance
Children	Baked fishcakes	Good source of protein — children need lots of it.
	Carrots, peas	Packed with vitamin C (and make up 2 of their 5 a day).
	Mashed potato	A starchy carbohydrate that is a healthier alternative to chips. Made with milk so includes calcium needed for healthy teeth and bones.

Make meals for children <u>visually interesting</u> by including different <u>colours</u> and <u>textures</u>.

	Ingredients	Nutritional importance
Teenagers	Grilled chicken breast	Protein for rapidly growing bodies.
	Wholewheat couscous	Lots of carbohydrate and fibre and low in saturated fat.
	Olives, spinach	Both good sources of iron — important for girls so they don't become anaemic.
	Red pepper	Adds colour and a good source of vitamin C too.

	Ingredients	Nutritional importance
Elderly	Lentil stew	Pulses are rich in protein and fibre. Fibre helps the weakening digestive system.
	Sweet potato	Lots of carotene (vitamin A) — helpful for healthy eyes.
	Soft tofu	Easy to chew and can be a good source of calcium to help maintain bone strength.
	Wholemeal bread roll	Another good source of fibre — much more than white bread.

Planning Meals for Different Groups

You may have to plan a meal for someone with a <u>dietary requirement</u> — <u>intolerances</u>, <u>allergies</u>, <u>ethical</u> and <u>religious beliefs</u>, and <u>diet-related health problems</u> all affect what people eat.

Intolerances and Allergies

Lactose Intolerance

People with <u>lactose intolerance</u> need to avoid food containing a type of sugar called <u>lactose</u>. Lactose is found in <u>milk</u>, so it's important to check labels for any <u>milk-based</u> ingredients.

Soya beans

- Consider <u>substituting</u> normal milk for <u>lactose-free</u> milk, e.g. <u>soya</u> or <u>almond</u> milk.
- <u>Dairy</u> products, e.g. cheese and yoghurt, have <u>lactose-free alternatives</u>.

Nut Allergy

People with <u>nut allergies</u> have to avoid <u>nuts</u> and foods that may <u>contain traces</u> of them. <u>Allergic reactions</u> can be <u>fatal</u>, so it's important you check labels very carefully — if you have any doubts about whether a product contains nuts it's safest not to use it.

- Nuts <u>aren't vital</u> for a balanced diet, so <u>substitutions</u> can be made.
- Some <u>biscuit</u> and <u>cake</u> recipes only use nuts to add flavour, so the nuts can just be <u>removed</u>.

Coeliac Disease

People with <u>coeliac disease</u> cannot eat food containing <u>gluten</u>. They must avoid <u>wheat</u>, <u>barley</u> and <u>rye</u> and products made with them.

- Many <u>basic foods</u> are fine for a <u>coeliac</u> — meat, vegetables and dairy products are all <u>naturally free</u> of gluten and should be included in their normal diet. However, you should check the label just in case.
- Use <u>alternative flours</u>, e.g. <u>coconut</u>, <u>tapioca</u> or <u>rice</u> flours are all <u>gluten-free alternatives</u> to <u>wheat flour</u>.

Ethical and Moral Beliefs

See p.63 for more on ethical and moral beliefs.

Vegetarians

A <u>vegetarian</u> is someone who <u>chooses</u> not to eat <u>any meat</u> (and sometimes <u>products</u> derived from <u>animals</u>, like milk and eggs) due to <u>personal</u> or <u>religious beliefs</u>.

Make sure you can plan meals for people with religious beliefs too (see p.62).

There are different <u>branches</u> of <u>vegetarianism</u>:

- <u>Pescatarians</u> will <u>not</u> eat <u>meat</u>, but <u>will</u> eat <u>fish</u> and <u>animal products</u>, e.g. eggs, cheese and milk.
- <u>Lacto-ovo</u> vegetarians will <u>not</u> eat any <u>meat</u> or <u>fish</u> but <u>will</u> eat milk, eggs and other <u>animal products</u>.
- <u>Lacto</u> vegetarians will <u>not</u> eat any <u>meat</u>, <u>fish</u> or <u>eggs</u>, but <u>will</u> eat milk and other <u>dairy products</u>.
- <u>Vegans</u> will <u>not</u> eat any <u>meat</u>, <u>fish</u> or <u>animal products</u>.

1) Dishes with vegetables are generally <u>healthy</u> and <u>nutritionally balanced</u>, but you will have to include protein from <u>alternative sources</u> other than meat (see p.1).

2) <u>Quorn</u>™ products are popular — they contain <u>mycoprotein</u> which is said to have a texture similar to meat (most Quorn™ products use <u>egg white</u>, so they are not all suitable for vegans).

3) Be careful of hidden animal-based ingredients, such as <u>gelatine</u> (used in jelly and marshmallows) and <u>rennet</u> (used in cheese).

Planning Meals for Different Groups

Diet-Related Health Problems

See p.19-20 for more on diet-related health problems.

Obesity and Cardiovascular Disease

People with <u>obesity</u> need to lower their <u>calorie intake</u> and amount of <u>saturated fat</u>.

- Use correct <u>portion sizes</u> to <u>control</u> the amount of <u>calories</u> in a meal.
- <u>Reduce</u> the amount of <u>saturated fat</u> by using <u>vegetable oils</u> when <u>frying</u> and opt for cooking methods that don't add extra fat (e.g. <u>grilling</u>).
- Include more <u>fruit</u> and <u>vegetables</u> to replace fatty and sugary foods.

Obesity is a <u>risk factor</u> of <u>cardiovascular disease</u>, so this advice should be followed for people with cardiovascular disease too.

Diabetes

People with <u>diabetes</u> need to control their <u>blood sugar</u> levels.

- Avoid adding <u>sugar</u> or use natural <u>sweeteners</u>, such as <u>xylitol</u> and <u>stevia</u>.
- Use <u>low GI</u> foods (see p.5) such as <u>brown rice</u> or <u>quinoa</u> because these foods are <u>digested slowly</u> and <u>gradually</u> raise blood sugar levels.

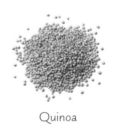

Quinoa

Anaemia

People with <u>anaemia</u> need good sources of <u>iron</u> in their diet (and <u>vitamin C</u> to help the body absorb it).

- Include foods high in <u>iron</u>, e.g. <u>red meat</u> and <u>dark-green leafy vegetables</u>.
- Include foods high in <u>vitamin C</u>, e.g. <u>tomatoes</u> and <u>citrus fruits</u>.

Bone Diseases

People with <u>bone diseases</u> (e.g. <u>rickets</u>, <u>osteoporosis</u>) need good sources of <u>calcium</u> in their diet (and <u>vitamin D</u> to help the body absorb it).

- Include foods high in <u>calcium</u>, e.g. <u>milk</u>, <u>cheese</u> and calcium-set <u>tofu</u>.
- Include foods high in <u>vitamin D</u>, e.g. <u>tuna</u> and <u>salmon</u>.

Tooth Decay

People with <u>tooth decay</u> need to limit their intake of <u>sugary foods</u>.

- Use less <u>free sugar</u> in recipes or use <u>natural sweeteners</u> instead (some evidence suggests that the natural sweetener <u>xylitol</u> may help <u>prevent</u> tooth decay).
- Offer <u>fluoridated water</u> or <u>unsweetened</u> tea or coffee with meals rather than <u>sugary drinks</u>, e.g. fruit juice or fizzy drinks.

Make sure your adapted recipes are still nutritionally balanced...

By now you should be confident adapting recipes to make them suitable for different groups and know how to cost things correctly — alternative ingredients (e.g. gluten-free) can often be more expensive than regular foods.

Warm-Up and Worked Exam Questions

That's almost Section One all wrapped up — make sure you're familiar with all the factors you need to consider when making a meal, and then work through this set of questions.

Warm-Up Questions

1) List the factors that can affect a person's BMR.

2) Calculate the daily energy requirement for someone with BMR of 2000 calories and PAL of 1.5.

3) According to government guidelines, what percentage of our total energy should come from:
   a) carbohydrates   b) fat   c) proteins?

4) How can nutritional analysis software help design food products that meet healthy eating guidelines?

5) Name an alternative ingredient for each of the following:
   a) Milk (for someone with lactose intolerance)   b) Flour (for someone with coeliac disease)

Worked Exam Questions

1 The ingredients and **nutritional content** for a cheese and onion sandwich are shown below.

a) Give one reason why the food label gives the nutritional content per 100 g.

So customers can make an informed choice by comparing the nutritional information of similar products.

[1 mark]

Ingredients
Wholemeal bread
Cheddar cheese
Spring onions
Butter
Flavourings
(chives, pepper, salt)

Nutrient	100 g contains
Energy	287.3 kcal
Fat	16.5 g
Saturates	5.4 g
Carbohydrates	24.5 g
Sugars	2.1 g
Fibre	3.3 g
Protein	10.2 g
Salt	1.0 g

b) Suggest **one** way the saturated fat content of the sandwich could be reduced.

There are other examples here —
Use a low-fat spread instead of butter. e.g. you could use a reduced-fat cheese.

[1 mark]

2 Complete the table below by suggesting **one** dish that uses minced beef and explaining why it is suitable for that age group.

	Dish that uses minced beef	Why is this dish suitable for this age group?
Children	Mini burgers with baked potato wedges and salad.	'Mini' burgers would be an appropriate portion size for children.
Teenagers	Beef moussaka with Greek salad.	Moussaka is made with a cheese sauce, which is high in calcium for healthy bone and teeth development.
Elderly adults	Cottage pie with sweet potato mash	This dish has a distinct aroma, which is important as the senses of taste and smell diminish with age.

[6 marks]

There are lots of answers here — as long as your dishes are appropriate for each age group, you'll get the marks.

Exam Questions

1   Your **PAL** is needed to calculate your daily energy requirement.

a)   Describe what is meant by PAL.

....

....
[2 marks]

b)   Why may an injured athlete have to change their diet to maintain a healthy weight?

....

....

....

....
[3 marks]

2   The ingredients for a pasta bake are shown in the table below.
Sammy wants to modify the pasta bake to meet healthy eating guidelines.

Suggest how he could modify the ingredients below to meet these guidelines.
The modification for plain flour has been done for you.

Ingredient	Amount	How could he modify this ingredient?
Full fat milk	1 litre	....
Garlic, crushed	Two cloves	
Dried pasta	500 g	....
Butter	75 g	....
Plain flour	75 g	Use a wholemeal flour or a nutritious alternative, e.g. coconut flour.
Parsley	Small bunch	
Mustard powder	1 tbsp	
Cheese, grated (Cheddar or Gruyère)	200 g	....

[4 marks]

Revision Questions for Section One

That's your lot for <u>Section One</u> — go back and revise any tricky bits before attempting these questions.

- Try these questions and <u>tick off each one</u> when you <u>get it right</u>.
- When you've done <u>all the questions</u> for a topic and are <u>completely happy</u> with it, tick off the topic.

Protein, Fats and Carbohydrates (p.1-6) ☐

1) Give three reasons our bodies need proteins. ☑
2) Describe the health problems caused by a) an excess of protein   b) a deficiency of protein ☑
3) Name four 'alternative proteins'. ☑
4) Give three reasons our bodies need fats. ☑
5) Explain the difference between saturated and unsaturated fats. ☑
6) What are the functions of omega-3 and omega-6 fatty acids in the diet? ☑
7) Describe four effects caused by   a) an excess of fat   b) a deficiency of fat ☑
8) Describe three effects caused by a) an excess of carbohydrates   b) a deficiency of carbohydrates ☑

Vitamins, Minerals, Fibre and Water (p.10-13) ☐

9) For each fat-soluble vitamin, A, D, E and K: a) Give an example of a food it can be found in
   b) Explain why the body needs it   c) Explain a risk of having a deficiency of it ☑
10) List five foods that are rich in B-vitamins. ☑
11) Explain the importance of the following vitamins in our diet:
    a) B1 (thiamin)   b) B2 (riboflavin)   c) B9 (folic acid)   d) B12   e) C (ascorbic acid) ☑
12) Explain the importance of these minerals in our diet:
    a) Calcium   b) Iron   c) Sodium   d) Phosphorous   e) Potassium   f) Magnesium ☑
13) Why is fibre needed for our digestive systems? ☑
14) Explain why it's important to keep the body hydrated. ☑

Healthy Eating Guidelines and Nutritional Needs (p.16-18) ☐

15) Sketch and label each section of the 'Eatwell Guide'. ☑
16) Describe the nutritional needs for:
    a) babies and toddlers   b) children   c) teenagers   d) early adulthood   e) late adulthood ☑

Diet-Related Health Problems (p.19-20) ☐

17) Describe the causes and health problems for the following:
    a) obesity   b) cardiovascular disease   c) anaemia   d) type 2 diabetes ☐
18) Explain what the following health problems are and how you could prevent them:
    a) rickets   b) osteoporosis   c) tooth decay ☐

Energy Needs, Nutritional Analysis and Planning Meals (p.23-28) ☐

19) What is: a) basal metabolic rate (BMR)   b) physical activity level (PAL)? ☑
20) What is nutritional analysis? Where can you find nutritional data? ☑
21) Give one example of how you can modify a recipe to:
    a) reduce sugar   b) reduce salt   c) reduce saturated fat   d) increase fibre ☑
22) Draw a table that could be used to calculate the cost of a recipe. ☑
23) Give two examples of equipment used to control portion size. ☐
24) Plan a meal for each dietary requirement below. Explain why you chose each ingredient.
    a) lactose intolerance   b) cardiovascular disease   c) coeliac disease   d) lacto-ovo vegetarian ☑

Why Food is Cooked

We all love food — we even have at least three moments in the day dedicated to it. This section explains <u>why</u> we cook food, the <u>different ways</u> we cook it and the <u>science</u> behind these methods — let's get started...

Food is Cooked for Many Different Reasons

<u>Different cooking methods</u> change our food in <u>different ways</u> — these include changes to <u>sensory properties</u> (<u>appearance</u>, <u>texture</u>, <u>flavour</u> and <u>smell</u>) and changes to <u>nutritive value</u>. Below are some of the reasons why we cook — keep them in mind as you read this section, as lots of the information relates back to these points:

To make it safe to eat

1) Many food sources (including <u>meat</u>, <u>poultry</u> and <u>eggs</u>) can contain <u>harmful bacteria</u> that can make us ill. Luckily, bacteria can be <u>killed</u> if food is cooked long enough at a <u>high temperature</u> (see p.51).

2) Some foods contain <u>harmful toxins</u> that are <u>destroyed</u> when the food is cooked — e.g. <u>red kidney beans</u> have to be soaked, boiled and simmered before they are safe to eat, crikey!

To improve shelf life

1) When foods are cooked at high temperatures, <u>bacteria</u> and <u>mould</u> are <u>destroyed</u> (see p.51).

2) This is one of the ways that food can be <u>preserved</u> during the manufacturing process.

3) E.g. milk is <u>pasteurised</u> (heated to a high temperature and cooled) — this helps it stay <u>fresh</u> for <u>longer</u>.

To develop flavour

1) <u>Chemical reactions</u> take place during cooking that <u>change</u> the <u>flavour</u> of the food. E.g. <u>caramelisation</u> can occur when onions are cooked, making them taste <u>sweeter</u> (see p.41).

2) <u>Roasting</u> meats and vegetables creates more <u>intense flavours</u>. The food becomes <u>browner</u> and <u>crispier</u> with more <u>fat added</u> to it and as <u>water evaporates</u> from inside the food.

3) Cooking also allows the flavours of <u>different foods</u> to <u>combine</u>, e.g. when braising a meat in a pot of <u>liquid</u> and <u>veg</u> (see p.35).

To improve texture

1) Cooking usually makes it <u>easier</u> for us to <u>chew</u>, <u>swallow</u> and <u>digest</u> our food.

2) Some foods become <u>softer</u> when they're cooked. E.g. vegetables like broccoli and carrots become <u>more flexible</u> and foods like rice and pasta swell as their <u>starch molecules soften</u> (see p.41).

3) Meats become more <u>tender</u> (softer, more succulent and easier to chew) as <u>solid fats</u> in the food <u>melt</u> and <u>proteins</u> in the food <u>denature</u> (see p.40).

4) Other foods become <u>firm</u> when they're cooked. E.g. the <u>proteins</u> in egg whites <u>coagulate</u> (see p.40) — this turns the food <u>opaque</u> and more <u>solid</u>.

5) However, meats can become <u>tough</u> and egg whites <u>rubbery</u> if they are <u>overcooked</u>.

6) A change in texture can also make food <u>more pleasant</u> to eat — e.g. roast potatoes have a <u>soft centre</u> but a <u>crispy outside</u>, and baked bread has a <u>light-textured</u> inside but a <u>crusty</u> outside.

To give variety in the diet

1) Foods can be cooked in <u>different ways</u> to create <u>variety</u>.

2) For example, if you had a craving for beef you could satisfy it with <u>grilled steak</u>, <u>roast beef</u>, <u>beef stew</u>, <u>pan-fried minced beef</u> for a spaghetti Bolognese or a <u>barbecued burger</u> to name only a few.

Sensory properties include the look, taste, texture and aroma of food...

Changing the sensory properties of our food is all about making it more palatable (appealing) — if I had to choose between a delicious, tender roast chicken or a tasteless, tough one I know which I would choose.

Heat Transfer

Now it's time for a page of <u>hard-boiled science</u> — it's all about the different ways we use <u>heat</u> when <u>cooking</u>.

Heat can be Transferred in Three Different Ways

Food is cooked using <u>heat energy</u>. Transferring heat energy means <u>moving</u> it from one place to another — this happens in <u>three</u> different ways:

Conduction

1) <u>Conduction</u> is the <u>transfer of heat energy</u> through the <u>vibration</u> of particles.

2) In a solid, the particles are held tightly together. So when one particle <u>vibrates</u>, it <u>bumps into</u> other particles nearby and quickly passes the vibrations on.

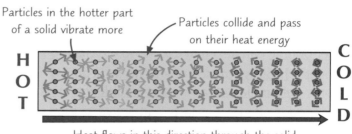

Particles in the hotter part of a solid vibrate more

Particles collide and pass on their heat energy

H O T

C O L D

Heat flows in this direction through the solid.

3) When a pan is placed on a hob, <u>heat energy</u> from the hob causes particles in the pan to <u>vibrate</u> more and gain heat energy.

4) When these particles <u>collide</u> with nearby particles, they <u>pass</u> some of their extra <u>heat energy</u> on to them.

5) This process continues throughout the pan until the heat has passed <u>all the way</u> through.

6) When food is placed into the hot pan, <u>heat energy</u> is transferred from the particles in the <u>pan</u> to the particles in the <u>food</u> in a similar way until the food is cooked through.

7) <u>Metals</u> are <u>good conductors</u> of <u>heat</u>. This is why most pans are made out of metal — so energy from the cooker is <u>quickly</u> transferred to the pan and its contents.

Convection

1) <u>Convection</u> is the <u>transfer of heat energy</u> through <u>gases</u> (e.g. air) or <u>liquids</u>.

2) When you <u>heat</u> up a liquid, the liquid near the heat source warms up <u>faster</u>.

3) The <u>warmer liquid rises</u> above its colder surroundings — like a hot air balloon does.

4) As the warm liquid rises, <u>colder liquid</u> takes its place.

5) This colder liquid is <u>heated</u> and when it starts to rise, colder liquid takes its place.

6) As this process continues, you end up with a <u>circulation</u> of fluid (<u>convection currents</u>) — after a while, this circulation of heat results in the <u>whole fluid</u> being <u>heated</u>.

7) Convection also occurs in <u>ovens</u> — <u>hot air rises</u> and <u>cooler air falls</u> in the same way.

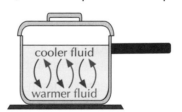

cooler fluid
warmer fluid

Radiation

1) <u>Radiation</u> is the <u>transfer</u> of <u>heat energy</u> through <u>waves of radiation</u> — it's like how radiation from the Sun heats up the Earth.

2) Unlike conduction and convection, there is <u>no direct contact</u> between the <u>heat source</u> and the <u>food</u>.

3) Cookers like <u>grills</u> and <u>toasters</u> use radiation to cook food.

4) They emit waves of radiation — when these waves reach the food, they are <u>absorbed</u> and <u>heat</u> the food up.

Bread being toasted. The glowing heating elements emit radiation.

5) <u>Microwaves</u> use radiation to heat up the <u>fat</u>, <u>sugar</u> and <u>water molecules</u> in our food.

EXAM TIP

We often use a mixture of these methods when cooking...

If you get an exam question asking how heat is transferred in a specific context, make sure you think about all three methods, and consider if a combination of them would be needed.

Cooking Methods — Water-Based

I don't know about you, but all this talk of cooking is starting to make me feel just a tiny bit <u>peckish</u>...

Water is Used to Cook in Lots of Different Ways

Boiling

- Boiling involves cooking food by heating it in a pan of <u>boiling liquid</u>, usually <u>water</u>.
- The types of food that are boiled include: tougher cuts of <u>meat</u>, <u>potatoes</u>, <u>rice</u>, <u>pasta</u> and <u>veg</u>.
- It's quite a <u>harsh</u> method of cooking and can't be used on delicate foods because the bubbles would break up the food — <u>over-boiling</u> can also make foods like pasta <u>too soft</u>.
- Boiling is a <u>healthy</u> way to cook as <u>no fat</u> is added. However, if veg is boiled for too long, <u>colour</u>, <u>flavour</u> and <u>water-soluble vitamins</u> (see p.11) are <u>lost</u> in the water.
- Boiled food is often not as <u>tasty</u> / <u>attractive</u> as food cooked by methods like roasting.
- However, boiling foods in a small amount of water with a <u>lid</u> covering the pan uses <u>less energy</u> than other methods, e.g. roasting or simmering.

When boiling, heat is transferred by <u>conduction</u> (from the pan to the liquid and through the food) and <u>convection</u> (through the liquid).

You can use the water from boiled food to make a tasty and nutritious stock or gravy.

Steaming

- Steaming means cooking food with <u>steam</u> from <u>boiling water</u> or <u>stock</u>.
- Foods you can steam include: <u>fish</u>, <u>rice</u> and <u>vegetables</u>.
- <u>No fat</u> is added and because there is <u>no direct contact</u> with <u>water</u>, the veg keep more of their <u>taste</u>, <u>texture</u>, <u>colour</u> and <u>nutrients</u> than if they'd been boiled — this makes it the <u>healthiest</u> way to cook. However, food may not have as much <u>flavour</u> compared to, say, <u>fried</u> or <u>roasted</u> food.
- Steaming is a <u>gentle</u> way to cook — so it's a good method for <u>delicate</u> foods such as fish, but not for tough meats.

When steaming, heat is transferred through <u>conduction</u> (from the pan to the water and through the food) and <u>convection</u> (through the steam).

Blanching

- Blanching involves <u>part-cooking</u> food in <u>boiling water</u> for a very short time before putting it in <u>cold</u> (or iced) <u>water</u>.
- The cold water <u>stops</u> the <u>cooking process</u> — this helps to preserve <u>colour</u>, <u>texture</u> and <u>vitamins</u>.
- Blanching can be used to <u>remove harsh flavours</u> in food, e.g. <u>raw onions</u> are blanched to give them a <u>milder taste</u>.
- Blanching foods like <u>tomatoes</u> and <u>almonds</u> makes their skins shrivel up, making the skins much <u>easier to remove</u>.
- It's also used to prepare <u>fruit</u> & <u>veg</u> for <u>freezing</u> (see p.50).

Simmering

- Simmering is like boiling, but more <u>gentle</u> as the <u>temperature</u> is slightly <u>lower</u> than boiling point (but still higher than when poaching).
- It's a very common cooking method for <u>soups</u> and <u>curries</u>.
- Simmering <u>preserves</u> more <u>nutrients</u> than boiling.

Poaching

- Poaching involves cooking food in a pan of liquid <u>below boiling point</u>, usually around <u>80 °C</u>.
- The types of food that are poached include: <u>eggs</u>, <u>fruit</u> and <u>fish</u>.
- Poaching is a <u>gentle</u> way to cook and it helps keep the food <u>tender</u>.
- Like with boiling, <u>nutrients</u> and <u>flavours</u> are transferred to the liquid, lowering the <u>nutritional content</u> and <u>tastiness</u> of the food.
- However, if food is poached in a <u>tasty sauce</u> (e.g. fish poached in a white sauce), the food can absorb <u>flavours</u> and give <u>variety</u>.

When poaching, heat is transferred through <u>conduction</u> (from the pan to the liquid and through the food) and <u>convection</u> (through the liquid).

Cooking Methods — Water-Based and Fat-Based

Braising

- Braising involves <u>slowly</u> cooking food in an ovenproof pot that has the lid on and contains <u>liquid</u> (usually water, stock or wine) and often <u>herbs</u> and <u>vegetables</u>.
- Food is cooked in the covered pot by a mixture of <u>simmering</u> and <u>steaming</u>.
- It's a great method for <u>big</u> or <u>tough</u> joints of <u>meat</u> because the gentle cooking of the meat helps to <u>tenderise</u> it.
- Before meat is braised, it's usually lightly fried to <u>brown</u> and <u>seal</u> it — this helps to keep <u>juices</u> inside the meat and gives it a <u>caramelised</u> flavour (see p.41).
- The <u>flavours</u> from the <u>liquid</u> and any <u>vegetables</u> and herbs in the pot are also <u>absorbed</u> by the joint — tasty.

When braising, heat is transferred through <u>conduction</u> (from the dish to the liquid and through the food) and <u>convection</u> (through the liquid and steam).

Frying Uses Hot Fat or Oil to Cook Food

When frying, <u>fat</u> or <u>oil</u> is heated to a <u>very high temperature</u>. Different types of frying use <u>different amounts</u> of <u>fat</u>:

Hot oil or fat can cause <u>serious burns</u>, and it's <u>highly flammable</u> — so using a large amount can be dangerous.

Stir-Frying

- Stir-frying tends to be done in a <u>wok</u> (a large round-based frying pan) coated in a <u>small amount</u> of oil, making it pretty healthy.
- Stir-fried foods include <u>noodles</u>, <u>vegetables</u>, <u>tofu</u> and small pieces of <u>meat</u> and <u>fish</u>.
- Food cooks <u>very quickly</u> and needs to be <u>moved</u> around the wok all the time so it doesn't burn — because they're cooked quickly, <u>vegetables</u> keep <u>more</u> of their <u>nutrients</u>.
- Stir-fried meals tend to have <u>more vegetables</u> than meat (some use no meat at all), making them a <u>healthy option</u>.

When frying, heat is transferred to the food by <u>conduction</u> (from the pan to the fat and through the food).

Stir-frying and shallow frying both increase the flavour of food because some of the fat is absorbed by the food as it cooks. Foods like onions also caramelise when they're fried, making them taste sweeter (see p.41).

Shallow Frying

- Shallow frying uses a frying pan coated in a <u>medium amount</u> of fat or oil.
- Shallow-fried foods include: <u>meat</u> (like chops, bacon and sausages), <u>fish</u>, <u>eggs</u> and <u>pancakes</u>.
- <u>More fat</u> is used when shallow frying than stir-frying, so it's a <u>less healthy</u> method of cooking. Solid fats in the food also <u>melt</u> into the pan as the food cooks, increasing the amount of fat in the pan even more.
- Shallow frying gives foods a <u>crispier texture</u> than stir-frying.

Another fat-based method of cooking is <u>sweating</u>. This method <u>releases moisture</u> from food, making it more <u>tender</u> and <u>sweet-tasting</u>. Sweating is most often used for <u>vegetables</u> such as onions, and uses a <u>small amount of oil</u> over a <u>low heat</u> — it's this low heat that allows the food to release moisture <u>without browning</u>. While the food is sweating, it's usually <u>covered with a lid</u> to help the moisture (in the form of steam) <u>circulate</u> around the food.

You're really steaming through this...

A key thing to remember is that the longer you cook with a water-based method, the more water-soluble vitamins (vitamins B & C) are transferred from the food to the water, lowering the nutritional value of the food.

Cooking Methods — Dry Methods

The next two pages of cooking methods focus on the <u>dry methods</u>: <u>baking</u>, <u>roasting</u>, <u>grilling</u> and <u>dry frying</u>.

Baking Uses Dry Heat to Cook Food

1) Baking cooks food using <u>dry heat</u>, usually in an <u>oven</u>.

2) Lots of different types of food can be baked, including:
   - <u>bread</u>, <u>pastries</u>, <u>cakes</u>, <u>pies</u> and <u>tarts</u>
   - <u>potatoes</u>
   - whole <u>fishes</u>, like sea bass or salmon

3) <u>Meat</u> is also baked, e.g. in meatloaf or casseroles, although <u>large pieces</u> of meat are usually <u>roasted</u> (see next page).

4) Because <u>hot air rises</u>, the <u>top</u> of an oven is often <u>hotter</u> than the bottom — that's why food cooks <u>quicker</u> on the top shelf than on the bottom shelf.

5) Modern <u>electric ovens</u> are usually <u>fan-assisted</u> (or "<u>convection ovens</u>") — they have a fan inside that helps to <u>circulate</u> the hot air around the oven. They're much more useful because...

   - food bakes more <u>evenly</u> because all parts of the oven are at a <u>similar temperature</u>.
   - the oven <u>heats up quicker</u> and your food <u>cooks quicker</u> — so they use <u>less energy</u>.

Heat is transferred around an oven by <u>radiation</u> and <u>convection</u>, and through the food by <u>conduction</u>.

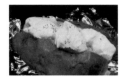

Baking food like fish or potatoes inside foil helps to keep the moisture in, making them nice and tasty.

Advantages	**Disadvantages**
• A <u>wide variety</u> of food can be baked. • The outside of the food <u>browns</u> and <u>crisps</u> up, which <u>looks</u> and <u>tastes nice</u>. • It's <u>quite healthy</u> because <u>no extra fat</u> is added, and solid fats in the food often leave as the food is baked.	• Baking food can take a <u>long</u> time. • Food can become <u>dried out</u>. • It uses a lot of <u>energy</u> as it requires the oven to be kept at a <u>high temperature</u> for a <u>long time</u>.

Fat Can Drip Off Food as It's Grilled

1) Grilling uses a <u>dry heat</u> at a <u>higher temperature</u> than baking or roasting to cook food.

2) As food is grilled, fats <u>drip out</u> of the food and the outside of the food becomes <u>golden</u> and <u>crisp</u>.

3) <u>Barbecuing</u> is similar to grilling, but heat radiates from <u>hot coals</u> and food is cooked at <u>lower temperatures</u> for <u>longer</u>.

4) You can grill many foods, such as: <u>smaller bits of meat</u> (like steaks and sausages), <u>vegetables</u> (like courgettes and aubergines) and <u>cheeses</u> (like halloumi or goats' cheese).

When grilling, heat is transferred to food through <u>radiation</u> (heat radiation from a grill, or hot coals when barbecuing) or <u>conduction</u> (if using a griddle pan).

In summer, we often grill food on a barbecue instead of "barbecuing" food in this slow way.

Advantages	**Disadvantages**
• Food cooks <u>quickly</u> at a high temperature. • It's fairly <u>healthy</u> as <u>no fat</u> is <u>added</u> and fat from the food <u>drips off</u> when cooked. • Just like roasting and baking, the golden outside of the food <u>looks</u> and <u>tastes</u> nice, and can have a lovely <u>crispy texture</u>. • Grilling on a <u>barbecue</u> gives food a <u>smoky flavour</u> which is very <u>popular</u>.	• The <u>high heat</u> used when grilling can make it hard to cook the food <u>evenly</u>. • It's easy to <u>burn</u> the food, or to end up with the outside cooked but the inside still <u>raw</u> — this could lead to food poisoning (see p.54). • Handling both raw and cooked meat on a barbecue might lead to <u>cross-contamination</u> (see p.53).

Cooking Methods — Dry Methods

Fat is **Added** to Food When It's **Roasted**

Heat is transferred around an oven by <u>radiation</u> and <u>convection</u>, and through the food by <u>conduction</u>.

1) Like baking, <u>roasting</u> uses dry heat from an <u>oven</u>.

2) Roasting is usually done at a <u>higher temperature</u> than baking, so foods cook and brown more quickly.

3) <u>Fat</u> is often added to the outside of the food, e.g. potatoes or veg, to help it <u>brown</u> and stay <u>moist</u>. Fat can be added or the fat that has melted from the food (e.g. chicken) can be put back on top — this is called <u>basting</u>.

4) Common types of food that are roasted include: <u>large cuts of meat</u> (such as a leg of lamb, a cut of beef or a whole chicken), <u>potatoes</u>, <u>vegetables</u> (e.g. root vegetables, peppers and onions) and <u>chestnuts</u> (on an open fire...)

Advantages

- Extra fat and a high temperature helps to <u>brown</u> and <u>crisp</u> the outside of food, which <u>looks</u> and <u>tastes delicious</u>.
- The fat from roasted meat can be used to <u>cook other food</u>, e.g. potatoes or fried bread.
- Roasted food can be tasty and <u>moist</u>.
- Roasting can produce meat with a <u>rare</u> (undercooked) centre, which a lot of people like.

Disadvantages

- Roasted food isn't always that <u>healthy</u>, as extra <u>fat</u> is often added.
- Just like baking, it takes a <u>long time</u> to roast food and uses a lot of <u>energy</u>.

Only certain types of meat (e.g. beef steak) can be served rare because of the dangers of food poisoning and parasites.

Dry Frying Does **Not** Use **Added Fat**

1) Dry frying means cooking food in a pan <u>without fat</u> or <u>oil</u>.

2) You can dry fry foods that contain <u>natural fat</u>, e.g. <u>minced meats</u>, and <u>bacon</u>. As the food heats up, the fats inside the food <u>melt</u> into the pan and begin to cook the food.

3) <u>Nuts</u>, seeds and <u>spices</u> can also be cooked in this way, although this method is usually called "<u>dry roasting</u>". This helps to release oils and bring out more flavour in the food.

4) Using a <u>medium heat</u> is important at the start of cooking to allow the fats to melt <u>without burning</u> the food — when the fat melts, the temperature can be increased as the fat starts to fry the food.

When dry frying, heat is transferred by <u>conduction</u> from the pan to the food.

Advantages

- <u>No extra fats</u> or oils are added, making this method <u>healthier</u> than other frying methods.
- Dry roasting can be used to give a more <u>distinct aroma</u> to <u>nuts</u>, seeds and <u>spices</u>.

Disadvantages

- It takes <u>longer</u> than other frying methods to cook meat thoroughly, because <u>lower temperatures</u> are needed at the start.
- It can only be used for a <u>small range</u> of food types compared to other cooking methods.

Time for a break, my brain's fried after all these methods...

Ahhh, there's nothing quite like the smell of baking wafting through the house... Apparently, a good way to remember something is to associate it with a smell. So get cooking and revising — perfect.

Warm-Up and Worked Exam Questions

A great way to learn how cooking methods affect food is to get in the kitchen and have a go at using them. You won't be able to cook in the exam, but luckily these questions will test that your knowledge is up to scratch.

Warm-Up Questions

1) Give one example of how cooking food can improve its flavour.
2) Explain the methods of heat transfer used to bring a pan of water to the boil.
3) Which method, boiling or steaming, is more suitable for cooking finely diced carrots?
4) Why is braising used to cook tough pieces of meat?
5) Which methods of heat transfer are used when baking a potato?
6) Give one benefit and one drawback of grilling food.

Worked Exam Questions

1   A cooker can transfer heat energy to food in different ways.

Try to visualise each cooking method (or sketch a quick diagram) to help you picture how heat energy is transferred.

Explain how heat energy is transferred when grilling halloumi.

Heat energy is transferred directly from the grill to the halloumi by (waves of) radiation, which are absorbed by the halloumi and heat it up.

[2 marks]

2   Benjamina has decided to **blanch** some broccoli.

a)   Describe the process of blanching.

Blanching involves part-cooking food in boiling water for a very short time before quickly putting the food into cold or iced water.

[2 marks]

b)   Blanching the broccoli will help to preserve vitamins. Give **one** other benefit of blanching the broccoli.

You could have given a different answer here — e.g. it helps to preserve colour / texture.

It will prepare the broccoli for freezing (and so extend its shelf life).

[1 mark]

3   Many people have roast turkey as part of their festive celebrations.

Give **one** benefit and **one** drawback of roasting turkey.

Benefit: *Extra fat is added to the turkey, which makes it look and taste better as it becomes browner and crispier.*

Drawback: *Roasting the turkey makes it less healthy, as extra fat is added.*

You'd get the marks for any suitable benefits and drawbacks of roasting turkey.

[2 marks]

Exam Questions

1 Lexie is using minced beef to make spaghetti Bolognese.
The recipe suggests she 'dry fries' the minced beef.

    a) Which method of heat transfer is used when dry frying?

....

[1 mark]

    b) Explain why minced beef is suitable for 'dry frying'.

....

....

[2 marks]

2 Meredith is cooking a roast chicken dinner for a group of friends.
She checks that the chicken is thoroughly cooked so it is safe to eat.

    a) Why will the chicken be safer to eat after Meredith has thoroughly cooked it?

....

....

[1 mark]

    b) Give **three** reasons why the chicken will be more appealing to eat after it has been cooked.

      1. ....

      2. ....

      3. ....

[3 marks]

3 Healthy eating guidelines suggest we reduce the amount of saturated fat in our diet.

Explain why stir-fried dishes are often healthier than those cooked with other frying methods.

....

....

....

....

....

[4 marks]

Changing Properties — Proteins

I hope you like <u>eggs</u>, because they're a great way to look at the <u>functional</u> and <u>chemical properties</u> of <u>proteins</u>. <u>Functional</u> = <u>how</u> they change food, <u>chemical</u> = the <u>science</u> behind these changes.

Proteins Denature During Preparation and Cooking

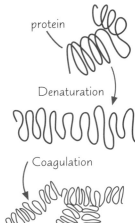

protein

Denaturation

Coagulation

1) Proteins (p.1) have a <u>complex structure</u>. When food is cooked, proteins <u>denature</u> — this means the <u>chemical bonds</u> holding their structure together <u>break down</u>.

2) The proteins <u>unravel</u> and their shape <u>changes</u> — in <u>most cases</u> this is <u>irreversible</u>.

3) Proteins can be denatured in different ways, including:
   - Physical <u>agitation</u> (e.g. whisking, beating and kneading)
   - Changes in <u>temperature</u> (e.g. heat)
   - <u>Acids</u> (e.g. lemon juice and marinades)

— Acidic marinades denature the protein in meat before cooking — this makes the meat more tender before you start cooking it.

Denatured Protein Molecules Coagulate

1) Once they have been <u>denatured</u>, protein molecules collide with other protein molecules and <u>coagulate</u> (join together).

2) During this process, <u>water</u> becomes <u>trapped</u> between the protein molecules.

3) Coagulation also changes the <u>appearance</u> and <u>texture</u> of the food. E.g. egg white turns from a <u>see-through liquid</u> into a <u>white solid</u>, while steak becomes <u>brown</u>, <u>firmer</u> and <u>easier to eat</u> as you cook it.

4) However, if food is <u>overcooked</u> and coagulation happens too much, the protein <u>tightens</u>. This forces <u>water out</u> of the molecules, making it <u>dry</u> and <u>chewy</u>.

When eggs are added to breadcrumb coatings and quiche mixtures, the process of protein coagulation helps hold everything together.

Foams are Formed When Air is Trapped

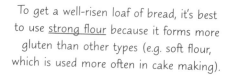

1) <u>Foams</u>, e.g. <u>chocolate mousse</u>, <u>whipped cream</u> or <u>cappuccino foam</u>, form when <u>gas</u> becomes <u>trapped</u> (aeration) inside <u>liquid</u>.

2) When liquids containing <u>proteins</u> are <u>agitated</u> (e.g. egg whites are whisked), the proteins inside the liquid <u>denature</u> — this causes them to <u>stretch</u> and <u>air</u> becomes <u>trapped</u> in the liquid.

3) When the proteins <u>coagulate</u>, this air becomes <u>trapped</u>, creating a foam.

4) However, <u>over-whisking</u> causes these new protein bonds to break — air escapes and the foam <u>collapses</u>.

5) Some foams form a <u>solid</u> structure when they are cooked, e.g. egg white foams become <u>meringues</u>.

Gluten Allows Doughs to Stretch and Rise

1) <u>Gluten</u> is a <u>protein</u> found in <u>wheat flours</u> (e.g. those made from <u>wheat</u>, <u>barley</u> and <u>rye</u>).

2) It's <u>formed</u> when <u>water</u> is mixed with the <u>flour</u> to make <u>dough</u> and can be found in foods like <u>bread</u>, <u>pasta</u>, <u>cakes</u> and <u>pastries</u>.

3) Molecules of gluten are <u>coiled</u> — this means they are able to stretch and bend — this gives all doughs <u>elasticity</u> (stretchiness).

4) Doughs need to be <u>kneaded</u> to 'work' the gluten — this causes gluten strands to get <u>longer</u>, <u>stronger</u> and <u>stretchier</u>.

5) When it reaches a high temperature, gluten <u>coagulates</u> (see above) and the <u>dough stays stretched</u>. This gives foods like well-risen bread a <u>light</u>, <u>airy texture</u>.

To get a well-risen loaf of bread, it's best to use <u>strong flour</u> because it forms more gluten than other types (e.g. soft flour, which is used more often in cake making).

REVISION TASK

Who knew proteins and eggs could be so useful?...

Draw a mind map of the ways proteins change during cooking — include changes to their chemical properties (e.g. molecules coagulate) and how this affects their functional ones (e.g. food gets firmer).

Changing Properties — Carbohydrates

For the exam you'll need to know about <u>three ways</u> in which <u>carbohydrates</u> change in food during cooking. If you need a <u>quick refresher</u> on carbohydrates before we get going, have a quick flick back to <u>pages 5-6</u>.

Starch **Gelatinisation** Thickens Liquids

1) <u>Gelatinisation</u> helps to <u>thicken</u> foods that contain starch, e.g. <u>sauces</u>, <u>custards</u> and <u>gravies</u>.

2) When <u>starch granules</u> are first mixed with liquid, they become <u>suspended</u> in it — if you don't stir the liquid these granules will sink to the bottom.

3) When the <u>granules</u> are heated with water, the bonds between starch <u>molecules</u> start to break, allowing <u>water molecules</u> to enter. As water is absorbed, the starch granules <u>swell</u> in size and <u>soften</u>.

4) Between <u>62 °C</u> and <u>80 °C</u>, the starch granules <u>burst open</u> and <u>release</u> their <u>starch</u> into the liquid.

5) This release of starch causes the liquid to <u>thicken</u>. How thick the liquid becomes depends on the ratio of starch to liquid in the mixture — the <u>higher</u> the <u>concentration of starch</u>, the <u>thicker</u> the <u>liquid</u>.

6) When it cools, the liquid <u>solidifies</u> and a <u>solid gel</u> is formed — this is useful for making 'set' desserts like <u>custards</u> and <u>lemon pie filling</u>.

Custards can also be set using gelatine or by the process of protein coagulation (see previous page).

7) Gelatinisation also happens when you cook starchy foods like <u>pasta</u> and <u>rice</u> — they swell, soften and release starch into the water as they cook.

Dextrinisation Occurs when **Starch** is Exposed to **Dry Heat**

1) When starchy foods such as <u>bread</u> or <u>biscuits</u> are cooked with <u>dry heat</u>, e.g. toasting or baking, the <u>starch molecules</u> in the food <u>break down</u> into smaller molecules called <u>dextrins</u>.

2) This breakdown is called <u>dextrinisation</u> and it gives food a <u>browner colour</u> and <u>crispier texture</u> as well as a <u>different taste</u> (imagine the difference in taste between bread and toast).

3) The <u>longer</u> the food is cooked, the <u>more starch</u> is converted into <u>dextrin</u> and the darker and crispier the food becomes.

Sugar **Caramelises** When it's Heated

1) Sugar molecules <u>break down</u> when they reach a <u>high temperature</u> — this causes sugar to turn <u>brown</u> and change <u>flavour</u>. This process is called <u>caramelisation</u>.

2) The sugar goes through various stages:
   - At first the liquid is runny and has a <u>very sweet</u> taste.
   - As time passes, it becomes more like a smooth <u>caramel</u>.
   - Eventually, it turns harder and as it cools it becomes more like a <u>candy</u>.

3) Caramelised sugar can <u>burn</u> very quickly, turning <u>black</u>, <u>brittle</u> and <u>bitter to taste</u>.

4) To avoid this, <u>water</u> is often added during the early stages of heating.

5) Caramelisation gives <u>desserts</u> such as a <u>crème brûlée</u> and <u>apple pie</u> extra sweetness.

6) Even <u>savoury foods</u> that contain <u>sugars</u> (e.g. onions) can <u>caramelise</u>. The sugars in the food are broken down and released, turning the food brown and adding sweetness.

The sugar doesn't actually caramelise until the water has evaporated, but the water helps to increase the temperature of the sugar without it burning.

These processes can occur in both sweet and savoury foods...

While it might be tempting to gloss over the tricky words on this page, it's important that you can spell them correctly in the exam — especially <u>gelatinisation</u>, <u>dextrinisation</u> and <u>caramelisation</u>.

Changing Properties — Fats and Oils

Fats and oils get a bad rap, but they're actually really useful for a variety of cooking situations...

Fats and Oils Have Lots of Different Uses

Aeration Means Incorporating Air

1) When fats such as butter are beaten with sugar (this process is called creaming) air becomes trapped in the mixture. This air makes the mixture fluffier and lighter in colour.

2) This aeration gives cakes a spongy and light texture when they're cooked.

3) Foods can be aerated in many different ways, e.g. whisking egg whites with a whisk or quickly beating ingredients with a spoon — there's more about this on p.44.

Oils don't trap air as easily as fats — oil-based doughs need something else to add air, e.g. baking powder (see page 44).

Shortening Gives Foods a Crumbly Texture

1) When you rub fat into flour, you cover the flour particles with fat — this gives the flour particles a waterproof coating.

2) This coating prevents long gluten molecules forming when water is added to the flour.

3) This means the dough cannot become stretchy and baked goods like shortbread keep a 'short' (firm and crumbly) texture — hence the name shortening.

4) Shortening is also used when making filled pies and tarts — it's helpful because the base doesn't rise and forms a solid case.

5) Some fats are called 'shortening' — they have 100% fat content (contain no water) which helps stop gluten formation and prevents steam from raising the food.

Plasticity Means Ability to be Spread and Shaped

1) Fats have 'plasticity' — we're able to spread and manipulate them.

2) This is possible because fats contain a mixture of different triglycerides (see p.3). These different triglycerides all melt at different temperatures — so fats gradually soften over a range of temperatures rather than melting at just one.

3) The more plasticity a fat has, the easier it is to spread.

Butter can be hard in the fridge, soft at room temperature and melty when it's heated.

4) You'll remember from p.3 that unsaturated fats tend to be soft or liquid at room temperature, while saturated fats tend to be solid — this means that the more unsaturated fatty acids a fat or oil contains, the more plasticity the fat or oil will have (e.g. it will be easier to spread).

5) Plasticity is useful for a range of different reasons, including:

- Decorating cakes with buttercream
- Rubbing fat into flour to make shortened dough (see above)
- Spreading butter on sandwiches and toast
- Putting cream cheese on crackers

6) Some vegetable fat spreads are marketed as being 'easy to spread'. This is because they contain a mixture of triglycerides with low melting points, meaning you can spread it as soon as you take it out of the fridge.

Changing Properties — Fats and Oils

We're not quite done with fats and oils yet. Time for the grand finale — emulsions...

Emulsification Keeps Oil and Water in a Stable Emulsion

1) Emulsions are formed when oily and watery liquids are shaken together (the droplets of one spread out through the other).

2) Milk, margarine and mayonnaise are all examples of emulsions.

3) Usually, oil and water don't mix together and so emulsions separate out again unless you keep shaking or stirring them — or use an emulsifier.

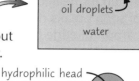
oil droplets
water

4) The molecules in an emulsifier have two different ends: one is hydrophilic (attracted to water) and the other is hydrophobic (repulsed by water).

hydrophilic head
hydrophobic tail

5) When you add an emulsifier, the water molecules bond to the hydrophilic side and the oil molecules bond to the hydrophobic side. This holds the oil and water together in a stable emulsion, preventing them from separating.

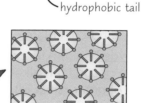

6) Emulsions can either be oil-in-water (e.g. milk, mayonnaise, salad dressings) or water-in-oil (e.g. margarine, butter).

7) Egg yolks contain a natural emulsifier called lecithin (also found in soya) — this is used as the emulsifier in margarine and mayonnaise.

> Mayonnaise is a stable emulsion of egg yolk, oil and vinegar. When making stable emulsions, you need to ensure you add the oil or water gradually and that you mix the ingredients for long enough.

You Can Use Emulsions for Sauces and Salad Dressings

1) Emulsions are often used as sauces (e.g. mayonnaise) and salad dressings (e.g. vinaigrette).

2) Hollandaise sauce is another example of an emulsion sauce — it's made from butter, water, egg yolks (the lecithin in it acts as an emulsifier) and lemon juice (for flavour).

3) Follow these steps to make a hollandaise sauce:

- Melt the butter in a pan.
- Mix the egg yolks and lemon juice in a bowl.
- Gently warm this mixture by placing the bowl over a pan of simmering water.
- Slowly add the melted butter to the mixture, constantly whisking as you do.
- Keep whisking the sauce until it's all mixed together smoothly.

> When making any oil-in-water emulsion, e.g. a sauce or dressing, it's important to add the liquid and emulsifier first, before very slowly adding the oil/fat while mixing vigorously.

It's important you know the various uses of fats and oils...

That's it for the functional properties of macronutrients — phew. It's tricky stuff, but make sure you understand it.

Raising Agents

Unless you're craving pancakes, a flat, dense cake is not a good thing — this is why we use <u>raising agents</u>. Raising agents add gas (to doughs and mixtures) which <u>expands when heated</u> to create the rise.

Some Raising Agents Produce **Carbon Dioxide**...

Chemical

- When it's heated, <u>bicarbonate of soda</u> breaks down to produce <u>carbon dioxide</u> bubbles that expand to make the mixture <u>rise</u>.
- It has an unpleasant <u>alkaline</u> (soapy) taste, so it needs to be used with a <u>strong flavour</u> to mask it. This is why it's used in things like <u>gingerbread</u> and <u>chocolate cake</u>.
- <u>Baking powder</u> is a mixture of <u>bicarbonate of soda</u> (an alkali) and <u>cream of tartar</u> (an acid). A <u>neutralisation reaction</u> takes place when baking powder is heated which gets rid of the horrid soapy taste.
- <u>Self-raising flours</u> contain a mixture of <u>plain flour</u> and <u>baking powder</u>.

Biological

- <u>Yeast</u> is a <u>biological</u> raising agent used in bread dough.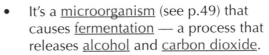
- It's a <u>microorganism</u> (see p.49) that causes <u>fermentation</u> — a process that releases <u>alcohol</u> and <u>carbon dioxide</u>.
- Doughs containing yeast are often <u>proved</u> (left in a warm place to allow fermentation to take place).
- This stage is important because it's when the carbon dioxide is released and trapped in the dough, causing it to rise — <u>fermentation stops</u> during <u>baking</u> as the yeast is killed by the heat.
- When the dough is baked, the <u>carbon dioxide</u> <u>expands</u>, causing the bread to <u>rise</u> even more — any <u>alcohol</u> produced by the yeast <u>evaporates</u> at this stage.

Using too much of a raising agent can actually cause cakes to sink — *see p.101 for more about sinking cakes.*

...Others **Add Steam** or **Air** to the Mixture

Steam

- When you use a very hot oven to cook a mixture that deliberately contains a lot of <u>liquid</u> (e.g. <u>batters</u>, <u>puff pastry</u> and <u>choux pastry</u>), water leaves the mixture as <u>steam</u>. As the <u>steam rises</u> it <u>raises</u> the mixture up.
- As the water leaves, the food bakes and becomes more <u>solid</u>. However, it's important to keep the oven door <u>closed</u> or the <u>cold air</u> from outside will cause the mixture to <u>sink</u>.

Mechanical

- We can <u>add air</u> into mixtures with just a little bit of good old-fashioned <u>elbow grease</u>:
- Air can be <u>folded</u> into mixtures and doughs in two different ways:

  1) To "fold" a <u>cake mixture</u>, you <u>carefully</u> use a spoon or spatula to repeatedly <u>pour</u> the liquid mixture over itself — <u>trapping air</u> each time.
  2) <u>Pastry doughs</u> can actually be folded into layers, trapping air <u>in between the layers</u> each time you fold.

- <u>Beating</u> is a more vigorous method where you use a spoon or fork to <u>mix ingredients</u> and <u>quickly</u> drive air into the mixture — e.g. beating eggs and sugar in a mixing bowl.
- <u>Whisking</u> is the same as beating, but you use a <u>whisk</u> instead.
- When you <u>sieve</u> flour, air becomes trapped between the individual <u>flour particles</u>.
- Air is also added when <u>creaming</u>, e.g. creaming butter and sugar, and between flour particles when you <u>rub fat</u> into flour (see p.42).

Some raising agents are more suitable for certain recipes...

Plan an investigation into the most suitable raising agent to use in a chocolate cake. You'll need to do some <u>research</u> using a range of resources, come up with a <u>prediction</u>, and explain how you could test if your prediction is true (there's more about planning tasks on p.109).

Warm-Up and Worked Exam Questions

Congratulations, that's it for this section. The only thing standing between you and the Food Safety section is this series of question pages to make sure that you're an expert in everything related to Food Science.

Warm-Up Questions

1) Name the processes that occur when frying an egg.
2) How are foams formed (in relation to food)?
3) Explain why onions can develop a sweet taste when they are fried in oil or fat.
4) Describe how shortening affects the texture of baked goods.
5) What is meant by 'hydrophilic' and 'hydrophobic'?
6) Why wouldn't you use bicarbonate of soda to raise a plain sponge cake?

Worked Exam Questions

1   The sensory properties of bread change when it is toasted.

   a)   Name the process that causes these changes.

   Dextrinisation

   [1 mark]

   b)   Explain what happens in this process.

   The more starch is converted into dextrin, the darker and crispier the bread becomes.

   Starch molecules in the bread break down into smaller molecules called dextrins

   when exposed to heat, giving the bread a browner colour and crispier texture.

   [2 marks]

2   Jen is making a quiche. After each step of the recipe she writes down some notes.
     Explain the changes Jen has noticed for each of the following steps.

Recipe	Jen's Notes	Why have these changes occurred?
Step 5: Place the quiche in the centre of a pre-heated oven and bake for half an hour at Gas Mark 5 (190 °C).	"After half an hour, the quiche mixture started to set around the edges. I will keep it in the oven a little longer to firm up."	The quiche set because the proteins in the mixture denatured when they were exposed to heat and then coagulated (joined together), making the mixture firmer.
Step 6: Remove the quiche from the oven when it has developed a golden colour.	"The quiche has developed a rubbery texture."	The quiche has been cooked for too long and the proteins have coagulated too much, forcing water out of the mixture (leaving it dry and rubbery).

[4 marks]

Exam Questions

1   When making a cake using the **creaming method**, fat and sugar are beaten together.

Why are fat and sugar beaten together in this method?

....
[1 mark]

2   **Gluten** is a protein that's formed when water is added to flour.

a)   Explain **one** role of gluten in bread-making.

....

....
[2 marks]

b)   Name the process that stops gluten from forming long strands.

....
[1 mark]

c)   Explain how rubbing fat into flour creates these short strands of gluten.

....

....
[2 marks]

3   The table below shows which raising agents are most commonly used in different products.

Product	Raising Agent
Baguette	Yeast
Chocolate eclair	Steam
Gingerbread man	Bicarbonate of soda

a)   Give **two** conditions yeast needs to work effectively:

1.   ....

2.   ....
[2 marks]

b)   i)   Why does choux pastry dough have a 'runnier' consistency than traditional dough?

....
[1 mark]

ii)   Why is this consistency needed to ensure the choux pastry rises properly?

....
[1 mark]

c)   Explain why bicarbonate of soda is suitable for gingerbread.

....

....
[2 marks]

Exam Questions

4 Different fats have different ranges of **plasticity**.

   a) What is meant by the plasticity of fats?

      ....

      [1 mark]

   b) Explain why margarine has more plasticity than lard.

      ....

      ....

      [2 marks]

5 **Hollandaise sauce** is an example of an **emulsion sauce**.
It is made from butter, water, egg yolks and lemon juice.

Outline the role of egg yolks in a hollandaise sauce.

....

....

....

....

      [3 marks]

6 A **roux-based sauce** is made using butter, plain flour and milk.

Explain how gelatinisation occurs in a roux-based sauce.

Psst... the key to gelatinisation is the starch in the flour.

....

....

....

....

....

      [4 marks]

7 George is making a cake for his friend's birthday. In addition to using a chemical raising agent, George plans to add air to the mixture by hand.

Discuss the methods George could use to mechanically aerate the cake mixture.

      [8 marks]

Revision Questions for Section Two

That's it for Section Two — put your Food Science knowledge to the test with a round of quick-fire questions.

- Try these questions and tick off each one when you get it right.
- When you've done all the questions for a topic and are completely happy with it, tick off the topic.

Why Food is Cooked and Heat Transfer (p.32-33) ☐

1) Give five reasons why food is cooked.
2) Explain in terms of particles how heat is transferred by conduction.
3) Which would be the most suitable material for a frying pan: metal or wood?
4) Explain how convection helps a liquid or gas to be heated.
5) Which method of heat transfer is used when toasting a slice of bread?

Cooking Methods (p.34-37) ☐

6) Boiling and steaming are two water-based methods of cooking.
   a) Which of these methods involves direct contact with food?
   b) Which of these methods produces the more nutritious food?
7) Explain why food is plunged into cold water during blanching.
8) Give one similarity and one difference between braising and poaching.
9) Give a benefit of poaching over boiling.
10) Which fat-based method of cooking is most suitable for cooking pancakes?
11) Explain the difference between grilling and roasting.
12) List the advantages and disadvantages of these cooking methods:
    a) simmering   b) baking   c) stir-frying   d) roasting   e) dry frying

Changing Properties (p.40-43) ☐

13) Give three ways proteins can be denatured.
14) Describe the process of protein coagulation and explain how it affects the texture of food.
15) Explain how foam formation happens in whisked egg whites.
16) What is the name of the protein that gives bread dough its elasticity?
17) Explain how starch can be used to thicken cheese sauce.
18) Name the process that makes biscuits browner and crispier when they're baked.
19) Name and describe the process that takes place when sugar is cooked at a high temperature.
20) What does the term 'aeration' mean?
21) Explain how you can prevent gluten molecules from forming long strands.
22) What is the name given to a fat's ability to be shaped?
23) Explain how emulsifiers can be used to keep oil and water in a stable emulsion.

Raising Agents (p.44) ☐

24) What are the differences between bicarbonate of soda, baking powder and self-raising flour?
25) Name one biological raising agent and explain how it can be used to raise bread dough.
26) Explain how a Yorkshire pudding (a food made from batter) is risen by steam.
27) Describe six ways you could mechanically incorporate air into a cake mixture.

Food Spoilage

Microorganisms are <u>tiny living things</u> found in <u>air</u>, <u>water</u>, <u>soil</u>, on <u>people</u>... basically <u>everywhere</u>. Most are <u>harmless</u>, but <u>pathogenic</u> ones can <u>spoil</u> food (make it <u>go off</u>) and cause <u>food poisoning</u>.

Microorganisms Grow in the Right Conditions

<u>Microorganisms</u>, e.g. <u>bacteria</u>, <u>moulds</u> and <u>yeasts</u> need <u>five conditions</u> to quickly grow and <u>multiply</u>:

1) A <u>warm temperature</u>
2) Plenty of <u>moisture</u> (water)
3) Plenty of <u>food</u>
4) The right <u>pH</u> (not too <u>acidic</u> or <u>alkaline</u>)
5) Enough <u>time</u>
   (in ideal conditions, bacteria split every <u>10-20 minutes</u>)

Temperature   Moisture

Food   pH   Time

<u>Pathogenic</u> microorganisms can <u>spoil</u> food (make it <u>go off</u>) and cause <u>food poisoning</u>.
Pathogenic means something that can produce disease.

Changing any <u>one</u> of these <u>conditions</u> will <u>slow</u> or <u>stop</u> the growth of microorganisms altogether. For example, you could:

- Use a <u>fridge</u> to change the <u>temperature</u> (see p.51).
- <u>Pickle</u> the food in <u>vinegar</u> to change the <u>pH</u>.
- Add <u>salt</u> — salt <u>absorbs water</u> (removes moisture) from the food, <u>drying</u> it out.

High Risk Foods Have Ideal Conditions for Bacteria

1) <u>High risk foods</u> are <u>ready-to-eat</u> foods that, if not <u>stored correctly</u>, could grow <u>harmful bacteria</u>.
2) They satisfy points <u>2 and 3</u> above — they're <u>moist</u> and <u>high in protein</u> (protein = <u>food</u> for bacteria).

High Risk Foods
- <u>cooked meat</u>, <u>fish</u> and <u>poultry</u>
- <u>dairy products</u> (eggs, <u>cheese</u>, etc.)
- <u>gravies</u>, <u>stocks</u> and <u>sauces</u>
- <u>shellfish</u>
- <u>cooked</u> rice

3) High risk foods have a <u>short shelf life</u> — you can't keep them for long, or the bacteria might multiply to <u>dangerous levels</u>.

The shelf life of a food is the length of time it can safely be kept for.

4) A <u>raw food</u>, e.g. <u>chicken</u>, might have lots of bacteria but it's <u>not</u> classed as a high risk food because you don't eat it <u>raw</u>. Once it's <u>cooked</u> and 'ready-to-eat' it can be described as <u>high risk</u>.
5) You can sometimes <u>identify</u> when a high risk food is <u>spoiling</u> — e.g. meat going <u>slimy</u>, milk smelling <u>sour</u> or cheese going <u>mouldy</u>...
6) ...but often <u>pathogenic bacteria</u> leave <u>no signs</u> — <u>taste</u>, <u>colour</u>, <u>odour</u> and <u>texture</u> aren't affected.
7) You can check there are no <u>visible</u> signs of spoilage when <u>buying food</u>:
   - <u>Fresh meat</u> should be brightly coloured, firm and have a fresh smell.
   - <u>Fresh fish</u> should have shiny skin, red gills, clear eyes and smell clean or slightly salty.
   It's best to source fresh food from <u>reputable suppliers</u> — they will have strict health and safety procedures for high risk foods.

Double, double, spoil and trouble...

Microorganisms, such as bacteria, multiply much more quickly in the right conditions. Luckily, you're able to slow the rate at which they do so by changing one or more of the factors above. Phew.

Food Spoilage

Fruit and vegetables <u>change</u> over time — e.g. <u>unripe</u> blackberries are <u>green</u> and <u>turn black</u> when they are <u>ripe</u>. This is the work of <u>enzymes</u>...

Enzymes are Biological Catalysts

<u>Enzymes</u> are <u>special proteins</u> that act as <u>biological catalysts</u> — they <u>speed up</u> chemical <u>reactions</u>. You can see the <u>effects</u> of enzymes in many <u>fruits</u> and <u>vegetables</u>:

Ripening
- <u>Enzymes</u> in fruit cause them to <u>ripen</u>, which affects the <u>sweetness</u>, <u>colour</u> and <u>texture</u> of the fruit.
- E.g. <u>Unripe</u> bananas are <u>green</u> and <u>firm</u> — enzymes <u>break down</u> <u>starch</u> inside them which makes the banana <u>softer</u> and <u>sweeter</u>.

Ripening enzymes

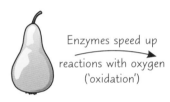

Enzymes speed up reactions with oxygen ('oxidation')

Browning
- When you <u>slice</u> fruits (apples, pears etc.), the <u>oxygen</u> in the air will turn the fruit <u>brown</u> (oxidation). Enzymes inside the fruit <u>speed up</u> this process.
- Leaving some fruit (bananas, avocados etc.) to <u>overripen</u> will give them a <u>brown colour</u> too.

These are examples of <u>enzymic browning</u>.

The <u>actions</u> of <u>enzymes</u> on food is a type of <u>natural decay</u> that causes <u>food spoilage</u>.

You Can Slow or Stop an Enzyme From Working

You can have some <u>control</u> over the <u>activity</u> of enzymes — here are a few <u>methods</u> that will <u>slow</u> or <u>prevent</u> the <u>unwanted</u> effects of enzymes:

- <u>Adding an acid</u> — enzymes <u>work best</u> at a <u>certain pH</u>. If you dip slices of fruit into <u>lemon juice</u>, the acidic conditions will <u>stop enzymic browning</u>.

- <u>Blanching</u> (plunging into <u>boiling water</u> for a short period — see p.34) is used to <u>prepare</u> vegetables for <u>freezing</u>. Natural <u>ripening enzymes</u> will cause veg to lose <u>colour</u>, <u>texture</u>, <u>flavour</u> and <u>nutrients</u> over time. Freezing will <u>slow down</u> the enzymes but not stop them completely. Blanching <u>destroys</u> the ripening enzymes, so the vegetables <u>retain</u> their colour, nutrients etc.

Mould and Yeast Can Spoil Food Too

1) <u>Moulds</u> and <u>yeasts</u> are both <u>microorganisms</u> (fungi) — this means in the right conditions (<u>warmth</u>, <u>moisture</u> etc.) they can <u>grow</u> and <u>spread</u> quickly.
2) Moulds spoil <u>bread</u>, <u>cheese</u> and <u>fruit</u> — they can change the <u>look</u>, <u>smell</u> and <u>taste</u> of the food. You can easily spot mould due to its 'fuzzy' appearance.
3) <u>Waste products</u> from moulds can cause <u>food poisoning</u> — even if you <u>scrape</u> it off, <u>toxins</u> may still remain.
4) <u>Yeasts</u> commonly grow on the surfaces of <u>fruit</u>, e.g. <u>grapes</u>, <u>blackberries</u> and <u>tomatoes</u>, and spoil fruit by <u>fermenting</u> the sugars into <u>alcohol</u> and <u>carbon dioxide</u>.
5) Mould and yeast growth can be <u>prevented</u> by <u>correctly storing</u> food, e.g. storing <u>bread</u> in <u>dry, cool conditions</u> and most <u>fruits</u> in the <u>fridge</u>.

For wine production (see p.55) this 'spoiling' has a <u>desirable</u> effect.

The action of enzymes and microorganisms both cause food spoilage...

Enzymic browning, mould and yeast growth aren't usually desirable in food. They can be useful though — e.g. different types of tea can be made by controlling the amount of browning on the tea leaves. Neat.

Storing Food Safely

I like to eat food straight away — but some people out there like to <u>preserve</u> it. Where's the fun in that...

The **Right Temperature** is **Vital** to **Storing Food Safely**

To <u>preserve</u> food, you need to keep it in <u>conditions</u> that <u>bacteria can't grow</u> in.
First up, there are some <u>critical temperatures</u> that affect bacterial growth:

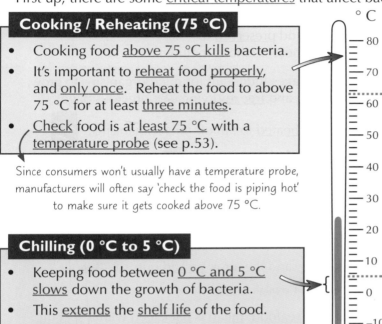

°C

Cooking / Reheating (75 °C)

- Cooking food <u>above 75 °C kills</u> bacteria.
- It's important to <u>reheat</u> food <u>properly</u>, and <u>only once</u>. Reheat the food to above 75 °C for at least <u>three minutes</u>.
- <u>Check</u> food is at <u>least 75 °C</u> with a <u>temperature probe</u> (see p.53).

Since consumers won't usually have a temperature probe, manufacturers will often say 'check the food is piping hot' to make sure it gets cooked above 75 °C.

The Danger Zone (5 °C to 63 °C)

- Bacteria grow and multiply <u>quickly</u> in temperatures from <u>5 °C to 63 °C</u>. This is called the <u>danger zone</u>.
- Hot food should be held <u>above 63 °C</u>.
- The <u>optimum temperature</u> for bacterial growth is <u>37 °C</u>.

This is your normal <u>body temperature</u>.

Freezing (−18 °C)

- Freezing food below <u>−18 °C</u> <u>stops bacteria growing</u> — they become <u>dormant</u>.
- Freezing <u>greatly extends</u> the <u>shelf life</u> of the food and the <u>nutrients aren't lost</u>.
- It <u>doesn't kill</u> the bacteria though. They become <u>active</u> again when the food defrosts.

Chilling (0 °C to 5 °C)

- Keeping food between <u>0 °C</u> and <u>5 °C</u> <u>slows</u> down the growth of bacteria.
- This <u>extends</u> the <u>shelf life</u> of the food.
- Chilling food doesn't change its properties much — chilled food <u>looks</u> and <u>tastes</u> the same — but it may have a <u>harder texture</u>.

Use a **Fridge** and **Freezer Correctly**

Fridges
- Fridges should be <u>0 °C to 5 °C</u>, ideal for <u>chilling</u> foods (especially <u>high risk</u> foods).
- Keep food <u>covered</u> or <u>stored in containers</u> to prevent <u>contaminating</u> other foods.
- Don't let the <u>blood</u> and <u>juices</u> of raw meat <u>drip</u> onto other food — <u>always</u> store raw <u>meat</u>, <u>poultry</u> and <u>fish</u> on the <u>bottom shelf</u> in the fridge.

Freezers
- Freezers are set at around <u>−18 °C</u>.
- Food should have <u>clear labels</u> with the <u>date</u> they were frozen.
- <u>Defrost</u> meat and poultry <u>thoroughly</u> in a <u>fridge</u> — if food is <u>partially frozen</u> the recommended <u>cooking time</u> may not be sufficient to <u>kill bacteria</u>...
- ...or if <u>cooking from frozen</u>, follow the '<u>cook from frozen</u>' time.

You should also not overstock a fridge or freezer — air can't circulate so heat can't be removed efficiently.

<u>Freezers</u> and <u>frozen foods</u> use a <u>star rating</u> to indicate how long to <u>store</u> food:

Storing in an ice box / freezer compartment of a fridge:
- * **1 week** (−6 °C)
- ** **1 month** (−12 °C)

Storing in a domestic freezer:
- *** **3 months** (−18 °C)
- **** Until '**best before**' end date on frozen foods (−18 °C or colder)

<u>Industrial processes</u> use special equipment to rapidly <u>chill</u> or <u>freeze</u> food:

If you're <u>not</u> doing the <u>OCR</u> course, you can skip to the next page.

- <u>Cook-freezing</u>: food is <u>cooked</u> and <u>rapidly frozen</u> to below <u>−18 °C</u>.
- <u>Blast-chilling</u>: a <u>blast chiller</u> (similar to a fridge) <u>rapidly cools</u> cooked food to <u>below 5 °C</u> within <u>90 mins</u>.
- <u>(Accelerated) freeze-drying</u>: food is <u>rapidly frozen</u> and <u>dehydrated</u> to <u>remove moisture</u> from the food. Adding water to the food <u>restores</u> the food to its <u>original texture</u> and <u>taste</u>.

Storing Food Safely

Temperature control is vital for storing food, so labels on food packaging will tell you whether you need to store it in a fridge, a freezer or just a 'cool, dry place'. (There's other information on labels too — see p.69.)

Some Food can be Kept in a Cool and Dry Place

Foods that are kept at room temperature are also called ambient foods.

1) Lots of food we buy from a supermarket doesn't need to be stored in a fridge or freezer.

2) Instead, they can be safely stored in a cool, dry place in their original packaging or an airtight container.

3) These foods contain little moisture or have been processed and preserved to make the conditions difficult for microorganisms to grow. These methods include:

- Drying — food is dehydrated. The lack of moisture makes it difficult for microorganisms to grow. Popular methods of drying include smoking and freeze-drying (see previous page).

- Canning/bottling — food is sealed in a can or jar and heated to kill off microorganisms.

- Pickling — food (e.g. gherkins, onions) is plunged in brine or vinegar, making it too acidic for microorganisms to grow quickly.

- Jam-making — fruit is boiled with sugar and pectin, and sealed in a glass jar (see p.94). The high sugar content prevents microorganism growth.

- Vacuum packing — food is put into plastic packaging, and the air is sucked out.
  ↳ Some microorganisms can't survive without enough oxygen.

- Modified atmospheric packaging (MAP) — food (e.g. seafood, meat) is packaged with a specific mixture of gases (different amounts of nitrogen, oxygen and carbon dioxide) depending on the food.

  You only need to know about MAP for the OCR course.

  Before being packaged, food may be kept in controlled atmosphere storage areas — the proportion of gases, temperature and humidity is controlled, which prevents pests and the growth of microorganisms.

4) These methods give foods a longer shelf life and make them safe to eat for many months or years.

Don't Let Food Go Past Its Best

All food will eventually spoil or lose its quality — date marks must be printed on the packaging of the food you buy to help you know when the food is likely to be unsafe to eat or not taste as good.

Use By Date

- The 'use by' date is shown on products with a short shelf life, e.g. high risk foods.
- It's given as a safety warning. If you use the food after this date, it might not be safe — you run the risk of getting food poisoning.

Best Before Date

- The 'best before' date is shown on products with a longer shelf life, e.g. tinned foods.
- It's given as a warning about quality. If you eat the food after this date, it's probably safe but might not be as nice as you'd expect, e.g. biscuits could be soft.
- Eggs, however, are risky to eat after their best before date — salmonella bacteria (see p.54) may have multiplied to dangerous levels.

REVISION TIP

GCSE Revision — [Best Before: day of exam]...

There's a key difference between 'use by' and 'best before' dates — make sure you remember that 'use by' dates are about food safety and 'best before' dates are about food quality.

Preparing Food Safely

If people eat food that's <u>contaminated</u> they could become very ill, so it's mega important that you handle food <u>safely</u> and <u>hygienically</u> to prevent bacteria spreading around the kitchen.

Avoid **Cross-Contamination**

When working with food, it's really easy to <u>pass bacteria</u> from <u>raw food</u> to <u>work surfaces</u>, <u>equipment</u> and your <u>hands</u>. Bacteria are then easily transferred to <u>other food</u> — this is called <u>cross-contamination</u>.

<u>Cross-contamination</u> can happen from a <u>variety</u> of <u>different sources</u>:

- <u>Other contaminated food</u> — raw meat juices can drip onto cooked food. High risk foods such as gravy can contaminate lower risk foods when added to a meal.
- <u>Utensils, equipment and work surfaces</u> — using unclean equipment, dirty cloths on work surfaces or the same work surface / chopping board for raw meat and ready-to-eat foods.
- <u>People</u> — poor personal hygiene (especially unclean hands) and sneezing or coughing.
- <u>Pests</u> — flies, rodents etc. contaminate food directly by walking over / eating it or by laying eggs and droppings on work surfaces. Waste bins will attract pests.

Follow **Safety** and **Hygiene** Procedures

You should take steps to <u>reduce</u> the <u>risks</u> when <u>preparing</u>, <u>cooking</u> and <u>serving</u> food:

Preparing
- Follow <u>personal hygiene procedures</u> — <u>wash your hands</u>, wear a clean <u>apron</u>, wear a <u>hat</u> or <u>hair net</u> to cover your hair, remove all <u>jewellery</u>, cover all <u>cuts</u>.
- <u>Separate</u> raw and cooked foods and use <u>coloured chopping boards</u> for different food groups, e.g. you could use red for <u>raw meat</u> and brown for <u>raw vegetables</u>.
- <u>Wash raw vegetables</u> thoroughly — even traces of <u>soil</u> contain bacteria.
- Use <u>clean equipment</u> and an <u>antibacterial spray</u> to <u>sanitise</u> work surfaces.
- <u>Defrost</u> frozen food <u>fully</u>, in the bottom of a <u>fridge</u> and away from other food.

Cooking
- Cook food at the <u>right temperatures</u> (see p.51) and for <u>the correct time</u>.
- Make sure food is <u>cooked all the way through</u> — e.g. cook <u>thicker</u> pieces of meat for <u>longer</u> than thin ones.
- Test the temperature <u>inside</u> food using a temperature <u>probe</u>.

- <u>Sterilise</u> the probe <u>before</u> and <u>after</u> use.
- Insert it into the <u>middle</u> of the <u>thickest</u> part of the food.
- Leave the probe in until the temperature <u>stabilises</u>.
- Check that the probe reaches at <u>least 75 °C</u>.

Serving
- Serve hot food <u>straight away</u> or keep it above <u>63 °C</u> for no longer than <u>2 hours</u>.
- If you're serving food <u>cold</u> or <u>storing</u> it, cool it down <u>within 90 minutes</u>.
- Keep food <u>covered</u> to prevent <u>flies</u> or other <u>pests</u> contaminating it — preferably put it in the <u>fridge</u>.
- Try to avoid <u>wasting food</u>, and check that waste bins are not <u>overfilled</u>.

I wouldn't cross with contamination if I were you...

It's dead easy for cross-contamination to happen. You have to be <u>very</u> careful and hygienic in the kitchen — especially if you're dealing with high risk foods that bacteria love.

Food Poisoning

Hope you're not eating your lunch... it's time to take a peek at the most common <u>types</u> of <u>bacteria</u> that cause <u>food poisoning</u> and their (rather unpleasant) <u>symptoms</u>.

Bacteria Can Cause **Food Poisoning**

1) The <u>general symptoms</u> of food poisoning include <u>sickness</u>, <u>diarrhoea</u>, <u>stomach cramps</u> and <u>fever</u>. In extreme cases, especially where people are <u>old</u>, <u>very young</u> or <u>vulnerable</u>, it can lead to <u>death</u>.

2) You can get food poisoning by eating <u>contaminated</u> food containing <u>pathogenic bacteria</u> — it can take a <u>few hours</u> to <u>several days</u> before you get any <u>symptoms</u>.

3) There are <u>many different</u> types of bacteria — you need to <u>learn</u> some of the <u>common</u> ones...

Remember These **Main Types** of **Bacteria**

Campylobacter

- The <u>most common</u> cause of <u>food poisoning</u> in the UK.
- Found mainly in <u>raw or undercooked poultry</u>, but also in other <u>raw meat</u>, and untreated <u>milk</u> / <u>water</u>.
- Symptoms include (bloody) <u>diarrhoea</u>, <u>stomach cramps</u> and <u>fever</u>.
- <u>Onset time</u>: 2–5 days.

> **Onset time** is the time it takes from ingesting the bacteria to when symptoms first appear.

E. coli O157

- E. coli live in the <u>intestines</u> of <u>animals</u> and can contaminate <u>raw beef</u>, untreated <u>milk</u> / <u>water</u>, unwashed <u>vegetables</u> and <u>salad leaves</u>.
- Most types are <u>harmless</u> but <u>E. coli O157</u> can cause <u>kidney damage</u> and <u>death</u>.
- <u>Onset time</u>: 1–3 days.

Salmonella

- Found in <u>raw poultry</u>, untreated <u>milk</u> and <u>eggs</u>.
- Symptoms include <u>diarrhoea</u>, <u>stomach cramps</u> and <u>vomiting</u>.
- <u>Onset time</u>: 6–72 hours.

Staphylococcus aureus

- S. aureus live on the <u>skin</u> and <u>hair</u>, and in the <u>noses</u> of <u>animals</u> and <u>people</u>.
- <u>Poor personal hygiene</u> can <u>contaminate</u> food.
- Symptoms include <u>diarrhoea</u>, <u>stomach cramps</u>, <u>vomiting</u> and <u>mild fever</u>.
- <u>Onset time</u>: 1–6 hours.

Listeria

- <u>Listeria</u> can be found in <u>soft cheeses</u>, <u>pâté</u> and <u>shellfish</u>.
- <u>Unlike</u> other bacteria it can <u>grow</u> in <u>cold temperatures</u>, such as in a <u>refrigerator</u>.
- <u>Pregnant</u> women are at a <u>higher risk</u> of infection — and it can lead to <u>miscarriage</u> or <u>health problems</u> in the child.
- <u>Onset time</u>: Up to 70 days.

If you're doing the <u>Eduqas</u> course, you can skip this box.

Controlling Bacteria

Two <u>common foods</u> that could be contaminated with bacteria are <u>untreated milk</u> and <u>eggs</u>, so there are <u>methods</u> in place to make these foods <u>safe</u> for us to eat:

- <u>Pasteurisation</u> — all milk sold in supermarkets is <u>pasteurised</u>. Milk is <u>heated</u> at around <u>72 °C for 15 seconds</u> to kill off any <u>pathogenic</u> bacteria before being <u>chilled</u>.
- <u>Vaccinations</u> — the <u>British Lion Quality</u> mark on egg shells and boxes is for hens that have been vaccinated against <u>salmonella</u>, so that it doesn't contaminate their <u>eggs</u>.

These bacteria have some scary names...

Think of ways to help you <u>spell</u> the names and remember the key <u>facts</u> for each of these bacteria. For example, S. aureus ends in 'us', so it's easy to remember you can find it in humans.

Uses of Microorganisms

The last page has probably left a <u>bad taste</u> in your mouth and you'll be forgiven for thinking that all microorganisms are bad for us... but hopefully this page will <u>convince</u> you that's <u>not the case</u>.

Yeasts Make Drinks Alcoholic and Bread Rise

<u>Alcoholic beverages</u> are made using the <u>fermentation</u> of yeast:

- During the <u>fermentation</u> process, <u>yeast</u> converts <u>sugar</u> into <u>carbon dioxide</u> and <u>ethanol</u> (also known as alcohol).
- For example, the sugars in <u>grapes</u> are fermented to produce <u>wine</u>.
- Sometimes the carbon dioxide is left to add '<u>fizz</u>' to the drink (e.g. with most ciders), but it can also be removed.

The production of many <u>varieties of bread</u> relies on the properties of <u>yeast</u> as a <u>raising agent</u>.

- Yeast is added to <u>flour</u> and <u>water</u> to form a <u>dough</u>. <u>Salt</u> is added for <u>flavour</u>, but also to <u>strengthen</u> the <u>gluten</u> in the dough.
- With the <u>ideal conditions</u> for growth (see p.49), the yeast quickly starts to <u>grow</u>. The yeast ferments the sugar to produce <u>carbon dioxide</u> — this gas is what causes the bread to <u>rise</u>.

Moulds can be Added to Cheese

1) The blue bits on <u>blue cheese</u> (e.g. Gorgonzola and Stilton) are due to the <u>moulds</u> that have been added.
2) The mould gives the cheese a <u>creamy texture</u> and a distinctive <u>sharp</u>, <u>tangy</u> taste.

Bacteria are Used in Yoghurt, Cheese and Fermented Meats

Bacteria are added to <u>pasteurised milk</u> to make <u>yoghurt</u>:

A similar process is used in the production of cheese (see p.93).

- The bacteria <u>ferment lactose</u> (milk sugar) and produce <u>lactic acid</u>.
- The lactic acid acts on the proteins in the milk to <u>thicken</u> it and gives it a <u>sour</u> or <u>tangy</u> taste.
- <u>Probiotics</u> and <u>prebiotics</u> may be added as supplements — probiotics are <u>live bacteria</u> which are <u>said</u> to give <u>health benefits</u>, while prebiotics are <u>non-digestible fibre compounds</u> which help the <u>growth</u> of probiotics.

<u>Lactic acid-producing bacteria</u> are also used to make <u>fermented meats</u> such as <u>salami</u> and <u>chorizo</u>:

Learn this only if you're doing the <u>Eduqas</u> course.

- Raw meat (usually pork or beef) is mixed with a combination of ingredients, including <u>salt</u>, <u>sugar</u>, <u>flavourings</u> and a '<u>starter culture</u>' of bacteria.
- The bacteria <u>ferment the sugar</u> and produce <u>lactic acid</u> — this lowers the pH of the meat, causing the <u>proteins</u> in the meat to <u>denature</u> and coagulate, forcing <u>water</u> out of the meat.
- This <u>low pH</u> and <u>lack of moisture</u> makes it much <u>harder</u> for pathogenic <u>bacteria</u> to <u>grow</u> (see p.49) — meaning the meat is safer to eat for longer.

Some microorganisms ne-ferment to hurt you...

There you have it — some marvellous uses of yeasts, moulds and bacteria. Make sure you are familiar with all of these examples before you head on over to the next page for questions on this section.

Warm-Up and Worked Exam Questions

Now that you've learned all there is to food safety, it's time to check that it's all sunk in.
Thankfully, there are a whole batch of questions coming up that I've handpicked just for you...

Warm-Up Questions

1) What is a high risk food? Give an example.
2) Identify one sign of food spoilage that could affect a tomato.
3) Explain the benefit of refrigerating cooked beef.
4) What is modified atmospheric packaging (MAP)?
5) How are each of the following a food safety risk:
   a) Preparing all meals on one chopping board.   b) Allowing pets on kitchen work surfaces?
6) Describe one positive use of a microorganism in food production.
7) What are probiotics? What are prebiotics?

Worked Exam Questions

1 Dominic is storing raw lamb mince in his fridge.

a) Which letter on the thermometer shows the
correct temperature range for a domestic fridge?

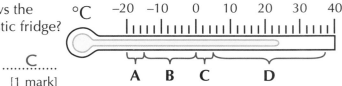

........C......
[1 mark]

b) Why should Dominic store the mince in its original packaging or a sealed container?

So blood or juices from the raw mince don't drip onto other foods and

contaminate them.

[1 mark]

2 A **temperature probe** is a useful piece of equipment to check that food is safe to eat.

Explain how to use a temperature probe correctly to check the core temperature of a food.

Sterilise the temperature probe before and after use. Insert it into the thickest part

of the food and wait until the temperature reading stabilises before checking the

temperature probe has reached at least 75 °C.

[3 marks]

3 Why do the following foods have a long shelf life?

Pickled onions: Pickling makes the onions too acidic for microorganisms to grow.

Dried pasta: Dried pasta lacks the moisture that microorganisms need to grow.

Food safety is all about preventing the growth of microorganisms [2 marks]
— make sure you know the conditions (see p.49).

Exam Questions

1 **Microorganisms** are able to grow more quickly in certain conditions.

State the **five** ideal conditions for microorganisms to grow and multiply.

1. ....   4. ....

2. ....   5. ....

3. ....

[2 marks]

2 Raw fruit and vegetables contain substances called **enzymes**.

a) Which of the following statements is **true**? Circle the correct answer.

A Enzymes are living microorganisms.

B Enzymes slow down chemical reactions.

C Enzymes help prevent fruit and vegetables from ripening.

D Enzymes are affected by high temperatures.

[1 mark]

b) i) What is meant by the term 'enzymic browning'?

....

....

[1 mark]

ii) Give **one** method that helps **prevent** enzymic browning.

....

[1 mark]

3 Food products have a '**best before**' or '**use by**' date on their packaging.

Explain the meaning of the information on the packaging of the following food products.

a) Hazelnut chocolates: ....

....

....

[2 marks]

BEST BEFORE 01.03.17

b) Cream-filled doughnuts: ....

....

....

[2 marks]

USE BY 01.01.17

Exam Questions

4   There are many types of bacteria that can contaminate the food we eat.

Complete the table below by filling in the blanks.

Type of bacteria	Onset time	**Two** food sources it might be found in
Campylobacter	....	1. Raw poultry 2. Untreated milk
E.coli	1 to 3 days	1. .... 2. ....
....	1 to 6 hours	(High risk foods handled by a person carrying this type of bacteria)
Salmonella	6 to 72 hours	1. .... 2. ....

[6 marks]

5   Many preserved foods can be safely stored in a **cool, dry place**.

   a)   Why can these foods be stored in this way?

   ....

   ....

[1 mark]

   b)   Outline how jam making can preserve fruit.

   ....

   ....

[2 marks]

6   Explain the role of non-pathogenic bacteria in the yoghurt-making process.

   ....

   ....

   ....

   ....

[3 marks]

7   A chef from a local buffet restaurant has asked you to write a set of safety procedures that the staff should follow to avoid cross-contamination in their kitchen.

   Write a list of safety procedures the staff should follow.   *Consider safety when preparing, cooking and serving buffet food as part of your answer.*

[8 marks]

Revision Questions for Section Three

That's <u>Section Three</u> over — tuck into these revision questions to see how you're doing.

- Try these questions and <u>tick off each one</u> when you <u>get it right</u>.
- When you've done <u>all the questions</u> for a topic and are <u>completely happy</u> with it, tick off the topic.

Food Spoilage (p.49-50) ☐

1) What is a pathogenic microorganism? ☑
2) Which five conditions are needed for the growth of microorganisms? ☑
3) What is a high risk food? List five types of food that would be classed as high risk. ☑
4) How do ripening enzymes change the properties of fruit and vegetables? ☑
5) Explain what enzymic browning is. ☑
6) Rhea is preparing a fruit salad. She says she can preserve it using lemon juice. Explain how lemon juice would help her preserve the fruit salad. ☑
7) How can you prevent mould and yeast growth on fruit? ☑

Storing & Preparing Food Safely (p.51-53) ☐

8) Give the temperature, or range of temperatures, at which you would:
   a) reheat food   b) chill food   c) freeze food ☑
9) What is meant by the danger zone? ☑
10) How does freezing affect the shelf life of food? ☑
11) What is the correct way of storing uncooked meat in a refrigerator? ☑
12) Describe five methods that can be used to preserve and extend the shelf life of food. ☑
13) How is a 'use by' date different from a 'best before' date? ☑
14) What is 'cross-contamination'? List four possible sources of it. ☑
15) Write a set of instructions to explain how to use a temperature probe correctly. ☑
16) Delphine is making beef bourguignon — a stew prepared with braised beef.
    Give three safety steps she should take for each of these stages:
    a) preparing the beef bourguignon
    b) cooking the beef bourguignon
    c) serving the beef bourguignon ☐

Food Poisoning p.54 ☐

17) List four general symptoms of food poisoning. ☑
18) For each type of bacteria, say where it can be found:
    a) Campylobacter   b) E. coli   c) Staphylococcus aureus ☑
19) What is an 'onset time'? Which type of bacteria has an onset time of less than 6 hours? ☑
20) Name two types of bacteria that could be found in raw minced beef. ☑
21) Explain the process of milk pasteurisation. ☑
22) How can you spot eggs from hens vaccinated against salmonella? ☑

Uses of Microorganisms p.55 ☑

23) Describe how microorganisms are used in the production of:
    a) alcoholic drinks   b) bread   c) blue cheese   d) yoghurt   e) salami ☐

Influences on Food Choice

There are loads of different things that affect your <u>food choices</u>.
Fortunately, this section will break them down into small, digestible, chocolate-coated chunks...

Many **Factors Influence** What **People Choose** to **Eat**

You need to learn these <u>10 factors</u> which influence people's food choices.

Physical Activity Level (PAL)

- Different people have different physical activity levels (PALs, see p.23).
  People with higher PALs need <u>more calories</u>.
- A person who has an <u>active</u> lifestyle (e.g. someone who walks 3 or more miles a day) will need to consume around 20% more calories per day than someone with a <u>sedentary</u> (inactive) lifestyle.
- Sportsmen/sportswomen may choose food to help <u>improve</u> their <u>performance</u>,
  e.g. <u>high protein</u> foods to help build <u>muscle</u>, or high carb foods to help with <u>endurance</u>.

Healthy Eating

- People trying to eat <u>healthily</u> will choose foods based on their <u>nutritional</u> value, e.g. foods <u>low</u> in <u>sugar</u> and <u>fat</u>, and high in <u>vitamins</u> and other nutrients.
- People with <u>allergies</u> or <u>intolerances</u> will need to avoid certain foods.

Cost of Food

- People choose food based on its <u>price</u>. Generally, they'll go for the <u>cheaper</u> option, unless they think it's worth paying more for <u>better quality</u> (see below).
- People will go for foods on <u>special offer</u> — everyone likes a bargain (see p.71).
- Supermarkets often show a <u>price per gram</u> to help people compare different products. Some people will buy food in <u>bulk</u> to get a lower price per gram.
- It can be <u>cheaper per portion</u> to <u>make</u> your own food than buy ready meals, but it'll usually cost more to buy the ingredients all at once than buy a single ready meal.

You should be able to cost your recipes. See p.26 for more information.

Income

- People on <u>high</u> incomes are more likely to buy <u>expensive</u> items, because a high price means (or at least suggests) it's of a higher <u>quality</u>.
- People on <u>low incomes</u> are more likely to go for the <u>cheaper</u> food option. Fresh meat, fruit and vegetables can be <u>pricey</u>, so it's more likely they'll opt for <u>cheaper</u>, <u>processed</u> foods (often high in fat and salt).
- In general, people on <u>lower</u> incomes tend to have <u>poorer</u> diets than high income groups.

Culinary Skills

- Some people are <u>great</u> cooks, some are more "<u>beans on toast</u>". Many people just lack the <u>confidence</u> to cook.
- People may not try <u>difficult-looking</u> recipes in case it all goes wrong or they just don't enjoy it. They may not want to risk <u>wasting</u> their money on ingredients, especially if a <u>ready-made</u> alternative is available.

Influences on Food Choice

What, more? Learn as many of these <u>influences</u> as possible, and the <u>reasons</u> behind them.

Lifestyle

- People who are feeling <u>stressed</u> or <u>bored</u> are more likely to go for <u>comfort food</u> (generally <u>high</u> in <u>fat</u> or <u>sugar</u>).

- People leading <u>busy</u> lives, e.g. long working hours or time-consuming hobbies, can <u>struggle</u> to find time to make a proper meal. This can make it tempting to just grab unhealthy food 'on the go'.

- People have different eating <u>patterns</u> — some have proper meals at set times of day, others tend to 'graze' throughout the day.

- Some people have <u>bad habits</u> like eating very late just before bed (not good for digestion) or regularly <u>skipping breakfast</u> (probably the worst sin of all).

Seasonality

- Certain UK grown foods are only available at <u>certain times</u> of year. For example, UK grown courgettes are available between June and September (see p.86).

- People worried about the environmental impact of <u>food miles</u> (see p.86) may buy <u>local foods</u> that are in season and <u>avoid</u> imports from around the world.

Availability

- People are more likely to buy and eat foods which are readily <u>available</u>. E.g. people in <u>rural</u> areas may have to shop at a <u>small local store</u> with <u>limited</u> food options.

- However, with <u>online shopping</u> on the rise, more and more people in rural areas are able to order online and have the supermarkets <u>deliver to them</u>. Handy.

Special Occasions

- Special occasions are often <u>celebrated</u> with a <u>large meal</u>. E.g. Fattening meals such as <u>turkey roast</u> and <u>suet pudding</u> are served at Christmas time in the UK, but they are far less common at other times of year.

Enjoyment

- Unsurprisingly, people tend to choose the food that they <u>enjoy</u>.
- You might think that it's all about <u>flavour</u>, but <u>smell</u>, <u>appearance</u> and <u>texture</u> all affect a food's <u>palatability</u> (how appealing it is).
- One downside of eating what you enjoy is it's often not very healthy. Humans are generally drawn towards <u>sweet</u> or <u>fatty</u> foods.
- People generally aren't drawn towards <u>bitter</u> foods, although some bitter foods are hugely popular once you get the 'taste' for them, e.g. coffee, dark chocolate, beer...

When I click my fingers you'll crave mashed potato...

Some of these influences may seem obvious, but some may surprise you. Have a go at writing a list of the ten factors and think about how each one affects your personal food choice.

Cultural, Religious and Moral Food Choices

Many cultures and religions have their own customs around what they do and don't eat.
In some there are strict rules, in others it's more guidance.

Different Religions Have Different Views on Food

If you're doing the OCR or AQA course, you'll need to learn this whole page.
If you're doing the Eduqas course, just learn the dietary laws for Islam, Hinduism and Judaism.

Christianity
1) There are no strict rules about foods in Christianity.
2) During Lent, Christians often choose to give up certain foods or drinks.
3) During various Christian celebrations, special foods are eaten.
   E.g. Hot cross buns on Good Friday (to represent the crucifixion of Jesus),
   and pancakes to mark the start of Lent (by using up excess ingredients).

Islam
1) The Qur'an states that meats eaten by Muslims must be halal — where
   the lawful animal is slaughtered in a specific way whilst being blessed.
2) Muslims cannot eat pork, nor any product made from pork products,
   such as gelatine. Muslims are also not allowed to drink alcohol.
3) During Ramadan (the ninth month of the lunar calendar),
   Muslims fast between sunrise and sunset.

In the lunar calendar, each month has 29-30 days and Ramadan falls at a different time each year.

Fasting is when no food is eaten for a period of time.

Hinduism
1) Many Hindus are vegetarian, but some tend to avoid certain vegetables
   that are considered harmful such as garlic, onion and mushrooms.
2) The Hindus that eat meat require that it be slaughtered using a quick, painless method called
   Jhatka. In Hinduism cows are considered sacred, so Hindus are not allowed to eat beef.

Judaism
1) Jewish dietary laws (kashrut) state that their food must be kosher (meaning fit for consumption).
2) Kosher animals are ones which have split hooves and chew cud (such as cows and deer), plus
   fish that have fins and scales (so no shellfish). These animals must be slaughtered using quick,
   painless methods which allow the blood to drain afterwards, as blood is considered non-kosher.
3) Jews are not allowed to eat pig, rabbit, hare, camel and many other animals.
4) Dairy and meats must not be cooked together or eaten together as a mixture.

Sikhism
1) Baptised Sikhs are prohibited from eating meat which
   is ritually slaughtered (such as halal or kosher meat)
2) Many Sikhs are vegetarians.
3) Sikhism teaches that its followers should only eat
   what they need to, and should avoid overindulging.

For more on planning food for groups, see p.26-28.

Buddhism
1) Buddhists believe that all living beings are sacred, so the majority of Buddhists
   are vegetarian or vegan (although there are no strict rules on this).
2) Most Buddhists avoid alcohol, as they believe it wrongly alters your view of the world around you.
3) Some Buddhists choose to fast from noon until sunrise the following day.

Rastafarianism
1) Eating pork is forbidden in Rastafarianism.
2) Many Rastafarians stick to an I-tal (clean and natural) diet, meaning the diets are mainly
   made up of fresh vegetables. Some eat fish, but the fish must be less than 30 cm long.
3) Many Rastafarians do not drink alcohol but will drink things made
   from natural, grown products, such as herbal tea or fruit juice.

Cultural, Religious and Moral Food Choices

There's more to <u>food choice</u> than just being <u>picky</u>. Some people choose their food based on <u>moral reasons</u>, whereas others must choose carefully to avoid getting <u>very ill</u>.

Food Choices Are Influenced by **Moral** or **Ethical Concerns**

'<u>Moral</u>' and '<u>ethical</u>' just mean 'what people think is <u>right or wrong</u>'. Loads of people choose food based on their idea of right and wrong, with reasons like the following:

Animal Welfare

Animal welfare is a concern for many people. People may choose to eat foods where they know the animals have been treated <u>ethically</u>, such as <u>free-range</u> products (p.79), or they may <u>avoid meat</u> altogether, e.g. <u>vegetarians</u>, <u>vegans</u> (p.27).

Working Conditions

- <u>Fairtrade</u> products, e.g. bananas, are popular with customers who want to make sure the farmers in developing countries get a <u>fair price</u> for their <u>produce</u> (see p.88).
- Fairtrade products are often slightly more <u>expensive</u> to buy than non-Fairtrade items.

Environmental Impact

- People may prefer to buy <u>British</u> or <u>local produce</u>, or foods that are in season, in order to support the local <u>economy</u> and to <u>reduce food miles</u> (see p.86).
- Some <u>fish</u> products say whether the fish were caught using <u>sustainable</u> fishing methods, to avoid damaging the ecosystem and stop fish from going extinct (see p.80).

Eating Naturally

- Some people prefer to eat <u>organic</u> foods (p.77) — ones that have been produced <u>without</u> the use of <u>synthetic chemicals</u>. Organic foods are grown using <u>natural fertilisers</u> and <u>natural pest control</u>.
- People may <u>avoid</u> buying genetically modified foods, over concerns about <u>unwanted effects</u> on the <u>consumer</u> and <u>environment</u> (p.78).

People with **Intolerances** or **Allergies** Must Avoid Certain **Foods**

1) Some people are <u>intolerant</u> to particular ingredients in food (p.27). Eating the food can lead to <u>illness</u>, and cause bloating, vomiting, pains etc.
2) Common intolerances are <u>lactose</u> (found in dairy products) and <u>gluten</u> (found in wheat, barley, oats and rye).
3) Food <u>allergies</u> may cause <u>serious illness</u> and can be <u>fatal</u> (p.27). Something that causes an allergic reaction is called an <u>allergen</u>.
4) The most common allergens are <u>nuts</u>, <u>eggs</u>, <u>dairy</u>, <u>wheat</u>, <u>fish</u> and <u>shellfish</u>.
5) It's important that food is <u>properly labelled</u> so that people with <u>allergies</u> know what they can safely eat.

Turns out our food choices are influenced by an awful lot...

Yup, there's a lot of factors to learn — go back and make sure you're familiar with them all.

British and International Cuisines

A <u>cuisine</u> is a style of cooking that is <u>representative</u> of a <u>particular country</u> or <u>region</u>. Different cuisines may have different <u>ingredients</u>, <u>serving styles</u> and <u>preparation techniques</u>.

Each Part of the UK Has Its Own Dishes

1) The United Kingdom has four countries — <u>England</u>, <u>Wales</u>, <u>Scotland</u> and <u>Northern Ireland</u>.
   Great Britain just consists of England, Wales and Scotland. Not a lot of people know that.

2) Traditional cooking techniques involve <u>stewing</u>, <u>roasting</u>, <u>baking</u>, <u>grilling</u>, <u>boiling</u> and <u>frying</u>.

3) Meals are eaten <u>three</u> times a day — breakfast, lunch and dinner (or breakfast, dinner 'n' tea if yer frum up North like us).

4) Main courses usually pair <u>meat</u> or <u>fish</u> with potatoes and other vegetables and are often served with a <u>sauce</u>, e.g. roast beef with gravy.

5) Here are some traditional <u>ingredients</u> and <u>dishes</u> from across the UK:

> <u>Meat and fish</u>: Beef, lamb, pork, haddock, eel, shellfish (e.g. crab, mussels, oysters).
> <u>Vegetables</u>: Potato, carrot, parsnips, cabbage, leek, onion, green beans, cauliflower.
> <u>Dairy and eggs</u>: Milk, cream, butter, cheese, chicken eggs.
> <u>Fruit</u>: Apples, pears, strawberries, blackberries, gooseberries, rhubarb, blackcurrants.

England

- <u>Cumberland sausage</u> — a coiled sausage flavoured with pepper and herbs.
- <u>Cottage pie</u> — beef mince, gravy and vegetables topped with grilled, mashed potato.
- <u>Cornish pasty</u> — pastry containing beef, potato, onion and swede.
- <u>Potted shrimps</u> — shrimps in melted butter.
- <u>Bread and butter pudding</u> — buttered bread soaked in milk, eggs, sugar and spices.

Northern Ireland

- <u>Crubeens</u> — boiled pigs' feet, which are battered and fried.
- <u>Soda bread</u> — bread made with bicarbonate of soda and buttermilk instead of yeast.
- <u>Potato farl</u> (Irish potato cakes) — a savoury Irish potato pancake.
- <u>Ulster fry</u> — a fried breakfast with soda bread, potato farls, bacon, sausage, egg and tomato.

Wales

- <u>Welsh rarebit</u> — toasted bread with a cheese sauce, often containing mustard, beer or wine.
- <u>Bara brith</u> — cake with dried fruit and spices.
- <u>Laverbread</u> — slow cooked seaweed paste.
- <u>Glamorgan sausage</u> — a vegetarian sausage made with cheese and leeks, and coated in breadcrumbs.
- <u>Welsh cakes</u> — small, round flat cakes with raisins baked on a griddle.

Scotland

- <u>Scotch broth</u> — soup made with red meat, root vegetables, barley and dried pulses.
- <u>Neeps and tatties</u> — swede and potatoes cooked in oil and mashed.
- <u>Haggis</u> — lamb (and sometimes beef), suet, onion, oatmeal, seasoning and spices.
- <u>Shortbread</u> — a buttery and crumbly biscuit made with butter, flour and sugar.

Modern British Cuisine Reinvents Popular Recipes

1) Modern takes on traditional recipes include <u>cottage pie</u> filled with <u>chilli con carne</u> and topped with <u>sweet potato</u>, salted-caramel <u>apple crumble</u>, and a <u>bread and butter pudding</u> made with <u>brioche</u> and <u>marmalade</u>.

2) Britain today is also a <u>multicultural</u> society that has <u>adopted</u> recipes from many other <u>cultures</u> — a very popular dish in the UK is <u>chicken tikka masala</u> (a variety of <u>curry</u>).

3) Even Britain's use of <u>common</u> 'staple foods' is changing — e.g. <u>potatoes</u> are still a <u>common ingredient</u>, but <u>rice</u> and <u>pasta</u> are becoming more <u>popular</u>.

> The <u>Eatwell Guide</u> (p.16) is the UK's most recent <u>healthy eating model</u> — it encourages people to swap <u>traditional</u> foods that are high in <u>saturated fats</u> for <u>alternatives</u>, e.g. <u>vegetable oils</u> instead of <u>butter</u> or <u>lard</u>.

British and International Cuisines

Now we'll show you a <u>couple of examples</u> of <u>different cuisines</u>, and the <u>type of things</u> you'd need to know about them. If you've studied different cuisines, make sure you learn <u>all this and more</u> about them.

Traditional Japanese Meals Consist of Rice and Okazu

1) Japanese cuisine mainly consists of <u>steamed rice</u> (gohan), combined with a number of <u>okazu</u> (dishes to eat with rice).

2) <u>Boiling</u>, <u>steaming</u> and <u>frying</u> are all popular cooking techniques.

3) <u>Rice cookers</u> and <u>woks</u> are used regularly in Japanese cooking. Bamboo steamers are used for steaming things like dumplings.

4) <u>Three</u> meals are eaten each day — in the morning, at midday, and in the early evening (the largest meal of the day).

5) Typical Japanese home-cooked dinners often have <u>one</u> course — in which multiple dishes are presented at once on separate plates or bowls.

6) Common <u>ingredients</u> in Japanese cuisine are:

> <u>Rice:</u> Rice is eaten with nearly every meal. It is also used to make desserts and sweets.
> <u>Noodles:</u> Strands of dough that are stretched and cut into shapes.
> <u>Seafood:</u> Such as salmon, mackerel, tuna, squid. Served raw (sashimi) or grilled.
> <u>Saké/Mirin:</u> Japanese rice-wines. Mirin is sweeter than saké, and also has a lower alcohol content.
> <u>Pickled vegetables:</u> Vegetables preserved in vinegar. Served as an appetiser, side or topping.
> <u>Matcha tea:</u> Powdered green tea. Used in hot drinks and as flavouring in cakes, ice cream etc.

7) Common <u>dishes</u> in Japanese cuisine are:

> <u>Sushi</u> — Sticky rice, often topped or rolled with raw fish (sashimi) and seaweed.
>
> <u>Tempura</u> — Seafoods, vegetables or meat coated with batter and deep-fried.
>
> <u>Gyoza</u> — Fried dumplings stuffed with meat or vegetables.
>
> <u>Ramen</u> — Noodles in a soup, topped with vegetables, meat, eggs etc.
>
> <u>Miso Soup</u> — a soup made from fermented soya beans, fungus and salt.

8) Desserts are less common in Japan than in the UK. Sweet <u>rice cakes</u>, served with green matcha tea, are very popular. Red bean paste is a common filling in desserts.

Japanese Meals are Eaten with Chopsticks

1) <u>Chopsticks</u> are often used to pick up food, rather than using hands or cutlery. Rice and soup bowls may be held <u>close to the mouth</u> to make them easier to eat from, but plates should be left on the table.

2) People traditionally <u>sit on floor mats</u> around low tables to eat, but many modern restaurants provide <u>Western-style tables</u> and <u>chairs</u>.

3) Soup can be <u>slurped</u> from the bowl — it shows the chef that the food is being enjoyed.

4) Raw or pickled <u>ginger</u> is used to 'cleanse the palate', e.g. with sushi.

5) Modern twists on Japanese foods include <u>fusing</u> Japanese and <u>Western</u> dishes, e.g. BBQ pulled pork gyoza, matcha tea frappés, wasabi-flavoured chocolate, and using teriyaki (a Japanese sauce) on roast meats.

> The <u>Japanese Food Pyramid</u> is Japan's most recent <u>healthy eating model</u> and is based on <u>traditional</u> Japanese foods. It recommends 5-7 servings of <u>grains</u> (rice, noodles etc.), 5-6 servings of <u>vegetables</u>, 3-5 servings of <u>fish</u>, <u>meat</u> or <u>eggs</u>, and 2 servings of both <u>milk</u> and <u>fruits</u> to be eaten each day.

British and International Cuisines

Here's another <u>international cuisine</u> for you. Again, if you've been taught about two different international cuisines, make sure you know <u>this type of stuff</u> about them.

In **Spanish** Cuisine **Lunch** is the **Largest** Meal of the **Day**

1) In Spain three main meals are eaten throughout the day. Smaller eats may occur between main meals.

2) Typical cooking methods in Spain are stewing, charcoal grilling, plate grilling and cooking in a sauce.

3) <u>Breakfasts</u> are <u>small</u> and <u>light</u>, and are eaten first thing in the morning. People often break for a larger snack at around 10 am.

4) The <u>largest</u> meal of the day is <u>lunch</u> (2-4 pm), which often consists of 3 courses — a <u>starter</u>, <u>main</u>, and <u>dessert</u> and/or coffee. <u>Dinner</u> is a <u>lighter meal</u> eaten around 9-11 pm.

5) The Spanish lunch <u>usually</u> has three courses, but can have up to six: Appetiser, first course, fish dish, meat dish, dessert and coffee.

6) Typical <u>ingredients</u> and <u>dishes</u> in Spanish cuisine are:

> <u>Meats</u>: Pork, chicken and seafood.
> <u>Herbs and spices</u>: Peppers, nutmeg, paprika, cumin and coriander.
> <u>Fruit and Veg</u>: Peppers, olives, garlic, tomatoes, oranges, lemons.
> <u>Other</u>: Almonds, olive oil, beans, wine (often served with meals).

<u>Churros</u>: thin strips or loops of fried dough, often dunked in hot chocolate or chocolate sauce.

<u>Serrano ham</u>: a type of cured ham.

<u>Chorizo</u>: a spicy cured pork sausage.

<u>Paella</u>: a rice dish made in a large flat plan, made with stock, seafood (such as squid, shrimp and mussels), chicken or other meats, and vegetables. It is commonly cooked in huge portions for festivals.

<u>Patatas bravas</u>: spiced, fried potato chunks served with a spicy tomato sauce.

<u>Tapas</u>: Small savoury dishes eaten as a snack or like a buffet (where many dishes are shared between a group of people). Examples include: king prawns in garlic and chilli, patatas bravas (see above), chorizo (see above), grilled fish, fried squid, filled tortillas, Spanish omelette.

7) Traditional Spanish recipes have been <u>modernised</u> in many ways, such as using quinoa or noodles in paella, and flavoured churros. Chorizo is often used in <u>non-Spanish</u> dishes like pasta or omelettes.

> The <u>NAOS Food Pyramid</u> is Spain's most recent <u>healthy eating model</u> which promotes a <u>Mediterranean</u> diet. It is divided into <u>three</u> sections to show the types of food that should be eaten <u>daily</u> (wholegrain cereals, fruits, vegetables), <u>weekly</u> (fish, red meat, eggs) and <u>occasionally</u> (sweets and snacks).

This is making me really want a holiday to Tokyo or Barcelona...

In the non-exam assessment you might have to plan a menu based on an international cuisine. Get ahead of the game — choose the international cuisine you're most familiar with and create a menu of three dishes to promote the main characteristics and ingredients of this cuisine.

Warm-Up and Worked Exam Questions

It's that time again — first, see if you've understood the basics by tackling these warm-up questions.
After that, follow the worked exam questions and see if you can do the questions on the next page yourself.

Warm-Up Questions

1) Explain how a low income can affect food choice and diet.
2) Explain how working long shifts can lead to weight gain.
3) Name five other factors that can influence food choice.
4) What dietary laws do Muslims follow?
5) Describe three traditional British dishes, stating the country that they came from.
6) Choose an international cuisine and:
   a) List four ingredients commonly used in it.
   b) Describe three traditional dishes associated with it.

Worked Exam Questions

1   In the UK, three meals are typically eaten a day, with dinner / tea as the largest meal.

Describe the eating patterns of an international cuisine of your choice.

In Spanish cuisine three meals are eaten a day. Lunch is the largest meal and dinner is a lighter meal.

If you had chosen a different cuisine, you'd be awarded a mark if you had written about the number of meals / meal times / size of meals in this cuisine.

[1 mark]

2   Food choice is limited for people with a food **allergy** or food **intolerance**.

What is the difference between a food allergy and a food intolerance?

A food allergy is an immune system reaction to certain foods, whereas a food intolerance is where a person has difficulty digesting certain foods.

This one is tricky. Food allergies and intolerances are <u>different</u>. It's vital to know all about allergies (for the exam and when cooking for others) as reactions can be fatal.

[2 marks]

3   Janet lives in a multicultural city.

Explain how Janet's location may affect her food choice.

Janet will have a wide variety of food to choose from because a multicultural city will cater for different cuisines.

[2 marks]

Exam Questions

1   Dana's diet is influenced by her concern over **animal welfare**.

State **two** ways that this concern might influence Dana's food choice.

1. ....

....

2. ....

....

[2 marks]

2   Many religions have **dietary laws** or **customs** that prohibit certain foods.

a)   What does it mean if meat is 'jhatka'?

....

....

[1 mark]

b)   Describe the dietary customs of the following religions:

i)   Judaism

....

....

....

[2 marks]

ii)   Buddhism

....

....

....

[2 marks]

3   The table below shows the lifestyles of two people.

Harriet	John
• Professional cyclist • Lives on a remote farm • Enjoys cooking	• Office worker • Trying to lose weight • Dislikes cooking

Discuss how their different lifestyles may affect their food choices.

[8 marks]

Food Labelling

Food labels can help people make informed choices about what they eat. There are tonnes of rules about what must appear on food labels and unfortunately you'll have to learn them.

Food Label Info is Controlled by Different Regulations

1) Countries in the European Union (EU) must follow the rules in the Food Information for Consumers regulations (FIC), updated in 2014.

2) The UK currently follows the regulations set out by the EU:

- Food labels must not be misleading, e.g. making claims that the food can cure illness.
- They must be clear and easy to read.
- Common allergens must be emphasised (e.g. highlighted, bolded) in the ingredients.

3) From December 2016 it is compulsory for nutritional information to appear on food labels (next page).

4) In the UK, the Food Standards Agency (FSA) is responsible for making sure that food manufacturers and businesses are following the regulations (correctly labelling foods, using safe, hygienic practices, etc.).

Labels Must Tell You Certain Information by Law

EU laws say that the labels on pre-packed food have to tell you all this stuff:

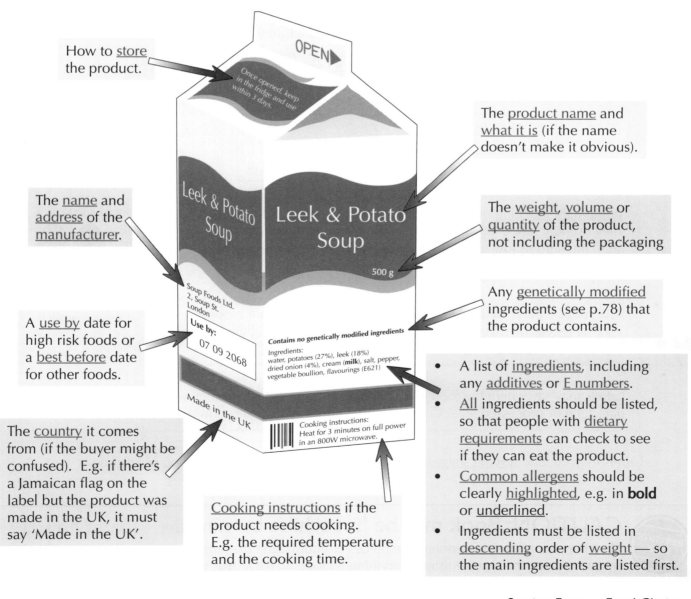

How to store the product.

The product name and what it is (if the name doesn't make it obvious).

The name and address of the manufacturer.

The weight, volume or quantity of the product, not including the packaging

A use by date for high risk foods or a best before date for other foods.

Any genetically modified ingredients (see p.78) that the product contains.

- A list of ingredients, including any additives or E numbers.
- All ingredients should be listed, so that people with dietary requirements can check to see if they can eat the product.
- Common allergens should be clearly highlighted, e.g. in **bold** or underlined.
- Ingredients must be listed in descending order of weight — so the main ingredients are listed first.

The country it comes from (if the buyer might be confused). E.g. if there's a Jamaican flag on the label but the product was made in the UK, it must say 'Made in the UK'.

Cooking instructions if the product needs cooking. E.g. the required temperature and the cooking time.

Label text: Once opened, keep in the fridge and use within 3 days. OPEN▶ Leek & Potato Soup 500 g. Soup Foods Ltd. 2, Soup St. London. Use by: 07 09 2068. Contains no genetically modified ingredients. Ingredients: water, potatoes (27%), leek (18%), dried onion (4%), cream (**milk**), salt, pepper, vegetable boullion, flavourings (E621). Made in the UK. Cooking instructions: Heat for 3 minutes on full power in an 800W microwave.

Food Labelling

Packaged food products should display certain <u>nutritional information</u>. This page will teach you all about it.

Nutritional Information must be Shown on Food Products

1) Since <u>December 2016</u>, manufacturers have had to include specific <u>nutritional information</u> on their packaging, although many have done this for years already.

2) Nutritional information should be shown in a <u>table</u> like this:

Energy is always given as kilojoules (kJ) and kilocalories, and the rest are given as grams.

NUTRITIONAL INFORMATION		
	per 100 g	per 55 g serving
Energy	2180 kJ/525 kcal	1199 kJ/289 kcal
Fat	33.0 g	18.2 g
of which saturates	15.0 g	8.3 g
Carbohydrate	50.0 g	27.5 g
of which sugars	2.0 g	1.1 g
Protein	6.5 g	3.6 g
Salt	0.7 g	0.4 g

Each nutrient must be given per <u>100 g</u> of the food.

3) Other nutrient details <u>may</u> be listed, such as the amount of <u>fibre</u>, <u>vitamins</u> and <u>minerals</u>. This is not necessary, so it's up to the manufacturer to decide.

Labels Have Non-Compulsory Information on Them Too

Lots of other information that <u>doesn't have to be there</u> is often found on food packaging...

Product labels often make claims about the product in order to make the product look more <u>attractive</u> and <u>improve sales</u> (see next page). This is stuff like:

- <u>High in protein</u>
- <u>Low in fat</u>
- <u>Free</u> from <u>artificial colours</u> and <u>preservatives</u>

Food labelling rules are very strict and claims about health benefits must be truthful and accurate.

<u>Traffic-light labelling</u> on a product shows how <u>healthy</u> it is <u>at a glance</u>. They use Reference Intake values to show whether a product has <u>high</u>, <u>medium</u> or <u>low</u> amounts of fat, salt and sugar. For example, a <u>pizza</u> might be red for fat and yellow for salt and sugar.

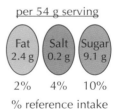

per 54 g serving

Fat 2.4 g	Salt 0.2 g	Sugar 9.1 g
2%	4%	10%

% reference intake of an average adult

Products often state whether they are suitable for certain groups, e.g. <u>vegetarians</u>, <u>vegans</u>, <u>muslims</u> (halal) and <u>coeliacs</u> (gluten-free) to make it <u>easier</u> for them to pick out the <u>correct</u> products.

Labels may say where the food / ingredients are <u>from</u> and where they were <u>packaged</u> or <u>processed</u>, e.g. 'Country of origin: Spain', 'Packaged in the UK'.

Labels may include <u>serving suggestions</u>, e.g. 'Try it with custard and a dollop of ketchup.'

CAUTION: Book may be hot whilst burning...

Sketch a pizza box and annotate the pieces of information that are required on its packaging by law. Check that you've listed everything by looking back over the previous pages.

Influences of Marketing

You find <u>food adverts</u> everywhere — from <u>TV ads</u> and <u>social media</u> to <u>magazines</u> and <u>posters</u>. There's more to marketing than just ads though. This page covers some of the <u>clever tricks</u> used to pull in customers.

Special Offers are a Common Marketing Technique

1) Special offers are used to <u>convince</u> customers to buy a product (or a quantity of it) that they wouldn't normally buy, by making it feel like they're getting a <u>bargain</u>.

> <u>Examples of special offers are:</u>
> - 'Buy one get one free' (BOGOF) or 'buy two, get the third free'
> - Reduced price (e.g. '30% off', or 'save £1.50')
> - Meal deals (e.g. main meal, dessert and a drink for £10)

2) <u>Loyalty card schemes</u> (where you get points for your shopping) allow supermarkets to record data about what you're buying, which they can use to send you offers <u>matched</u> to your <u>buying habits</u>.

3) <u>Point of sale marketing</u> is used near the till — <u>carefully chosen</u> items (chocolate, sweets, magazines, vouchers) are put on display in the hope that you'll <u>eventually</u> be tempted while you're queuing.

Celebrity or Brand Endorsement Can Increase Sales

1) Some companies use <u>endorsement</u> by <u>celebrity chefs</u> to <u>boost sales</u> — the chef's name is used to convince you that it's a quality product.

2) Food companies may partner up with big <u>film or TV brands</u> like 'Space Wars' — using 'Space Wars' on their products or adverts helps target certain <u>age groups</u>.

3) Food companies may <u>sponsor</u> sports and sportspersons, e.g. an energy drink company might sponsor a televised car rally. They'll <u>pay money</u> to put their name on advertising banners, cars, helmets, ... and benefit from it being seen by a <u>wide audience</u>.

Companies May Use Health Claims...

1) Food manufacturers may <u>promote</u> their food as having certain <u>health benefits</u> (e.g. high in vitamin C, 2 of your 5 a day). Claims that make a product appear <u>healthy</u> can <u>greatly increase sales</u>.

2) Manufacturers may also market a <u>low sugar</u> or <u>low fat</u> version of an <u>existing</u> product (e.g. diet cola), or one that only uses <u>natural</u> ingredients in order to attract buyers who are <u>health conscious</u>.

3) Special products such as <u>gluten-free</u> breads target customers who have specific dietary requirements.

...or Promote Their Ethical Values

1) Food companies may join ethical schemes like <u>Fairtrade</u> — it may cost them more to produce the food, but they can charge a <u>higher price</u> and the product will appeal to a <u>wider market</u>.

2) <u>Organic</u> food ranges may be produced to target certain groups — again, it'll cost more to produce, but the customers they're aiming at will probably be willing to pay a <u>higher price</u> for it.

3) Companies may advertise that they use <u>biodegradable</u> or <u>recycled materials</u> in their packaging, to attract customers concerned about the environment.

4) Product labels may use words like '<u>natural</u>' and '<u>fresh</u>' and use images of nature to make the product appear more natural (sometimes hiding the fact that they're actually full of artificial <u>chemicals</u>...).

Products use multiple marketing techniques...

Evaluate the marketing techniques used on the cereal box on the right.

Sensory Testing

We use a combination of <u>senses</u> to try and figure out what we should eat. What would you rather eat — a cupcake that <u>smells</u> like old cheese or a packet of <u>crunchy</u> roast-dinner <u>flavoured</u> mealworms?

Humans **Taste** by Using Their **Tongue** and **Nose**

1) Human tongues are covered in thousands of taste buds, which detect five different things — <u>salt</u>, <u>sweet</u>, <u>sour</u>, <u>bitter</u> and <u>umami</u> (savoury).

2) We use <u>taste buds</u> in conjunction with <u>olfactory receptors</u> in the nose (which detect <u>smells</u>) to identify the flavour of foods.

This is why you can't taste food properly when your nose is blocked.

Our **Senses Influence** Our **Choice** of **Food**

1) People use a combination of <u>senses</u> to decide whether a food is appetising.

2) Good food should appeal to the senses: <u>sight</u>, <u>smell</u>, <u>taste</u>, <u>touch</u> and <u>sound</u>.

3) Each sense influences choice in a different way:

Sight — We want food that <u>looks appealing</u>, e.g. that's colourful, looks fresh, is attractively presented... not a brown splodge on a plate.

Taste — Foods must have an enjoyable <u>taste</u>. The <u>method</u> of cooking, <u>freshness</u> of ingredients, choice of herbs, seasoning and flavour <u>combinations</u> all affect the overall taste.

Touch — Texture can make a surprising difference... we like our veg to be <u>crunchy</u> (not chewy and bendy), rice and pasta <u>firm</u> (not soggy), and 'wheat-biscuit' cereals with a little <u>crunch</u>.

Smell — Smell helps us to <u>taste</u> food, and can also make us <u>want to</u> eat it (think of the smell of bread baking in the oven... or of chips...). As above, how it's cooked and flavoured will affect the aromas that are given off.

Sound — Sound might seem unimportant at first, but some research suggests that <u>certain sounds</u> can make a food seem <u>crunchier</u>, <u>softer</u> or <u>sweeter</u> in the mouth.

4) For top marks, you'll need to use <u>sensory descriptors</u> to correctly describe the <u>sensory qualities</u> (how a food looks, tastes, feels and smells) for a <u>range</u> of foods and <u>combinations</u>.

Colourful Crispy Sour
Sweet Tender Crumbly
Firm Smooth Chewy

You might see sensory qualities referred to as <u>organoleptic properties</u> in the <u>OCR</u> course.

Sensory Tests Should be **Fair** and **Unbiased**

Behind many a great food product is a great <u>sensory test</u>. <u>Sensory testing</u> helps you <u>understand</u> how other people feel about the <u>sensory qualities</u> of your product, so you can go away and <u>improve</u> it.

Here is how a <u>fair</u> and <u>unbiased</u> sensory test should be set up:

1) Choose <u>enough</u> tasters for your tasting panel (e.g. 10).

2) Tasters should <u>not be told</u> what each sample is — this is known as a '<u>blind test</u>'.

3) Tasters should work on their <u>own</u>, so they cannot be <u>influenced</u> by others.

4) Tasters should be given <u>clear instructions</u> on what they <u>need to do</u>.

5) Only <u>small samples</u> should be given to the tasters, to stop them filling up before the final samples.

6) Tasters should be allowed to drink <u>water</u> between samples to <u>wash the taste away</u>.

7) The tests should be carried out in:
   - <u>Clean</u>, <u>hygienic</u> conditions.
   - A <u>quiet</u> area.
   - Similar testing areas with the same lighting, so that the food <u>looks</u> the <u>same</u> for each taster.

8) When testing is finished, the results can be <u>analysed</u> to see which sensory qualities of the product need <u>improving</u>.

Sensory Testing

This page covers some of the many different <u>sensory tests</u> that can be used — make sure you can use them correctly and choose the one that is most <u>appropriate</u> for your product.

Sensory Tests Compare Sensory Qualities of Food

Paired Preference Test

In a <u>paired</u> preference test, <u>two slightly different</u> foods, e.g. two cookies (one made with <u>butter</u> and one made with <u>margarine</u>), are tasted and the taster chooses their <u>favourite</u>.

Triangle Test

A <u>triangle test</u> is a type of '<u>discrimination</u>' test. <u>Three</u> food products are tasted, where <u>two</u> are the <u>same</u> and one has a <u>tweaked recipe</u>. The taster has to <u>identify</u> which product <u>differs</u> from the others.

Ranking Test

Foods are tasted, and the tasters put the foods in <u>order</u> from <u>lowest</u> to <u>highest</u> (e.g. 1-4) for a certain <u>characteristic</u>, e.g. spiciness, sweetness. The ranks for each food are <u>totalled</u> at the end.

Taster	Sample — Texture			
	S1	S2	S3	S4
A	1	4	3	2
B	2	4	3	1
C	1	3	4	2
D	1	4	2	3
Rank total	5	15	12	8
Rank place	4th	1st	2nd	3rd

Rating Test

In a <u>rating test</u>, people rate either the <u>characteristics</u> of a food or a <u>variety</u> of foods using a <u>scale</u>, e.g. 1-5, Hate-Love, or smiley face to sad face.

Characteristic	Taster Ratings			
	A	B	C	D
Sourness	5	3	2	4
Sweetness	2	3	2	1
Saltiness	0	1	1	2
Spiciness	5	3	2	3

Profiling Test

Tasters rate certain <u>characteristics</u> of a food and the <u>average</u> rating for each characteristic is worked out to create a <u>profile</u> of the food. This can be displayed visually, e.g. on a star diagram.

Characteristic	Taster Ratings				Average
	A	B	C	D	
Sourness	5	3	2	4	3.5
Sweetness	2	3	2	1	2
Saltiness	0	1	1	2	1
Spiciness	5	3	2	3	3.25

Overlapping two star diagrams lets you easily compare two different foods at a glance, e.g. here, food A is rated more sour, but less sweet and salty than food B.

Key:
Food A
Food B

And in first place... the runner beans...

If you're doing a sensory test, you need to make sure that you're not influencing the tasters' decisions. Go through everything on these pages, before jumping into the questions on the next pages.

Warm-Up and Worked Exam Questions

There was a lot of information on the last few pages — make sure you read anything you don't understand again and again, until it sticks. Now, onto the final warm-up questions of the section...

Warm-Up Questions

1) Why is it important that all ingredients are listed on the label of a food product?
2) Give two examples of non-compulsory information often given on food products.
3) How could a food product be advertised to promote ethical values?
4) List five examples of sensory descriptors.
5) Outline how a rating test can be used to test the characteristics of a food.

Worked Exam Questions

1   Retailers use **marketing techniques** to attract customers to certain products.

Give **three** techniques retailers use to influence customers.

1. Special offers, such as buy one get one free or half price
2. Meal deals
3. Loyalty card schemes

[3 marks]

2   A manufacturer uses peanuts in a cereal bar.

How should the manufacturer show that the cereal bar contains peanuts?

This is compulsory information — even if it is obvious, it has to be included on packaging.

The manufacturer should highlight the peanuts in the list of ingredients to make it obvious to the consumer (by underlining it or putting in bold).

[1 mark]

3   Shane's comment on how taste influences our food choice is shown below.

The only sense that matters when it comes to food is <u>taste</u>.

Do you agree with Shane? Explain your answer.

You might have mentioned that sound may be important here too.

I disagree with Shane. Taste is important, but smell, sight and touch also influence our food choice. Smell helps us taste and identify the flavours of food. We choose food that looks good, is colourful and is attractively presented, as well as food which has an enjoyable texture, such as crunchy crisps or soft bread.

[4 marks]

Exam Questions

1   The **nutritional information** below is from the label of a snack product.

NUTRITIONAL INFORMATION		
	(per 125 g)	(per 50 g serving)
Energy	2180 kJ	210 kcal
Protein	6.5 g	2.6 g
Fat	33.0 g	13.2 g
(of which saturates)	15.0 g	6.0 g
Salt	0.7 g	0.3 g

Identify **three** problems with the label.

1. ....

2. ....

3. ....

[3 marks]

2   Mei wants to find out if people prefer her homemade lemonade to a branded variety.
She gave the instructions below to each taster.

> **Instructions:**
> * You have two types of lemonade in front of you — one is labelled 'Lemonade A' and one is labelled 'Lemonade B'.
> * Drink 500 ml of each lemonade and mark in the box which you prefer.
> * You can discuss your opinions with the other two tasters if you want.
>
> Lemonade A ☐
>
> Lemonade B ☐

a)   Is Mei's test fair?
Circle the correct answer.

                    YES / NO

[1 mark]

b)   Explain your answer to part a).

....

....

....

....

....

[4 marks]

3   A manufacturer uses a **profiling test** to compare the characteristics of two fish pies.

Discuss how the manufacturer should carry out the test and how they could analyse the results.

[6 marks]

Revision Questions for Section Four

Well, that's <u>Section Four</u> all wrapped up — time to see <u>how much</u> you can remember.
* Try these questions and <u>tick off each one</u> when you <u>get it right</u>.
* When you've done <u>all the questions</u> for a topic and are <u>completely happy</u> with it, tick off the topic.

Influences on Food Choice (p.60-63) ☑

1) Briefly describe ten different factors that can affect what food you choose. ☑
2) Outline the dietary laws of:
   a) Hinduism   b) Islam   c) Judaism   d) Sikhism   e) Rastafarianism ☑
3) List four ethical factors that might affect the food people choose. ☑
4) Write down three symptoms of a food intolerance. ☑
5) Write down four common allergens. ☑

British and International Cuisines (p.64-66) ☐

6) For British, Japanese and Spanish cuisines (or two international cuisines of your choice):
   a) Describe the equipment / cooking methods used.
   b) Describe the eating patterns, e.g. when and how they eat.
   c) Describe five traditional foods or dishes.
   d) Describe two modern twists on traditional dishes. ☐

Food Labelling and Nutritional Information (p.69-70) ☐

7) List nine items of information that should be shown on a packaged food product by law. ☑
8) As of December 2016, what compulsory information must be shown in a table on food labels? ☑
9) What does each colour represent in traffic-light labelling? ☑

Influences of Marketing (p.71) ☐

10) Give two examples of special offers that may be used to increase food sales. ☑
11) Explain how data collected from loyalty card schemes can be used by supermarkets. ☑
12) Explain how celebrities and film / TV brands can be used to boost sales of food products. ☑
13) Why might a food company choose to sponsor a sporting event? ☑
14) How could a manufacturer modify an existing product to attract:
   a) health conscious customers
   b) customers worried about the environment? ☑

Sensory Testing (p.72-73) ☐

15) What are the five basic tastes? ☑
16) Describe how we identify flavours in food. ☑
17) What is meant by a 'sensory quality' of a food? ☑
18) Describe how you would make a sensory test fair and unbiased. ☑
19) Describe how to carry out the following sensory tests:
   a) ranking test   b) triangle test   c) paired preference test ☑
20) Draw a star diagram to visually represent the
    food profile shown in the table on the right. ☑

Characteristic	Taster Ratings				Average
	A	B	C	D	
Crunchiness	3	5	4	4	4
Bitterness	3	2	2	1	2
Dryness	5	4	4	5	4.5

Grown Food

Food provenance is all about where your food <u>originally comes from</u> — it can be <u>grown</u>, <u>reared</u> or <u>caught</u>.

Crops are Grown Intensively or Organically

<u>Grown food</u> includes <u>fruits</u>, <u>vegetables</u> and <u>cereals</u>, e.g. wheat, rice, barley, oats, rye. There are two methods of farming them which you need to know about — <u>intensive farming</u> and <u>organic farming</u>.

Intensive Farming Uses Chemicals to Achieve Maximum Yields

<u>Intensive farming</u> uses methods that will produce the <u>highest possible yield</u> (more food from the same area of land). Production is often <u>large-scale</u>, with huge areas all growing the <u>same</u> crop.

1) <u>Large mechanical equipment</u> is used to <u>save time</u> and <u>cut down</u> on <u>production costs</u>.

2) <u>Artificial (chemical) fertilisers</u> are added to the soil to <u>supply nutrients</u> for crops to grow.

Intensive farming is also known as <u>conventional farming</u>.

3) <u>Pesticides</u> are used. These are <u>chemicals</u> that <u>control pests</u> and <u>protect</u> crops and include <u>insecticides</u>, <u>herbicides</u> (<u>weedkiller</u>) and <u>fungicides</u>.

4) Some people are <u>concerned</u> about using artificial <u>fertilisers</u> and <u>pesticides</u>. They can harm <u>wildlife</u>, damage the environment, e.g. by <u>polluting rivers</u>, and some think they have a harmful effect on <u>human health</u> too.

Organic Farming Uses Natural Methods

Organic food is grown naturally <u>without</u> using artificial fertilisers and pesticides. This makes it more <u>expensive</u> to produce.

1) Farmers add <u>organic matter</u> like <u>manure</u> and <u>compost</u> instead of artificial fertilisers.

2) Techniques such as <u>crop rotation</u> (growing different crops) and leaving land <u>fallow</u> (growing nothing) are used to make sure the soil is <u>fertile</u> every <u>year</u>.

3) Some farmers may use <u>alternative methods</u> to control pests. Things like:

- Introducing a pest's <u>natural predators</u> (e.g. ladybirds to eat aphids).
- <u>Biological pesticides</u> (e.g. certain fungi).
- Spraying crops with <u>hot water</u>.

4) These alternatives are generally <u>better</u> for the <u>environment</u>, but can be <u>more expensive</u> and <u>less effective</u> than using chemical pesticides.

5) Organic farming has its share of <u>advantages</u> and <u>disadvantages</u>:

Advantages	Disadvantages
• It <u>reduces</u> the amount of <u>chemical pesticides</u> going onto the land, so it's <u>less harmful</u> to the <u>environment</u>. • Fewer <u>non-renewable resources</u> are used than in intensive farming, so it's more <u>sustainable</u>. • It <u>appeals</u> to <u>consumers</u> (see p.63) who are <u>concerned</u> about the use of artificial <u>chemicals</u> and their damage to the <u>environment</u>.	• Organic farming tends to produce a <u>lower yield</u>. • There are higher <u>production costs</u>, which mean <u>higher prices</u> in <u>supermarkets</u>.

Intensive and organic farming — learn the pros and cons of each...

There are advantages and disadvantages for both intensive and organic farming — you should be able to discuss how crop yields, production costs and environmental impact differ between these two farming methods.

Grown Food — GM Crops

People today are very concerned about <u>how</u> their food is <u>produced</u> and what <u>effect</u> it has on the <u>environment</u>. <u>Organic foods</u> are very popular, while lots of people are wary of <u>GM foods</u>.

Genetically Modified Foods Have Altered Genes

1) A genetically modified (<u>GM</u>) food is one that's had its <u>genes altered</u> to give it <u>useful characteristics</u>, such as improving its <u>growth</u> or changing its <u>colour</u>:

- GM plants are produced by inserting a <u>desirable gene</u> from another plant, an animal or a bacterium into the plant you want to <u>improve</u>.
- You plant modified <u>seeds</u> and up comes your GM crop.

2) For example, you can get GM maize that's <u>pest-resistant</u>. The <u>farmer</u> gets a <u>bigger yield</u> of maize because less of the crop is eaten or damaged by pests.

3) GM <u>weedkiller-resistant</u> crops can withstand chemicals that kill the <u>weeds</u> around the crop.

4) Currently, <u>no GM crops</u> are grown in the <u>UK</u>, but it's <u>popular</u> in other countries, e.g. the <u>USA</u> grows lots of GM <u>maize</u>, <u>cotton</u> and <u>soya beans</u>.

5) GM foods have both <u>advantages</u> and <u>disadvantages</u>:

Advantages

1) Crops can be made to <u>grow quicker</u>.
2) Producers can get <u>higher yields</u> of crops for the same amount of seed and fertiliser.
3) This makes food <u>cheaper</u> to <u>produce</u> so it's also <u>cheaper</u> for the <u>consumer</u> to buy.
4) Crops can be altered to have a <u>longer shelf life</u> — so less food is <u>wasted</u>.
5) Crops can be made to <u>ripen</u> earlier than normal, so <u>fresh foods</u> can be available for consumers <u>earlier</u> in the year.
6) Crops can be modified to contain <u>extra nutrients</u> which can improve <u>nutrition</u> in <u>poor countries</u>. E.g. <u>golden rice</u> has been genetically modified to contain carotene (which provides vitamin A).

Disadvantages

1) GM foods haven't been around for long — so their <u>long-term health effects</u> <u>aren't known</u>.
2) There are concerns that modified genes could get out into the wider <u>environment</u> and cause problems, e.g. the <u>weedkiller-resistance</u> gene could be transferred to a weed, making it an indestructible '<u>superweed</u>'.
3) GM producers can't sell their food everywhere — the <u>European Union</u> (EU) <u>restricts</u> the <u>import</u> of some GM foods.

Consumers Have Safety Concerns

1) Some people believe that we shouldn't <u>mess about with genes</u> because it's <u>not natural</u>.
2) In the European Union:

- All GM foods must undergo <u>strict safety assessments</u> and can only be sold if no health risks have been identified.
- All foods that are GM or contain more than <u>1% GM ingredients</u> must be <u>clearly labelled</u>.
- However, meat and dairy <u>products</u> from animals fed on <u>GM feed</u> are <u>not labelled</u>.

Not everyone thinks genetic modification is a good idea...

Genetic modification is a fairly new technology which can help food producers and consumers — make sure you understand the benefits of GM foods, but also the arguments surrounding the risks and ethics.

Reared Food

Reared animals are animals raised by humans specifically for their meat (and other products).
E.g. cows are reared for beef and milk, and poultry (birds) for meat and eggs.

Factory-Farmed Animals Don't Have Much Space

Factory-farmed animals don't have much room to move — they may be in cages with
lots of other animals in the same place. This is another form of intensive farming.

1) Animals are kept inside in warm sheds, so they don't waste much energy moving or keeping
   themselves warm. That means that more of their energy goes into producing meat or eggs for food
   — this maximises food production.

2) Animals are sometimes given things like growth hormones or are
   force-fed to speed up their growth — making it even quicker and
   cheaper to produce meat.

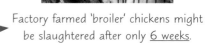

3) Factory-farmed food is generally cheaper than free-range (see below)
   — it's a more efficient way of farming, though it isn't as ethical.

4) People are becoming more concerned that intensively reared animals
   don't live very nice lives — they're more likely to suffer from nasty
   diseases, they can't behave naturally and are killed at a young age.

Factory farmed 'broiler' chickens might
be slaughtered after only 6 weeks.

5) Some people believe that meat from factory-farmed animals
   doesn't taste as nice as meat from free-range animals.

6) Battery cages for hens were banned throughout the EU in 2012. New 'enriched cages' provide
   slightly more space and nesting areas, but some people still argue that standards could be better.

Free-Range Animals Have More Space

Concerns for how reared animals are kept has led to an increase in people buying free-range food.

1) Free-range food (e.g. eggs) comes from animals that have more space
   to live than factory-farmed animals — they're often free to roam.

2) Free-range animals have different amounts of space depending on the
   brand you buy and aren't given hormones to speed up their growth.

3) They usually have nicer lives because of the higher standard of welfare.

4) Less food can be produced by rearing animals in free-range conditions — they use up
   energy moving around, so take longer to grow. The extra land needed also adds to the cost.
   This makes products more expensive and they might be beyond some people's budget.

5) Labels are added to foods to show they meet welfare standards. For example:

- The Red Tractor symbol on products lets consumers know that the
  producer meets standards of food safety, hygiene, animal welfare and
  environmental protection set by the Assured Food Standards scheme.
  Farm assured food can be traced back to the farms they came from.

- The RSPCA Assured symbol can be found on eggs, fish and meat — to
  get the logo, producers have to follow strict RSPCA welfare standards.
  These standards cover every part of an animal's life, including
  diet, lighting, bedding and how they're transported.

Remember — free-range animals are free to roam...

Now you know a handy way to remember what 'free-range' food means, but you'll also need to be
able to explain the reasons why they are generally more expensive than factory-farmed animals.

Caught Food

Fish are a super source of <u>protein</u> and really benefit the <u>human diet</u>. Sadly, some fish species are so <u>popular</u>, like <u>North Sea cod</u>, that they have almost <u>disappeared</u> from our seas due to <u>overfishing</u>.

There are **Different Fishing Methods**

Fish can be <u>caught</u> or <u>reared</u> — the fishing method used depends on the <u>type</u> of fish and where it's <u>found</u>.

Trawling
- <u>Trawling</u> is a very common method of <u>fishing</u> — <u>trawlers</u> are fishing boats that catch fish using <u>nets</u>. Large trawlers may process fish on-board (<u>factory trawlers</u>).
- There are <u>different methods</u> of trawling — some <u>drag</u> a net through the <u>open sea</u>, and others along the <u>surface</u> of the <u>seabed</u> (bottom trawling).
- <u>Dredging</u> is like bottom trawling but uses a <u>metal 'basket'</u> instead of a net.

Fish Farming
- Large numbers of fish are <u>raised</u> in <u>tanks</u> or <u>enclosures</u> in rivers and lakes or in <u>cages</u> in the <u>sea</u>. E.g. <u>salmon</u>, <u>carp</u> and <u>trout</u>.
- As with <u>factory-farmed</u> land animals, there is <u>overcrowding</u> — the fish are more likely to suffer from <u>diseases</u>.

When the fish are <u>caught</u> they may be <u>washed</u> and <u>gutted</u> on the boats before they are brought to shore. Fish are <u>chilled</u> (packed with ice) or <u>salted</u> to prevent <u>spoilage</u> on the way to supermarkets and fishmongers.

Sustainable Fishing Preserves Future Fish Stocks

There is concern over how fishing methods are <u>damaging</u> the <u>environment</u>...

Bottom trawling is <u>destructive</u>, e.g. the nets that drag across the seabed can <u>destroy corals</u>, which are a <u>habitat</u> for lots of <u>marine life</u>.

Trawlers can also catch <u>unwanted</u> animals, like <u>dolphins</u> or <u>turtles</u>, in their nets.

<u>Overfishing</u> is when <u>more fish</u> are <u>caught</u> than can be <u>replaced</u> by natural reproduction. E.g. the demand for <u>bluefin tuna</u> to make <u>sushi</u> has led to overfishing. Bluefin tuna are now endangered (at risk of going <u>extinct</u>).

...so there needs to be <u>methods</u> to <u>conserve</u> fish stocks and make fishing more <u>sustainable</u>.

<u>Alternative fishing methods</u>

E.g. <u>Longline</u> fishing uses a fishing line with <u>baited hooks</u> secured between two buoys. <u>Fewer</u> fish are caught and there is less chance of catching <u>unwanted</u> fish.

<u>Fishing quotas</u>

<u>Quotas</u> set by <u>governments</u> help <u>endangered</u> species of fish. They limit the <u>amount</u> and <u>sizes</u> of fish that can be caught.

<u>Regulating net size</u>

Holes in fishing <u>nets</u> have to be a certain <u>size</u>, so that <u>smaller</u>, <u>unwanted</u> fish can escape.

> A <u>sustainable method</u> is one that doesn't damage the environment or use up finite resources.

Sustainable fishing techniques help protect the environment...

There's not much to it — learn the various fishing methods and how fishing can be made sustainable.

Food Classification

Vegetables, fruits, meat and fish are classified (put into different groups) based on what they look like or where they come from. Don't memorise everything on this page, but learn at least one example for each classification.

Food can be Classified in Different Ways

Vegetables

Vegetables are classified depending on the part of the plant they come from, e.g. the stem, leaf or roots.

Classification	Examples
Bulb	Onion, shallot, leek
Root	Beetroot, carrot, parsnip
Flower	Broccoli, cauliflower
Stem	Celery, rhubarb, asparagus

Classification	Examples
Seeds / pods	Beans, peas, sweetcorn, mange tout
Tuber	Potato, sweet potato
Leaves	Brussels sprouts, spinach, watercress
Fruit vegetables	Tomato, cucumber, peppers

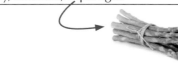

Fruits

Fruits typically develop from a flowering plant and contain seeds.

Classification	Examples
Hard	Apples, pears
Soft / berry	Raspberries, strawberries, blackcurrants
Citrus	Lemons, limes, oranges, grapefruit
Other	Banana, kiwi, melon

Meat, Poultry and Game

Meat is sourced from animals. The term poultry refers to meat from reared birds, and game refers to meat from wild animals.

Classification	Examples
Poultry	Chicken, turkey, goose, pheasant
Game	Rabbit, venison (deer), partridge

Meat can be described as white meat or red meat. Typically, white meat comes from poultry and fish, and red meat comes from mammals (e.g. beef, pork or lamb).

Offal refers to edible animal 'innards' including the liver, heart and tongue. Common offal dishes include pâté and sweetbread.

Animal intestines are usually used as a casing for sausages too.

Fish

Fish can be classified into three groups — oily fish, white fish and shellfish:

Classification	Examples
Oily	Herring, mackerel, trout, salmon, tuna, sardine
White (round)	Cod, haddock, whiting
White (flat)	Halibut, sole, plaice
Shellfish (crustaceans)	Crab, lobster, prawns, shrimps
Shellfish (molluscs)	Cockles, mussels, oysters, scallops

That's an odd looking fruit...

Classifying fruits can get a little strange — for example, tomatoes and cucumbers are technically fruits but chefs label them as vegetables because they are used in savoury dishes.

Warm-Up and Worked Exam Questions

That's the first part of food provenance covered — knowing where our food comes from and how it can be classified is important stuff, so check you've understood it all by doing some questions.

Warm-Up Questions

1) Give one benefit of intensive farming.
2) Give one benefit of organic farming.
3) What is a GM crop?
4) Describe what a sustainable method is.
5) Give an example of:
   a) a root vegetable   b) a bulb vegetable   c) a citrus fruit   d) a white, flat fish

Worked Exam Questions

1 GM crops are regulated throughout Europe.
Despite this, many people still have concerns over GM crops.

a) Give **two** EU regulations for GM crops.

1. GM foods have to pass strict safety tests before they can be sold.

2. Foods that contain GM ingredients (more than 1%) have to be clearly labelled.

[2 marks]

b) What concerns do people have over GM crops?
You could also say that people are worried that modified genes could get out into the environment.

Some people believe it is wrong to alter genes and are wary that there may be

long-term effects on our health.

[2 marks]

2 A farmers' market sells **organic** carrots and **intensively-farmed** wheat.
'Crop rotation' is something else you would get marks for here.

a) Describe the farming methods that are used to grow organic carrots.

Organic carrots are grown using manure or compost as a natural fertiliser.

Alternative methods of pest control, such as biological pesticides (e.g. types

of fungi) and introducing a pest's natural predator, can be used to kill pests.

[3 marks]

b) Give **three** methods that are used to intensively farm wheat.

1. Mechanical equipment is used to harvest the wheat.

2. Wheat is grown in large fields.

3. Artificial fertilisers supply the soil with nutrients.

[3 marks]

Exam Questions

1 Animals can be reared using **factory-farming** or **free-range** methods.

Describe the differences in living conditions between factory-farmed and free-range animals.

....

....

....

[2 marks]

2 Scientists noticed that many children in a developing country were suffering from a disease caused by a deficiency of a certain vitamin. The children's diet involved large quantities of rice.

Suggest how genetic modification could be used to help prevent the disease.

....

....

[1 mark]

3 **Sustainable** fishing methods help to prevent species of fish becoming endangered.

Explain **three** methods that can make fishing more sustainable.

1. ....

....

....

2. ....

....

....

3. ....

....

....

[6 marks]

Waste Food and Packaging

Millions of tonnes of food are thrown away each year — most of which could have been avoided. Households, food producers and retailers all contribute to food wastage.

We Throw Away Lots of Food at Home

Households are big culprits when it comes to wasting food — fruits, vegetables and bread are all thrown out unnecessarily.

Reasons for wasting food

1) Food has spoiled because:
   - It was overcooked or burnt
   - It wasn't covered or stored correctly
   - It wasn't kept at the right temperature
   - It had passed its use by date
2) Confusion over best before dates and other date marks — people wrongly think the food is no longer edible.
3) Too much food was cooked, and edible leftovers aren't frozen or reused.
4) Preparing food incorrectly — e.g. peeling vegetables too thickly.

Producers and Retailers Waste Food Too

A lot of food is wasted during production and by shops.

Reasons for wasting food

1) Retailers will reject food from producers if it is damaged or spoiled during transport.
2) Imperfect food (e.g. 'ugly' looking fruit) is often rejected by retailers too — the producer can't sell it, so it gets wasted.
3) To avoid running out of stock and disappointing their customers, supermarkets stock more than they can sell. The unsold stock gets binned, including stuff that is still safe to eat, like bread.
4) Offers from supermarkets encourage people to buy more than they can use or store.
5) Larger packs of food are better value for money — but again, it's often more than people need.

Reduce Waste and Save Money

Reducing food waste will not only help the environment, it will help people save money too.

1) Plan meals and correct portion sizes — only buy ingredients that you will use.
2) Correctly store food and pay attention to use by dates.
3) Use up the contents of your fridge before buying more food.
4) Use leftovers in meals the day after or freeze them for another time.
5) Use the whole food (e.g. bones can be used for stocks, peelings can be made into compost).
6) Donate unwanted food (cereals, pasta, beans etc.) to food banks. Some supermarkets are reducing their waste by donating unsold food.

Food waste costs the average household around £500 a year.

Waste not, want not — save money and the environment...

Waste food and packaging (there's more about that over on the next page) can damage the environment. Less food waste can reduce this impact and save us money, so it's a good idea to plan out your meals properly.

Waste Food and Packaging

Packaging is <u>pretty useful</u>, but like <u>waste food</u>, if it's <u>thrown away</u> it can damage the <u>environment</u>.

Packaging is **Great** for **Manufacturers**

Manufacturers use different <u>materials</u> to <u>package food</u> — each material has certain <u>benefits</u>.

- <u>Plastic</u> (cling film, vacuum-pack bags) — <u>transparent</u>, <u>lightweight</u> and can be <u>shaped</u> to the food.
- <u>Glass</u> (milk bottles, jars) — <u>transparent</u>, <u>heat-resistant</u>, gives food a <u>long shelf life</u> and is <u>reusable</u>.
- <u>Metal</u> (tins) — <u>heat-resistant</u> and gives food a <u>long shelf life</u>.
- <u>Paper</u> (pizza boxes, egg cartons, labels) — <u>lightweight</u>, can be <u>printed on</u> and is <u>biodegradable</u>.

Choosing <u>suitable</u> packaging <u>reduces waste food</u> (and saves the <u>manufacturer money</u>) because it:

- <u>Protects</u> food from being <u>damaged</u> while it's being <u>transported</u>, <u>displayed</u> and <u>stored</u>.
- <u>Preserves</u> the food and stops <u>contamination</u> from <u>bacteria</u> or <u>pests</u>.

Packaging also shows <u>useful information</u> to help customers (see p.69).

Packaging Can Be **Bad** for the **Environment**

<u>Excess</u> packaging is often used to make a product look more <u>appealing</u> to get a customer to buy it. But this <u>comes at a cost</u>...

1) <u>Manufacturing</u> the materials for packaging uses lots of <u>energy</u> and <u>natural resources</u> — some of which are <u>non-renewable</u> (e.g. <u>plastics</u> from <u>crude oil</u>).

2) Packaging often gets used <u>once</u>, <u>thrown away</u> and then just takes up space in Britain's already huge <u>landfill sites</u>.

3) Some packaging, like <u>plastics</u>, take a long time to <u>biodegrade</u> (decompose), and could <u>take up space</u> in a landfill site for decades.

4) Packaging adds to the <u>weight</u> of a product, so heavier materials, such as <u>metals</u> and <u>glass</u>, require more energy to <u>transport</u> them.

5) <u>Litter</u> is <u>hazardous</u> to animals too — e.g. <u>marine life</u> can get <u>entangled</u> in <u>plastics</u> or <u>eat it</u> by mistake.

Producing energy uses fossil fuels...
...which produce greenhouse gases...
...which add to global warming.

You Can **Reduce** the **Environmental Impact**

1) <u>Recycling</u> uses much <u>less energy</u> than manufacturing <u>new</u> packaging...

2) ...so always <u>recycle</u> <u>tins</u>, <u>glass</u>, <u>card</u> and <u>paper</u> — there are recycling <u>banks</u> all around the UK and local <u>councils</u> provide <u>recycling bins / bags</u> for homes.

3) Most <u>plastics</u> (bottles, pots, tubs and trays) can be recycled too. If in doubt, the <u>labels</u> on plastic packaging will tell you which <u>materials</u> are used and <u>whether</u> you can <u>recycle</u> them.

4) Buy products with little or no packaging and <u>refuse</u> ones with <u>excess packaging</u>.

5) Choose products with <u>biodegradable packaging</u> or packaging <u>made</u> from <u>recycled materials</u>.

6) Carry food in <u>reusable shopping bags</u> to reduce the need for <u>plastic bags</u>.

Since October 2015, large shops in England have to charge 5p for a plastic bag to encourage customers to re-use them instead.

Excess packaging is bad, but our food still needs to be packaged...

Without packaging, foods would spoil and get damaged during transport, causing food waste.
It's all about using the right materials, but not too much of them.

Food Miles and Carbon Footprint

Your food doesn't just magically appear in a <u>supermarket</u> — some of it's travelled <u>thousands of miles</u>.

Food Comes from **Different Countries**

Food Miles — the distance food travels from where it's produced to the consumer.

Kenyan   Spanish
4500 miles   1000 miles
Green Beans   Oranges

1) Some food is <u>transported a long way</u> to be sold, e.g. some <u>green beans</u> you buy in the UK have come from Kenya.

2) This is bad for the <u>environment</u> — planes, ships and trucks all burn scarce <u>fossil</u> <u>fuels</u> and release <u>carbon dioxide</u> into the atmosphere, contributing to <u>global warming</u>.

3) But consumers now expect food to be <u>available all year round</u>, not just when it's in season here. So shops and manufacturers buy food from <u>abroad</u> when it's out of season at home, e.g. asparagus has a very short season here. Also, some things <u>just can't be grown</u> here, like bananas.

4) Manufacturing costs are <u>different</u> in other countries, so <u>imported food</u> can sometimes be <u>cheap</u>.

Buy **Food** from **Local Markets** to Reduce **Food Miles**

1) <u>Local food</u> is often better for the <u>environment</u> as it has fewer <u>food miles</u>.

2) Local food is often <u>fresher</u> and <u>tastier</u> because it reaches you soon after it has been harvested.

3) Buying from <u>farmers' markets</u> and independent <u>greengrocers</u> etc. <u>supports local businesses</u> and their produce can be <u>cheap</u>.

4) <u>Check labels</u> on foods from <u>supermarkets</u> too — <u>food producers</u> often make it a <u>big deal</u> on their packaging if they use ingredients from the <u>UK</u>.

When planning your meals look to source local, seasonal ingredients that are in season and haven't been shipped from around the world.

It's <u>good</u> for the <u>environment</u>, but buying locally does have <u>downsides</u> too:

1) <u>Seasonal</u> food is <u>not available</u> all year round, e.g. strawberries are only available in the summer, so you have a <u>smaller selection</u> of products.

2) <u>Unpackaged</u> or <u>unpreserved</u> foods <u>spoil</u> faster — you have to use them <u>quickly</u>.

Carbon Footprint Measures **Environmental Impact**

1) Your <u>carbon footprint</u> measures the <u>impact</u> your lifestyle has on the <u>environment</u>.

2) It's given as the amount of <u>greenhouse gases</u> you <u>directly</u> and <u>indirectly</u> produce from burning fossil fuels for <u>heat</u>, <u>electricity</u>, <u>transport</u> etc. (usually expressed as <u>tonnes</u> of <u>carbon dioxide</u> per year).

3) <u>Foods</u> have a carbon footprint too — greenhouse gases are produced when <u>growing</u>, <u>processing</u>, <u>packaging</u> and <u>transporting</u> them.

The average UK person has a carbon footprint of over 10 tonnes a year.

You can <u>reduce</u> your carbon footprint:
- Buy food that is <u>in season</u>, with <u>lower food miles</u> and with <u>less packaging</u>
- Use <u>public transport</u>, <u>walk</u> or take up <u>cycling</u>
- <u>Waste less energy</u> in the home (e.g. turn TVs off standby, turn the heating down)

EXAM TIP

From plate to mouth — 0.0001 food miles...

In the exam, you might be asked a question about the environmental impact of a meal. Think about the food miles of each ingredient and how they may have been processed.

Global Food Production

A great challenge we face today is to provide the world's population with a steady, sustainable supply of food. You need to understand why this is such a challenge and the effects that food poverty can have.

Climate Change Can Affect Food Production

Climate Change

1) Processing, transporting and wasting food all lead to the production of greenhouse gases.
2) These greenhouse gases build up in the atmosphere.
3) Heat is 'trapped' — less heat can escape into space.
4) This effect is what is causing global warming — the Earth is getting slowly hotter.
5) Rising temperatures are changing our climate, causing more extreme weather (e.g. hurricanes, tornadoes) than usual.
6) Changes in the temperature and weather are affecting the crops and food that we rely on.

Layer of greenhouse gases

Heat tries to escape, but is trapped and redirected back — this is known as the greenhouse effect.

1) Just a tiny increase in average global temperature can massively affect the production of crops:
   - Many crops will have lower yields, e.g. maize production could be reduced by millions of tonnes.
   - Pests and microorganisms can reproduce more easily and can invade new regions that were too cold for them before.

2) Climate change can cause some extreme weather events which affect food production:

Drought
- A drought happens in an area that has had a lack of rainfall.
- Crops struggle to grow or fail completely.
- Rivers and lakes can dry up, killing fish and other wildlife.
- Drought can cause wildfires — uncontrollable fires spread through the countryside, destroying fields and reared animals.

Flooding
- Severe rainfall, cyclones etc. can cause major flooding.
- Floods directly damage and destroy crops.
- Soil and nutrients useful for crop growth are washed away.
- Sewage can pollute fields and spread disease in animals.
- Reared animals may drown.

3) In parts of the world, food shortages are common due to droughts (e.g. Ethiopia) or flooding (e.g. Bangladesh).
4) The lack of food leads to malnutrition (due to a diet without the right balance of nutrients), ill health and even death from starvation.

Some colder countries may benefit from a warmer climate — they can grow things that they couldn't before. E.g. more land is being used for wine grapes in southern England due to recent warm summers.

Food Poverty is Where a Person Can't Obtain Nutritious Food

Even in a relatively rich country such as the UK, millions of people live in food poverty:

Food poverty is where a person isn't able to access or afford nutritious food.

1) People can live in food poverty if they don't earn enough money to spend on food or have no choice but to spend it on other things, e.g. fuel bills, debts or loans.
2) Low income households in rural areas might find it difficult to access nutritious food — households without a car or with insufficient access to public transport may have to shop in more expensive local shops, with less choice.

You only need to know this bit for the Eduqas course.

3) People in food poverty may buy cheap and unhealthy foods. These foods can lead to malnutrition (due to a diet without the right balance of nutrients) and diet-related health problems such as obesity and diabetes.
4) Families may rely on food donations from the local community (e.g. food banks), and parents may even go hungry so their children can eat.

Global Food Production

Food Security is Where People Have Access to Food They Need

People have food security when they have access to enough nutritious food to stay healthy and active.

1) You can talk about the food security of a person, a community, a country or the world:

   - A country that can produce a lot of food or is rich enough to import the food it needs has food security.
   - An African community where the people can't produce enough food or buy what they need does not have food security.

2) In 1996, the World Food Summit stated that global food security will be achieved when everyone, at all times, has access to sufficient, safe and nutritious food for an active and healthy life.

3) The World Health Organisation describes three things we need to address to achieve global food security:

   Availability: Sufficient food needs to be produced by countries to feed their populations and excess food should be exported to countries that need it.

   Access: Food needs to be affordable to all, or sufficient land and resources should be available for people to grow their own food.

   Utilisation: Educating people on food and nutrition means people can use a greater variety of foods, reduce food waste, retain the nutritional value of foods and prevent illness from cross-contamination.

4) Many factors affect food security:

   - Climate — some countries have unsuitable climates for farming (e.g. too hot or little rainfall).
   - Insufficient land — people living in poverty often don't have their own land to grow food.
   - Growing industrial crops — more farmland that previously grew crops for food is now being used to grow non-food crops, e.g. crops for biofuels (fuels from plant material).
   - Wealth — wealthier people have more disposable income to spend on food, often more than they need. People with lower incomes may not be able to afford nutritious food.
   - Rising population — the more people there are, the less food there is to go around.

With global demand for food increasing, we need to increase food supplies.

   - Using new technologies — e.g. GM crops can be given pest-resistance, higher nutritional values and higher yields.
   - Eating less meat — animals that are reared for their meat are fed crops that we grow. It's more efficient if we directly eat those crops instead.
   - Reducing food waste — if less food is wasted, more is available to eat.

Fairtrade is About Improving Conditions for Farmers

1) The Fairtrade Foundation was established to support farmers and workers in less developed countries and encourage sustainable food production.

2) Raw ingredients (such as tea leaves, coffee beans etc.) are used in expensive products — but the farmers often receive very little money for their produce.

3) Fairtrade aims to make it fairer for these smaller businesses by making sure they get a decent price and by improving working conditions.

4) The farmers themselves become more food secure — they have more money to spend on food for themselves and their families.

Look for the FAIRTRADE mark on products like coffee and tea.

The weather has a big impact on food production...

A question about climate change might pop up in the exam — make sure you are prepared to explain the various ways in which it can affect food production.

Warm-Up and Worked Exam Questions

Global food production is a difficult topic — once you think you've mastered it, work through these warm-up questions to get you in exam mood, and then attempt the questions on the next two pages.

Warm-Up Questions

1) Describe one advantage of using plastic to package food.
2) Give some benefits of 'pick your own' strawberries over buying from a supermarket.
3) Give an example of a food product that has a high carbon footprint, and say why it is high.
4) Briefly describe what the 'greenhouse effect' is.
5) Give one way that rising sea levels could affect food production.
6) Explain how food poverty can increase a person's risk of developing a diet-related health problem.
7) Describe the following things which are needed to address global food security:
   a) Availability   b) Access   c) Utilisation
8) What does the FAIRTRADE Mark on products mean?

Worked Exam Question

1 All food products have a **carbon footprint**.
   Buying and consuming food contributes to your personal carbon footprint.

   a) i) What is meant by the 'carbon footprint' of a food product?

   The amount of greenhouse gases directly or indirectly produced during

   the life cycle of the food product.

   [2 marks]

   ii) List **two** things that contribute to the carbon footprint of a food product.

   1. *Growing or rearing the raw ingredients*

   2. *Transporting the food product*

   There are lots of options here — processing, refrigerating or   [2 marks]
   packaging the food product are other acceptable answers.

   b) Louis wants to **reduce** the impact food has on his carbon footprint.
       Suggest ways that he could do this.

   Louis could eat more in season, locally produced food and aim to buy food products

   that have less excess packaging. He could also try to cut down on wasting food.

   He could do this by freezing leftovers and using them in other meals, and by using

   all parts of a food (such as bones for stocks).

   [3 marks]

Exam Questions

1 Packaging has many functions that are valuable to food **manufacturers**, but excess packaging can be harmful to the **environment**.

a) Give **one** benefit of packaging for manufacturers.

....

....

[1 mark]

b) Outline why some packaging has a negative impact on the environment.

....

....

....

[2 marks]

2 Scientific reports suggest the Earth's average temperature is **rising**.

Give **one** benefit and **one** drawback of increased global temperatures for food producers.

Benefit: ....

....

Drawback: ....

....

[2 marks]

3 **Food waste** has a **financial** impact on households.

a) Suggest **two** reasons why households throw away food.

1. ....

....

2. ....

....

[2 marks]

b) Suggest **two** ways households can reduce food waste.

1. ....

....

2. ....

....

[2 marks]

Exam Questions

4   Supermarkets may choose to source both **locally produced food** and food **imported** from other countries.

a)   Why might a supermarket choose to import food?

....

....

[1 mark]

b)   Explain **one** advantage of producing food locally rather than importing it from other countries.

Remember to use correct terminology in your answer, e.g. 'food miles'.

....

....

....

[2 marks]

5   **Food security** is a problem that affects local communities and entire countries.

a)   What is meant by 'food security'?

....

....

[1 mark]

b)   Explain how each of the following factors affect food security.

Population growth: ....

....

....

[2 marks]

Population growth

Food security

Wealth: ....

....

....

[2 marks]

Wealth   Biofuels

Biofuels: ....

....

....

[2 marks]

Primary Food Processing

All food goes through stages of processing before it reaches our plate. It's important so that food is safe to eat, is easier to transport, doesn't spoil as quickly and looks nice for the consumer.

Primary Processing Changes Raw Foods

Primary processing prepares raw foods (straight from being picked, harvested or slaughtered) so they're ready either to be eaten or cooked immediately or used as ingredients to make other food products.

Primary stages of processing include transporting food from its point of origin (the place where it's grown or reared), as well as cleaning, sorting, milling etc. For example:

Fruit / Vegetables

- Pits (stones) are removed from fruit, e.g. peaches and cherries.
- Fruits are squeezed for fruit juices or dried, e.g. grapes are sun-dried to make raisins.
- Fruits and vegetables are washed with water to remove dirt, insects and chemical sprays.
- Fruits and vegetables are sorted into different sizes and shapes.
- Fruits and seeds are crushed or pressed to extract oils, e.g. olive oil.

Meat / Poultry

- Some meats (e.g. beef) are hung and dried to make them more tender and improve flavour.
- Feathers and internal organs of poultry are removed.
- The wings and legs of poultry are tied (trussed) so it cooks evenly.
- Meat is chopped, sliced or cut.

Flour is Made by Milling Wheat Grains

A wheat grain
Bran (mostly fibre)
Endosperm (mostly starch)
Germ (vitamins, protein and fat)

1) A wheat grain contains different parts — the bran, endosperm and germ.
2) Wheat grains (seeds) are harvested and then cleaned to remove any stones, dust etc.
3) The grains are stored in dry conditions to prevent moulds from growing on them.
4) The grains are put into a hopper and are crushed between rollers that crack open the grain.
5) Different types of flour can be made by sieving and removing parts of the grain:

- Wholemeal flour — 100% of the grain is used, nothing is taken out.
- Wheatmeal (Brown) flour — about 85% of the grain is used, some of the bran and germ are removed.
- White flour — about 70% of the grain is used (only the endosperm is used).

6) Important B group vitamins are lost when making white flour, so they're added back in (p.95).
7) The Eatwell Guide recommends wholemeal products as we get the nutritional benefit of the whole grain.

Milk is Heat Treated to Kill Bacteria

Milk is heat treated to destroy pathogenic bacteria, but other non-harmful bacteria are also lost.

- Pasteurisation — milk is heated quickly to 72 °C for 15 seconds and then rapidly cooled.
- Ultra Heat Treatment (UHT) — milk is heated to at least 135 °C for 1-4 seconds and packed in a sterile container — the milk can last at an ambient (see p.52) temperature for several months. UHT milk has slightly less nutritional value and a slightly different taste than pasteurised milk.
- Sterilisation — bottled raw milk goes through a steam chamber at 110 °C for 10-30 minutes. ALL bacteria are killed, so it tastes different, and many B group vitamins and vitamin C are lost.
- Microfiltration (MF) — bacteria that turn milk sour remain after pasteurisation. Microfiltration forces milk through a membrane which separates the milk from the souring bacteria. This extends the shelf life of the milk and doesn't have much effect on the flavour or nutritional content.

Secondary Food Processing

Secondary Processing Uses Primary Processed Foods

After primary processing comes, surprisingly, secondary processing. Primary processed foods are turned into other food products by altering them in some way or combining them with other ingredients.

Raw food

↓

Primary processing

↓

Secondary processing

Milk can be Turned into Lots of Dairy Products

Milk contains a natural fat called butterfat (or simply milk fat) — the fat content is important to make different dairy products:

Cream

1) Milk fat is less dense than water and naturally rises to the top of the milk — this layer of fat is known as cream, and can be 'skimmed off' the top.

2) This process can be sped up by centrifugation — this is where milk is rotated at high speed by an electric motor, which forces the milk fat droplets to separate from the denser liquid.

3) Whipped cream is made by whisking cream (or by using an electric mixer) — this agitates and incorporates air (see p.40) into the cream, forming a foam and making it light and fluffy.

Different types of cream have different amounts of milk fat — e.g. single cream has around 18% milk fat content, whipped cream has around 35%, and double cream around 48%.

In the UK, whole milk contains around 3.5% milk fat, semi-skimmed milk contains around 1.5% milk fat, and skimmed milk (where the cream is removed entirely) contains only around 0.1% milk fat.

You'll only need to remember this stuff if you're doing the OCR course.

Butter

1) Butter is made by churning cream.
2) Churning agitates the cream until the fat droplets begin to stick together.
3) The cream becomes thicker and thicker until it forms a solid mass of butter.
4) Any leftover liquid (buttermilk) is drained away.

Butter has a milk fat content of around 80%.

Cheese

(1) For most types of cheese, raw milk is pasteurised to kill off any pathogenic bacteria.

Bacteria   Rennet

(2) 'Friendly' bacteria sour and thicken the milk, and rennet from calf stomachs is added. A vegetarian alternative to rennet can be used.

 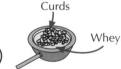

Curds

Whey

(3) Rennet causes the milk to coagulate into solid cheese curds. The liquid remaining is called whey.

(4) The whey is removed by either draining, cutting, cooking, salting or stacking curds on top of each other (cheddaring).

(5) The curds are pressed to form blocks of cheese and placed in temperature-controlled storage to 'mature' and develop taste and texture.

(6) Bacteria or moulds may be added to change the flavour of the cheese (see p.55).

Milk can also be made into yoghurt — see p.55 for more details.

Secondary Food Processing

Flour can be Turned into Pasta and Bread

Flour goes through <u>secondary</u> stages of processing to turn it into <u>pasta</u> and <u>bread</u>:

Pasta
- Flour is <u>mixed</u> with <u>water</u> or <u>eggs</u> to make a dough.
- The dough is <u>shaped</u> by forcing it through a <u>metal die</u> and then <u>folded</u> / <u>twisted</u> etc.
- <u>Colourings</u> may be added to dye the pasta (e.g. <u>spinach</u> makes it <u>green</u>, <u>beetroot</u> makes it <u>purple</u> and <u>carrot</u> makes an <u>orange</u> pasta).
- Pasta can be sold <u>fresh</u> or <u>dried</u>. Dried pasta has a much longer shelf life — all the <u>moisture</u> in the pasta is taken out.

Pasta usually uses <u>semolina</u> flour — it comes from milling a type of wheat known as <u>durum</u> wheat.

Bread
- Flour is <u>mixed</u> with <u>water</u> and <u>yeast</u> to make a dough.
- The dough is <u>kneaded</u> to 'work' the gluten (see p.40).
- The dough is <u>proved</u> to let the yeast <u>ferment</u> (see p.44).
- The dough is <u>baked</u> in an oven.

Fruit can be Turned into Jam and Jellies

E.g. filtering, pasteurising and packaging.

Fruit goes through <u>secondary</u> stages of processing to turn it into <u>juice</u>, <u>jam</u> (a <u>fruit preserve</u>) and <u>jelly</u>:

Jam
- <u>Crushed fruit</u> is mixed with <u>sugar</u>.
- The mixture is <u>boiled</u> (to at least <u>105 °C</u>) and left to cool.
- <u>Pectin</u> (a gelling substance in the fruit) <u>thickens</u> the jam as it cools.
- Jam is <u>poured</u> into glass jars which are <u>sealed</u> to extend its shelf life.

Jelly
- <u>Fruit juice</u> is mixed with <u>sugar</u> and heated.
- <u>Gelatine</u> (a gelling substance from animal products) is soaked in <u>cold water</u> to <u>soften</u> and then added to the hot mixture.
- The mixture is <u>sieved</u> to remove <u>lumps</u> or <u>pips</u>.
- The mixture is <u>refrigerated</u> — the gelatine <u>thickens</u> and <u>sets</u> the jelly.

Pectin must be added if low-pectin fruits are used, e.g. raspberries, so that the jam sets properly.

Processing Affects Sensory and Nutritional Properties

Processing a food can change how it <u>looks</u> and <u>tastes</u>, as well as its <u>nutritional content</u>. For example:

- <u>Fish</u> and <u>meat</u> products might be <u>salt-cured</u> (preserved with salt) — this gives them a <u>salty taste</u>.
- <u>Colourings</u> might be added to pasta (see above) to alter the <u>colour</u> of the pasta.
- <u>Milk</u> can be <u>heat treated</u> (see p.92), which can alter its <u>taste</u>.

- There's <u>lots of fibre</u> in the <u>skin</u> of a potato — peeling the skin removes this <u>important source</u> of fibre.
- <u>High temperatures</u> can <u>destroy vitamins</u>, e.g. when using <u>UHT</u> for milk or <u>boiling fruit</u> for jam.

Food processing can have lots of complex stages...

Grab a piece of paper and draw a mind map to show the primary and secondary processes that are used to turn raw milk into different dairy products (whipped cream, butter, cheese and yoghurt). *The following words may help you:*

Pasteurisation   **Agitation**   **Butterfat**   **Bacteria**   **Coagulation**   **Moulds**

Food Fortification and Modification

Today's technology allows manufacturers to add vitamins and minerals to food products — some people claim that this is an effective method of improving our health and preventing deficiencies in the diet.

Fortification Adds Nutrients to a Food

Take a look through p.1–6 and p.10–13 to see why we need nutrients in our diet.

1) Fortification is where nutrients are added to a food.

2) It improves the nutritional value of foods.

3) Fortification is done for different reasons — sometimes it's to replace nutrients lost during processing, or to add extra nutrients to make a food more nutrient-rich.

4) Here are some common foods that are fortified:

White Flour

- Iron, thiamin (B1), niacin (B3) and calcium are lost during the production of white flour (p.92).
- By law, these nutrients have to be added back in — they aren't added to wholemeal flour because the nutrients are naturally present.

Breakfast Cereals

- Cereals can be fortified with iron, thiamin and folic acid.
- Cereal is eaten by lots of people — if manufacturers choose to fortify their products it helps the population get the recommended amounts of these nutrients.

Butter Alternatives

- Many people use butter alternatives, e.g. margarine and low-fat spreads.
- Butter naturally contains vitamins A and D — by fortifying butter alternatives, consumers don't miss out on these important vitamins.
- Margarine and low-fat spreads are usually fortified on a voluntary basis by manufacturers.

Cholesterol Lowering Spreads

- Some vegetable fat spreads have added plant sterols.
- These substances help reduce cholesterol for people with high cholesterol only — they don't benefit people with normal cholesterol levels.

5) Manufacturers may fortify processed foods as a 'marketing tool' — it can give the impression that their products are healthy.

6) You should be careful eating excessive amounts of fortified foods — you may get too much of some vitamins or minerals in your diet.

Multivitamin supplements are hugely popular:

- Multivitamin supplements are full of vitamins and minerals your body needs — they're handy if you don't get enough from your normal diet but should never replace a healthy, balanced diet.
- They are more useful for certain people, e.g. elderly adults (see p.18) and pregnant women.
- However, it's debatable whether they make any difference for most people and taking too many could be harmful to your health.

Fortifying a food doesn't necessarily make it healthy...

Fortification is used in loads of different foods. You might think that you could just add vitamins to junk food to make them healthier, but unfortunately these foods are still packed with sugar, salt and fats.

Food Fortification and Modification

There are other ways of <u>modifying</u> food products so they're nicer than ever — read on...

Additives Change the **Properties** of Food

1) An <u>additive</u> is something that's <u>added</u> to food to <u>improve its properties</u>.
2) Some additives occur <u>naturally</u> and some are made <u>artificially</u>.

Preservatives

<u>Preservatives</u> are additives that <u>prevent bacteria from growing</u> — so the <u>food lasts longer</u>.
- Natural preservatives include <u>vinegar</u>, <u>lemon juice</u>, <u>salt</u> and <u>sugar</u>. ⎫ Important in food
- Artificial preservatives include things like <u>nitrates</u> and <u>sulphites</u>. ⎭ safety — see p.49.

Colourings

<u>Colourings</u> make food look more <u>attractive</u> and more <u>appealing</u> to eat. They can be used to <u>add colour</u> to something that is <u>colourless</u>, or to <u>return</u> food to its natural colour if it's <u>lost</u> during <u>processing</u>.
- <u>Caramel</u> is a <u>natural</u> food colouring — it can make products darkish brown, e.g. <u>cola</u>.
- <u>Tartrazine</u> is an <u>artificial</u> food colouring — it's used to make products a <u>yellow</u> colour, e.g. <u>custard powder</u>, <u>syrups</u>, <u>sweets</u>. | Tartrazine combined with a blue colouring produces the green used for mushy peas.

Flavourings

<u>Flavourings</u> add <u>new flavours</u> and <u>flavour enhancers</u> improve the <u>existing flavour</u> of a product.
- <u>Natural</u> flavourings include <u>herbs</u> and <u>spices</u>, e.g. <u>basil</u>, <u>chillies</u> and <u>vanilla</u>. | Natural sugar alternatives like xylitol and stevia are becoming more popular now, e.g. in soft drinks.
- <u>Artificial sweeteners</u>, e.g. <u>aspartame</u>, are used as <u>substitutes</u> for <u>sugar</u>. →
- <u>Monosodium glutamate</u> (MSG) is an example of a <u>flavour enhancer</u> — it boosts the existing flavour of a product and gives it a <u>savoury taste</u>.

Emulsifiers / Stabilisers

<u>Emulsifiers and stabilisers</u> help to <u>preserve</u> the <u>shape</u> and <u>texture</u> of food products (see p.43).
<u>Emulsifiers</u> help <u>mix together</u> ingredients that <u>don't usually mix</u>, e.g. <u>oily</u> and <u>watery liquids</u>.
<u>Stabilisers</u> stop mixed ingredients from <u>separating</u>.
- <u>Lecithin</u> is a <u>natural emulsifier</u> found in <u>egg yolks</u> and <u>soya beans</u>.
- <u>Pectin</u> is a <u>natural stabiliser</u> found in <u>berries</u>, <u>apples</u> and many other <u>fruits</u>.

<u>Thickeners</u> are another type of additive, and are used to <u>thicken liquids</u>. Common thickeners include <u>xanthan gum</u> and <u>egg whites</u>.

Additives Have **Disadvantages** Too

1) Additives, such as <u>sulphites</u> (found in <u>bacon</u> or <u>salami</u>), can cause <u>allergic reactions</u> and worsen <u>asthma</u>.
2) Some <u>natural</u> additives, like <u>sugar</u> and <u>salt</u>, are <u>bad</u> for our <u>health</u> in <u>large amounts</u>.
3) They can disguise <u>poor quality ingredients</u>, e.g. processed meat products may not contain much meat but can be made to <u>taste good</u> by using additives.
4) Additives must pass a <u>safety test</u> before they can be used in food — when an additive passes it gets an <u>E number</u> and can be used throughout the <u>European Union</u>, e.g. caramel colouring is E150a...
5) ...but there are concerns about possible <u>long-term health effects</u>. Some research <u>suggests</u> that some colourings, e.g. <u>sunset yellow</u> (E110) and <u>tartrazine</u> (E102), cause <u>hyperactive behaviour</u> in children.

EXAM TIP

This sentence needs an emulsifier...

Don't worry about memorising a list of E number codes for the exam — it's more important that you understand the functions of the different types of additives and can name a few examples for each.

Warm-Up and Worked Exam Questions

Alright, that's everything covered in Section Five — as always, try the warm-up questions to start and check that the worked exam questions make sense, then delve into the exam questions on the next few pages.

Warm-Up Questions

1) Suggest two primary processes that a walnut might undergo.
2) Give a brief explanation of how these dairy products are made: a) cream   b) butter
3) Explain why a milk substitute like soya milk might be fortified.
4) Give a reason why a manufacturer might add a colouring to sweets.

Worked Exam Questions

1   The ingredients for a caramel and vanilla slice are shown on the right.

> - Flour
> - Egg
> - Milk
> - Butter
> - Salt
> - Sugar
> - Caramel
> - Aspartame
> - Vanilla essence

   a)   Identify the artificial sweetener from the list.

Aspartame

[1 mark]

   b)   i)   Identify a natural preservative from the list.

Sugar is another correct answer here.

Salt

[1 mark]

      ii)   Describe the function of a preservative.

Preservatives prolong the shelf life of a food because they prevent microorganisms from growing and can prevent enzymic browning.

[1 mark]

2   Secondary food processing is essential to make some food products, such as bread.

   a)   What is meant by secondary food processing?

It is where primary processed foods are changed or mixed to make other products.

[1 mark]

   b)   Outline the processing stages that turn flour into bread.

Bread is made by mixing flour, water and yeast together to form a dough. The dough is kneaded to 'work' the gluten and make the dough more elastic, and is left in a warm place to let the yeast ferment. This is called proving and it causes carbon dioxide to be released and trapped in the dough, causing it to rise. Finally, the dough is baked, which causes the bread to rise even more as the carbon dioxide expands.

[4 marks]

Exam Questions

1   By **law**, manufacturers must fortify white flour with certain nutrients.
They may **choose** to fortify margarine or low-fat spreads.

   a) Name **two** nutrients that are added to the following fortified foods:

     i) White flour

       1. ....   2. ....

[1 mark]

     ii) Margarine

       1. ....   2. ....

[1 mark]

   b) Give **one** reason why manufacturers may voluntarily choose to fortify processed foods.

....

[1 mark]

   c) What is the role of plant sterols in fortified vegetable fat spreads?

....

....

[1 mark]

2   All manufactured food products go through **primary** food processing.

For each row in the table below, name **one** primary process and state why it is carried out.
Do not repeat the same process.

	Primary process	Why is this process carried out?
Vegetables	....	....
Poultry	....	....
Fruit	....	....

[6 marks]

Exam Questions

3 Milk is heat treated to kill any harmful bacteria.

a) Outline **one** example of a heat treatment used for milk.

....

....

....

[2 marks]

b) Name **one** food product that is made from the secondary processing of milk.

....

[1 mark]

4 Processing can alter the **nutritional** and **sensory properties** of foods.

a) Give **two** examples of how processing can change the **nutritional** properties of a food.

1. ....

2. ....

[2 marks]

b) Give **two** examples of how processing can change the **sensory** properties of a food.

1. ....

2. ....

[2 marks]

5 Some consumers are wary of food products that contain lots of **E numbers**.

a) What is an 'E number'?

....

....

[1 mark]

b) Discuss why some consumers have concerns over the use of additives.

[8 marks]

Revision Questions for Section Five

Section Five is done and dusted — try these questions to see how much you can remember.
- Try these questions and tick off each one when you get it right.
- When you've done all the questions for a topic and are completely happy with it, tick off the topic.

Grown, Reared and Caught Food (p.77-81) ☑
1) What is meant by 'intensive farming'? ☑
2) Give one disadvantage of using pesticides. ☑
3) What is meant by 'organic farming'? ☑
4) Describe an alternative to using a pesticide as a method of controlling pests. ☑
5) What is a 'genetically modified' food? ☑
6) List five advantages and three disadvantages of growing GM foods. ☑
7) Explain the difference between a 'factory-farmed' and a 'free-range' animal. ☑
8) What does the 'Red Tractor' symbol mean on food packaging? ☑
9) Describe two different fishing methods. ☑
10) Explain how unsustainable fishing can damage the environment. ☑
11) What three groups can fish be classified into? ☑

Waste Food and Packaging (p.84-85) ☑
12) List lots of ways that food is wasted: a) in the home   b) by producers and retailers ☑
13) Explain why using excessive packaging is bad for the environment. ☑
14) List three ways that we can help to reduce food packaging waste. ☑

Food Miles, Carbon Footprint and Global Food Production (p.86-88) ☑
15) What is meant by 'food miles'? ☑
16) Give a reason why bananas are imported to the UK. ☑
17) List four advantages and two disadvantages of only buying local food. ☑
18) Name three things that increase your carbon footprint. ☑
19) Briefly describe how food production contributes to climate change. ☑
20) For each weather event, explain how it affects food production: a) drought   b) flooding ☑
21) What is meant by 'food poverty'? ☑
22) What is meant by 'food security'? Describe five factors that can affect food security. ☑
23) Describe what the Fairtrade Foundation is. ☑

Food Processing, Fortification and Modification (p.92-96) ☑
24) Give two examples of primary processing for: a) vegetables   b) meat ☑
25) Describe the following procedures used in the primary processing of milk:
    a) pasteurisation   b) UHT   c) sterilisation   d) microfiltration ☑
26) Explain how these food products are made: a) pasta   b) jam   c) cheese ☑
27) What is meant by food 'fortification'? List four food products that are commonly fortified. ☑
28) Give an example for each type of additive and say what it does:
    a) preservatives   b) colourings   c) flavourings   d) emulsifiers   e) stabilisers ☑
29) List four disadvantages of using food additives. ☑

Practical Skills

A note about this section

On these pages we'll cover all the <u>practical skills</u> you need to learn.
You should have practised all these skills during your course — this is just a <u>brief reminder</u>.
If there are any that you're <u>rusty</u> on, it's time to do some <u>brushing up</u>.

- Make sure you have a <u>detailed knowledge</u> and <u>understanding</u> of all of these skills for your <u>exam</u>.
- You'll also need to <u>demonstrate a good range</u> of these skills in your <u>non-exam assessment</u>.

General Practical Skills

Prepare Your Workspace

1) It's a good idea to <u>organise</u> all your ingredients and equipment <u>before</u> you start <u>cooking</u> (e.g. weighing and measuring out your ingredients).

2) You can also <u>grease</u>, <u>oil</u>, <u>line</u> or <u>flour</u> equipment like tins — this not only makes removing the food easier, but it also helps with cleaning up after.

Select and Adapt Cooking Times

1) <u>Cooking time</u> is affected by different factors, including the <u>type of food</u> (e.g. fish cooks a lot faster than red meat) and <u>portion size</u> (e.g. a thick piece of steak needs cooking for longer than a thin one).

2) Select an <u>appropriate</u> cooking time, but be prepared to <u>adapt</u> it — e.g. if your food is cooking quicker than expected, reduce the cooking time (but make sure that you cook it thoroughly all the way through to the middle).

Cakes can sink if you remove them from the oven before they're cooked, if you open the oven during cooking (letting cold air in) or if you put too much sugar in the mixture. These can be prevented by making sure the oven is up to temperature before baking and that each ingredient is measured precisely.

Weigh and Measure Ingredients Accurately

1) <u>Dry ingredients</u> (e.g. flour) and <u>solid ingredients</u> (e.g. butter) are usually measured using <u>electronic</u> or <u>balance weighing scales</u>.

2) <u>Liquids</u> are measured in <u>measuring jugs</u> or <u>cups</u> (some dry ingredients are measured in cups too).

3) You can use <u>measuring spoons</u> (e.g. a teaspoon) for small amounts.

Test Food to See If It's Cooked

You need to be able to tell if food is <u>cooked through</u> properly. Luckily, there are ways to check this:

- <u>Temperature probes</u> are placed into the middle of food to check if it's <u>hot enough</u> (see p.53).

- You can pop <u>knives</u> or <u>skewers</u> into food such as cake mixtures — if they come out <u>clean</u> then the mixture is cooked.

- You can also cut into <u>meats</u> and apply a little pressure — if the <u>juices</u> come out <u>clear</u> (without blood) the food is cooked.

- You can <u>gently press</u> cakes to see if they're cooked. The cake is done if it <u>springs back</u> when you poke it.

- When cooking foods like pasta, you can <u>bite</u> into a small piece to see if it's cooked to your liking. But be warned — too much use of the bite test can quickly result in small meals.

- If you've ever baked biscuits until they were '<u>golden brown</u>', you've successfully completed a <u>visual colour check</u>.

- You can also perform a <u>sound check</u> by knocking on the bottom of baked bread — if it's baked correctly you should hear a hollow sound.

Practical Skills

Change How Food Affects the Senses

1) You can change the flavour of foods with <u>salt</u>, <u>pepper</u>, <u>sugar</u>, <u>herbs</u> and <u>spices</u>, but also by using:

- <u>Pastes</u> (e.g. garlic paste)
- <u>Reductions</u> (see p.105)
- <u>Jus</u> (a thin sauce made from the juices of cooked meat)
- <u>Infused oils</u> (oils that have absorbed the flavour of herbs)

When cooking, try a small amount of your food to see how it tastes. You can then adjust it until the flavour is right.

2) The <u>texture</u> of food can be changed by adding <u>crust</u>, <u>crispiness</u> and <u>crumbs</u>, e.g. coating chicken in breadcrumbs, adding seeds to bread dough or breadcrumbs on top of a dish, e.g. macaroni cheese.

3) <u>Browning</u> changes the <u>flavour</u> and <u>appearance</u> of food:

- Both <u>dextrinisation</u> and <u>caramelisation</u> brown food (see p.41).
- You can even use a cook's <u>blowtorch</u> to brown the tops of foods, e.g. a crème brûlée.
- You can <u>glaze</u> foods (e.g. pies) by <u>brushing egg</u> over the food. When it cooks, the pie will have a nice golden brown colour.

Add Garnishes and Decorate Your Dishes

1) <u>Garnishes</u> are small <u>additions</u> to your dish and can <u>add extra colour</u> and/or <u>flavour</u>. These can be as <u>simple or complicated</u> as you want, from a slice of lemon or a piece of lettuce to a piped balsamic sauce or a flower made out of a radish.

2) Other <u>decorative techniques</u> can be used, such as <u>piping</u> icing onto a cake, or creating a decorative <u>pattern</u> on top of a pie.

3) Styling your food using these techniques can make your dish look <u>more appealing</u>.

Knife Skills

Different Knives Are Used for Different Jobs

You need a variety of <u>knives</u> for all the <u>different skills</u> you use when preparing food:

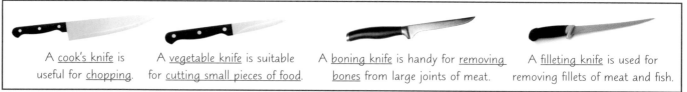

A <u>cook's knife</u> is useful for <u>chopping</u>.

A <u>vegetable knife</u> is suitable for <u>cutting small pieces of food</u>.

A <u>boning knife</u> is handy for <u>removing bones</u> from large joints of meat.

A <u>filleting knife</u> is used for removing fillets of meat and fish.

It's <u>REALLY IMPORTANT</u> to <u>take care</u> when using these knives as they can cause serious harm.

There are Different Ways to Cut Fruit and Vegetables

1) When cutting <u>smaller fruits and vegetables</u> (e.g. apples or potatoes) use a <u>bridge hold</u>.

2) When cutting <u>longer fruits and vegetables</u> (e.g. carrots or cucumbers) use a <u>claw grip</u>. It's really important that your <u>fingers</u> are <u>tucked under</u> here so they don't get sliced off.

3) You can use a knife to <u>peel</u>, <u>slice</u> and <u>dice</u> (chop into small cubes) your fruit and veg. Or cut them into <u>batons</u> (thick sticks) or, to be fancier, <u>julienne</u> strips (thin sticks).

Practical Skills

Cutting **Meat** and **Fish** Is More Complicated

1) Cutting meat and fish is more complicated and requires a different approach to cutting fruit and veg. It also requires a different type of knife, e.g. a <u>boning</u> or <u>filleting knife</u> (see previous page).

2) You can <u>divide</u> a <u>whole chicken</u> into eight portions (two of each of the following: drumsticks, thighs, breasts and wings). The chicken breasts are then often <u>filleted</u> (this removes the skin and tenderloin).

There are loads of video tutorials online that show you how to portion and fillet various foods with step-by-step instructions.

3) Different methods of filleting are needed for <u>round</u> fish (e.g. mackerel) and <u>flatfish</u> (e.g. plaice) due to the position of the backbone. You'll typically get 2 fillets (pieces) from round fish, and 4 from flatfish.

4) Knives can be used to remove <u>fat</u> and <u>rind</u> (the thick skin of foods such as pork).

Preparing **Fruit** and **Vegetables**

1) You probably already know (and use) lots of the different ways you can prepare fruit and veg.

2) Some of the <u>most common</u> include: <u>mashing</u>, <u>crushing</u>, <u>shredding</u>, <u>grating</u>, <u>peeling</u>, <u>de-seeding</u> and <u>blending</u>.

3) Other methods include:

- <u>Segmenting</u> — e.g. <u>dividing an orange</u> into segments.
- <u>Piping</u> — e.g. <u>piping mash</u> to create decorative patterns.
- <u>Blanching</u> — placing the fruit or veg into <u>boiling</u> then <u>cold water</u> (see p.34).
- <u>De-skinning</u> — this can be done by blanching tomatoes (after blanching, the skins can be <u>peeled off</u> easily just using your fingertips).
- <u>Scooping</u> — this is used when <u>balling melons</u> or making <u>equal portions</u> of <u>mash</u>.
- <u>Juicing</u> — e.g. using a <u>lemon squeezer</u>.
- <u>Preparing garnishes</u> — e.g. <u>tomato roses</u> that go alongside a main dish.
- <u>Scissor snipping</u> — e.g. when <u>snipping herbs</u>. You can use special <u>herb scissors</u> that have <u>multiple blades</u> to make snipping even quicker.

4) You can also <u>prevent enzymic browning</u> while preparing fruit and veg, e.g. by <u>blanching</u> them or adding an <u>acid</u> like lemon juice (see p.50).

Use of the **Cooker** and **Cooking Methods**

The technical side of the <u>cooking methods</u> below have been covered in <u>Section 2</u>, but here's a quick recap on how you can use your cooker's <u>grill</u>, <u>oven</u> and <u>hob</u>:

Grill
- The cooker can grill food such as <u>meat</u>, <u>fish</u>, <u>veg</u> and <u>firm cheese</u> like <u>halloumi</u> (see p.36).
- You can also use the grill to <u>char</u> (blacken the outside) and <u>toast</u> foods, e.g. seeds and nuts.

Oven
- The <u>oven</u> can be used for <u>baking</u> (p.36), <u>roasting</u> (p.37) and <u>braising</u> (p.35).
- You can also use it to cook <u>casseroles</u> and <u>tagines</u>. Both are <u>slow-cooked</u> to <u>tenderise</u> the meat inside. Like braising, they cook food in a mix of liquid, vegetables and herbs. A <u>tagine</u> is a <u>slow-cooked North African dish</u> that's cooked in a covered pot which (confusingly) is also called a tagine. Both casseroles and tagines are <u>covered</u> during cooking to trap moisture.

A tagine

Hob
- <u>Water-based</u> hob methods include <u>steaming</u>, <u>boiling</u>, <u>simmering</u>, <u>blanching</u> and <u>poaching</u> (p.34).
- <u>Fat-based</u> hob methods include <u>stir-frying</u> and <u>shallow frying</u> (p.35).
- The hob is also used for <u>dry frying</u>, sometimes called <u>dry roasting</u> (p.37).

Practical Skills

Use of Equipment

Equipment Can Be Used to Save Time

1) <u>Blenders</u> are used to <u>blend</u> (chop and mix) different ingredients together. This makes them good for <u>soups</u> and <u>smoothies</u>. They come in many different forms: some are a jug with a rotating blade, while with others you lower the blade into the food <u>by hand</u>.

2) <u>Food processors</u> are similar to blenders but they can be used for <u>mixing</u>, <u>slicing</u>, <u>chopping</u>, <u>grinding</u> and <u>dicing</u> food. Using the <u>same settings</u> will give you the <u>same results</u> each time. They're good for making burgers, meatballs, quickly chopping onions or (with an attachment) grating carrots.

3) <u>Food mixers</u> (unsurprisingly) mix food. They're often used for making <u>cake mixtures</u> and <u>batters</u>. Like blenders, they can be <u>hand-held</u> or come as a worktop appliance with a mixing bowl attached.

4) <u>Pasta machines</u> have <u>rollers</u> that turn your <u>pasta dough</u> into flat <u>sheets of pasta</u>. They can usually be adjusted to change the <u>thickness</u> of the pasta and create <u>different types</u> of pasta.

5) <u>Microwave ovens</u> use <u>radiation</u> (see p.33) to <u>quickly</u> cook foods such as baked potato and to heat up foods such as baked beans. They're also good for quickly <u>melting</u> foods like chocolate and cheese.

Prepare, Combine and Shape

1) You can <u>shape</u> and bind <u>wet</u> mixtures <u>by hand</u>, e.g. shaping burgers, fish cakes, meatballs, or doughs for biscuits or bread buns — it's quick, but your results might not be very consistent.

2) You can also <u>combine</u> different foods in a variety of ways to make your dishes more interesting:

- You can <u>wrap</u> foods around each other — e.g. wrapping bacon around chicken or sausages.

- Foods including meat, vegetables and fruit can be <u>skewered</u> together to make <u>kebabs</u>.

- Different types of <u>rolls</u> can be made — e.g. sushi, sausage rolls and spring rolls.

- You can <u>coat</u> foods with different ingredients — e.g. coating chicken pieces, fish or cheese by covering them in flour, then egg, then breadcrumbs.

- Foods can also be combined by <u>layering</u> them. A popular example is <u>lasagne</u>, although layering can also be achieved more simply — e.g. the mashed potato on the top of a <u>shepherd's pie</u>.

Mixtures for burgers, fish cakes and meatballs often include eggs — when the food is cooked, the proteins in the eggs coagulate (see p.40) and bind the mixture together.

Bacon wrapped around chicken

Vegetable kebab

Maki roll

Chicken in breadcrumbs

Lasagne

Combining foods is a great way to bring together different flavours...

Experimenting with how you can shape, combine and cook food is a heck of a lot of fun. Without the invention of unusual ideas, we wouldn't have some of the delicious food combinations we have today.

Practical Skills

Now if this stuff doesn't get you excited, I don't know what will. Seriously though, this stuff is <u>dead useful</u>.

Making Sauces

Sauces can be Made in Lots of Different Ways

Sauces are used in both savoury and sweet dishes — as an <u>accompaniment</u> (e.g. custard, ketchup) or as <u>part</u> of the dish (e.g. in lasagne). You can put pretty much anything you like in a sauce, but they usually contain at least one of these: <u>flour</u>, <u>butter</u>, <u>eggs</u>, <u>cornflour</u>, <u>stock</u>, <u>milk</u>, <u>cream</u>, <u>sugar</u>. Here are three ways you can make a sauce:

> When making a sauce, heat is transferred by <u>conduction</u> (from the pan to the sauce) and <u>convection</u> (through the sauce) — see p.33.

Gelatinisation Thickens Starch-Based Sauces

Starch-based sauces thicken by <u>gelatinisation</u> (see p.41). They can be made in different ways:

> You can make a <u>roux</u> as a base for your sauce by mixing equal weights of <u>melted butter</u> and <u>plain flour</u> in a pan — stir until the flour is <u>cooked</u> (to add colour and get rid of the raw flour taste). Gradually add <u>liquid</u> (e.g. milk) to make a sauce, stirring to avoid lumps the whole time. <u>Simmer</u>, then add the rest of your ingredients. The roux will help to give your sauce a good <u>consistency</u> (thickness) and <u>flavour</u>.

> To make a <u>blended sauce</u>, you mix <u>cornflour</u> with a small amount of <u>water/milk</u> to form a paste (a blend of starch and liquid). You then heat up additional liquid and add it to the paste to make a sauce. <u>Heat</u> the sauce until it <u>thickens</u>.

> Or you can just make an <u>all-in-one</u> sauce by putting all your ingredients into a saucepan. <u>Stir</u> over a medium heat, until your sauce starts to bubble and thicken.

You can adapt a plain roux sauce to make an <u>infused velouté</u> sauce or a <u>béchamel</u> sauce:

- A <u>velouté sauce</u> is made by adding <u>white stock</u> (e.g. chicken or fish stock) to the roux <u>instead of milk</u>.
- For a <u>béchamel sauce</u>, you simmer the milk with foods such as <u>peppercorns</u>, <u>onions</u>, <u>cloves</u> and <u>bay leaves</u>.

The <u>thickness</u> of your sauce depends on the <u>ratio of starch to liquid</u> in it, e.g. the more milk you add to your roux, the thinner your sauce will become. This has many different uses, such as using a <u>thick</u> roux sauce to <u>bind ingredients</u> together in a fish cake, or making a <u>thin pouring sauce</u>, e.g. a cheese sauce.

Starch-based sauces can often become lumpy, e.g. if liquid is added too quickly or the mixture isn't stirred (agitated) enough, so it's important to add the liquid gradually and stir thoroughly. You can sometimes save lumpy sauces by using a sieve to get rid of any larger lumps.

Reduction Sauces Thicken by Evaporation

1) Reduction is a process that <u>thickens liquids</u> such as <u>sauces</u> and soups by <u>simmering</u> them and causing water to <u>evaporate</u> — this also <u>concentrates</u> the <u>flavour</u> of the sauce, making it more <u>intense</u>.

2) Common reduction sauces include <u>tomato pasta sauce</u>, <u>curry sauce</u> and <u>gravy</u>, although they can also be sweet-tasting — such as apple or raspberry <u>coulis</u>.

You can include liquids like cooking juices, stock and wine in reduction sauces.

Emulsion Sauces Contain Oil and Water

There's loads of stuff about <u>emulsion sauces</u> (e.g. hollandaise) on p.43.

Tenderise and Marinate

1) <u>Marination</u> involves <u>soaking</u> vegetables, meat, fish or alternatives such as tofu in a <u>liquid</u> before they're cooked. This liquid often contains <u>herbs</u>, <u>spices</u> and <u>acid</u> (e.g. lemon juice).

2) The <u>acid</u> in <u>marinades</u> makes meat <u>more tender</u> by <u>denaturing protein</u> (see p.40).

3) Marinades also add <u>flavour</u> and <u>moisture</u> to food. It's common for foods such as chicken to be paired with <u>barbecue</u>, <u>sweet chilli</u> or <u>tandoori marinades</u>.

Tofu changes colour as it absorbs marinades.

Practical Skills

Making Dough

Dough Making Uses Lots of Technical Skills

1) You need to make doughs whenever you make foods like <u>bread</u>, <u>pastry</u> and <u>pasta</u>.

2) Most doughs are made by combining <u>flour</u>, <u>water</u> and a bit of <u>salt</u>.

3) If you're making <u>pasta dough</u>, you can <u>change the water for eggs</u>.

4) <u>Bread doughs</u> also include <u>yeast</u> to give the final product a nice <u>rise</u> (p.44).

5) <u>Fat</u> or <u>oil</u> is added to change the <u>texture</u> of the dough —
loads of it is used in pastry, and just a little in bread or pasta.

6) Making doughs can show you've learned lots of <u>technical skills</u>, including:

- <u>Shortening</u> (see p.42), e.g. if you were making shortcrust pastry.
- <u>Forming gluten</u> (see p.40), e.g. if you were kneading bread dough.
- <u>Proving</u> (see p.44), e.g. if you were making risen bread.

Different Types of Pastry Have Different Properties

When making <u>pastry dough</u>, you need to choose which one gives you the right <u>taste</u> and <u>texture</u>:

Type of pastry	Properties of finished pastry	Used for...
Shortcrust	A 'short' texture (see p.42)	pies, quiches, tarts and pasties
Sweet	Sweeter than other pastries	sweet pies and tarts
Puff	Has flaky, puffed up layers	sausage rolls, pies, fruit turnovers
Choux	Light texture and hollow centre	profiteroles and eclairs
Filo	Light, crisp and fragile	strudels and pastry parcels

Each dough is different, and you need to think about different things for each one. E.g. when making <u>choux pastry</u> (for which the dough is more like a paste than other doughs), you need to <u>cool</u> the hot flour/butter mixture <u>before</u> adding your <u>eggs</u> (to avoid protein coagulation), and make sure you use enough water and a hot oven so that steam can be created and make the dough rise.

Shaping and Finishing Your Dough

When it comes to adding <u>shape</u> and <u>finishing touches</u> to your dough, there are a lot of options. Here's a big list of ways you could shape and finish your dough. You should know what each one is and be ready to <u>demonstrate some</u> in your <u>non-exam assessment task</u>.

- You can <u>roll out</u> doughs to get the right <u>shape</u> and <u>thickness</u>. Use a <u>rolling pin</u> to get an even thickness, and <u>flour</u> to stop the mixture sticking to surfaces.
- <u>Folding</u> a dough creates layers. This helps to trap air (p.44) and is used to make foods like puff pastries and palmiers.
- You can <u>line cases</u> with pastry dough (press the dough into the shape of the case — the dough then bakes into this shape, giving your pie a solid <u>pastry case</u>. You can prick the pastry with a fork to release any air and keep a flat base.

Palmiers

Lining a pastry tin

- <u>Bread rolls</u> can be shaped in a <u>huge variety</u> of ways, including: baguettes, bloomers, rings, bagels, cobs, braids, breadsticks, rolls etc...
- You can make different types of <u>flatbread</u> — lots of them don't use yeast (e.g. <u>tortillas</u>), although it's sometimes added to give them a relatively small rise (e.g. <u>naan bread</u>).

Practical Skills

- Choux pastry is used to make foods like profiteroles and chocolate eclairs — you can pipe it in different ways and shapes to create different products.

- Pasta dough can be shaped in lots of different ways to give us pasta like: ravioli, lasagne, cannelloni, tagliatelle, tortellini etc...

- Dough can be made into pinwheels by rolling it (not with a rolling pin, but in the same way you'd roll up a carpet). Cinnamon buns and cheesy pinwheels are made this way — you can even make coloured swirls by adding fillings.

- The most common shape for a pizza base is circular with thicker crusts around the outside. You can also make a calzone by folding the pizza over, completely covering the filling with dough.

- The shape of doughs change during proving as they rise and increase in size.
- Brushing your doughs with egg wash (egg mixed with water, milk or cream) creates a nice glaze that turns the food golden brown during baking.
- You can also finish the tops of pies and tarts using decorative patterns (p.102).

Raising Agents

Raising agents (see p.44) come in many different forms:

- Chemical (bicarbonate of soda, baking powder and self-raising flour), biological (yeast), mechanical (folding, beating, whisking, sieving, creaming and rubbing in) and steam.

- Eggs can be used as a raising agent as their proteins stretch and trap air when they are whisked — this creates a gas-in-liquid foam that solidifies when the food is cooked (p.40).

Remember, using too little (or too much) of a raising agent can cause a cake to sink.

Setting Mixtures

Gelation Sets Mixtures by Removing Heat

1) Foods such as custard or ice cream set when they are chilled or frozen.
2) This process is called gelation — this also happens with unbaked cheesecakes, as they need to be left in the fridge overnight to set.
3) It's easy to get confused between gelation and gelatinisation (p.41) — remember, gelation involves chilling, while gelatinisation involves heating.

Protein Coagulation Sets Egg-Based Mixtures

1) Mixtures that contain egg (e.g. quiches or egg custards) can be set by heating.
2) This is because when they're cooked, heat causes the proteins in the eggs to denature and coagulate (see p.40).
3) It's this coagulation of proteins in the mixture that causes it to set — it also traps the other ingredients in the mixture, e.g. bacon in quiche.

Try to practise as many practical skills as possible when making dishes...

There are a lot of ways you can make, shape and finish your dough — these might seem a little overwhelming at first, but go through them one at a time (and maybe make a few of them) and it will get easier.

108

Skills Checklist

So long <u>Section Six</u> — there are a lot of practical skills on these pages, but it's important you can use them.

- Go through this list of practical skills and <u>tick off each one</u> when you <u>can do it</u>.
- When you can do <u>all the parts</u> of a skill section and are <u>completely happy</u> with it, tick it off.

General Practical Skills (p.101-102) ☑

1) I can organise all my ingredients before cooking. ☑
2) I can select and adapt cooking times. ☑
3) I can weigh and measure ingredients accurately. ☑
4) I can test food in a variety of ways to see if it's cooked. ☑
5) I can change how food affects the different senses. ☑
6) I can add garnishes and decoration to my food. ☑

Knife Skills (p.102-103) ☑

7) I can safely use different knives for different uses. ☑
8) I can cut fruit and vegetables in different ways. ☑
9) I know how chicken and fish can be portioned. ☑

Preparing Fruit and Vegetables (p.103) ☑

10) I can prepare fruit and vegetables in many different ways. ☑

Use of the Cooker and Cooking Methods (p.103) ☑

11) I can use the oven, grill and hob on the cooker for a range of cooking methods. ☑

Use of Equipment (p.104) ☑

12) I can use different equipment to speed up food preparation processes and save time. ☑

Prepare, Combine and Shape (p.104) ☑

13) I can prepare, shape and combine foods in a variety of ways. ☑

Making Sauces (p.105) ☑

14) I can make a roux, blended and all-in-one sauce. ☑
15) I can adapt a roux sauce to make a velouté and béchamel sauce. ☑
16) I can make a stable emulsion sauce. ☑
17) I can make both sweet and savoury reduction sauces. ☑

Tenderise and Marinate (p.105) ☑

18) I can make marinades to tenderise and flavour food. ☑

Making Dough (p.106-107) ☑

19) I can make a variety of different doughs using shortening, gluten formation and fermentation. ☑
20) I can select the right type of pastry dough for my dish. ☑
21) I can shape and finish my dough in lots of different ways. ☑

Raising Agents (p.107) ☑

22) I can use different raising agents to make my food rise. ☑

Setting Mixtures (p.107) ☑

23) I can set mixtures using gelation. ☑
24) I can set mixtures using eggs. ☑

Section Six — Food Preparation and Cooking Skills

Non-Exam Assessment Advice

In Food Preparation & Nutrition you'll have to do some cooking — and it's worth a good portion of the marks.

The **Non-Exam Tasks** Are Worth **50%** of the **Total Marks**

1) During the final year of your GCSE, you'll have to do some <u>non-exam</u> tasks.
They allow you to show off your <u>culinary knowledge</u> and <u>cooking skills</u>.

2) The non-exam work is split into <u>two</u> parts — a <u>Food Investigation task</u> worth 15% of the overall marks, and a <u>Food Preparation task</u> worth 35% of the overall marks.

Their <u>functional</u> and <u>chemical</u> properties (see p.40-43)

The **Food Investigation Task** Involves Some **Experimenting**

1) In the Food Investigation task, you'll have to investigate and write a <u>report</u> about <u>how</u> and <u>why</u> ingredients work in a chosen task, e.g. "Investigate the ingredients used in sweet scone baking."

2) You'll be marked on three main things — <u>research</u>, <u>investigation</u> and <u>analysis</u>.

A — Research

1) Start by reading your task <u>thoroughly</u>, then draw out a <u>mind map</u> of the things you want to research — particularly how ingredients work, and why.

2) Use a <u>range of sources</u> to research your ideas, including textbooks, the internet and your own knowledge.

3) Use this research to make a <u>prediction</u> you can investigate — e.g. "Self-raising flour will be the best raising agent to use for making sweet scones."

Types of flour · Types of sugar · Types of filling, e.g. raisins, cherries · Amount of sugar · **Ingredients in scone baking** · Types of raising agent · Gluten content of different flours · Effects of using fresh / old milk · Essential scone ingredients

B — Investigation

1) To test your prediction you'll need to plan some <u>practical investigations</u>. You need to carry out <u>several experiments</u> (e.g. making scones with different flours, mechanically aerating scones in different ways).

2) It's important that these experiments have <u>clear methods</u> and are <u>fair</u>.

3) Prepare any <u>tables</u> or <u>graphs</u> to record your results in beforehand — this will make it clear what you need to write down during the experiments.

4) You should also take <u>photos</u> throughout your experiments to prove what you did.

- E.g. Cook all at the same temperature, for the same length of time.
- Make sure all ingredients are weighed accurately.
- Make all scones the same size by using a cutter or weighing scale.

C — Analysis / Evaluation

1) You'll then need to <u>analyse</u> and <u>evaluate</u> your <u>findings</u> (interpret what you've discovered).

2) You can do this by <u>linking</u> your findings to the <u>research</u> you did at the start of the task (explaining how and why your ingredients worked the way they did), discussing your <u>results</u>, and deciding whether your findings support your <u>prediction</u> (is what happened what you expected?).

3) You need to show that you've done all this by producing a <u>written report</u>. This will include:

- A <u>summary</u> of your <u>research</u> (including how it helped you understand the task).
- Your <u>prediction</u> (including how your research led you to this decision).
- The <u>aims</u> of your different experiments (what you hoped to achieve).
- The <u>methods</u> you used in your experiments and how you made each one a <u>fair test</u>.
- The <u>ingredients</u> you used in your experiments.
- The <u>results</u> of your experiments (include any tables/graphs/charts here).

You really want to show off your knowledge here, so remember to use correct technical terms.

- Any <u>photos</u> you took during the task.
- An <u>analysis</u> of your results (this should fully explain what you have learned from them).
- A <u>conclusion</u> — this should sum up what you've learned, looking at your original predictions, results, how you'd apply what you've learned to future cooking projects, and any further research you'd do if you had the chance.

Non-Exam Assessment Advice

The **Food Preparation Task** Involves Lots of **Cooking**

1) In the Food Preparation task you'll have to cook a range of dishes to fit a chosen task, as well as producing a portfolio to show the following things:

> - Your research (finding out more about your chosen task).
> - Your use of planning and practical skills (e.g. different technical skills/cooking techniques).
> - Your ability to prepare, cook and present three dishes within a period of 3 hours.
> - An analysis and evaluation of your chosen dishes.

2) During the practical tasks you should take photographs of each stage in the preparation and cooking. You will use these photographs in your portfolio.

Part 1 — Doing the Research

1) First, make sure you've read all the tasks properly, then choose the one you find most appealing. Each task on the brief has a certain research focus, such as 'life stages', 'dietary requirements', 'cuisines' or 'specific contexts'. E.g. "A local school is planning a week where only vegan meals are served in the canteen. Research, prepare and cook three dishes the canteen could serve that week."

2) Decide what you need to research. This could be stuff like:

> - Advantages and disadvantages of a vegan diet.
> - Meat and dairy-free alternatives to everyday food products, and their nutritional values, e.g. soya milk, sunflower spread.
> - Surveying vegans to ask about their personal food choices and / or the availability of vegan products.
> - Nutritional guidelines for vegans.

Always make sure your research is relevant to the brief.

3) Carry out your research, then summarise what you've found on a page of your portfolio. You can then use this research to help you plan your dishes.

Part 2 — Making Trial / Technical Skill Dishes

1) In this part, you'll need to plan and cook 3 or 4 dishes using the information you found in Part 1.

2) It's helpful to start by making a plan of action / mind map of dishes that fit your task. You can narrow down your choices by making a list of important things your dishes should achieve, such as:

> - Do my dishes agree with my task and research findings?
> - Am I capable of making the dishes to a high standard under timed conditions?
> - Do the dishes show off enough technical skills? E.g. making a dough, making a sauce.
> - How much will the dishes cost to make, and will I be able to find the ingredients?
> - Do the dishes follow nutritional guidelines?

3) When you've chosen your dishes, write a brief summary of the technical skills required for each.

4) You should avoid using ready-prepared ingredients in this task — preparing "fiddly" ingredients yourself (e.g. making pasta, preparing meat / fish off the bone) is a great way to show technical skill.

5) Make sure you take plenty of photographs whilst you're making the dishes (especially when carrying out technical skills) — you'll need to put these in your portfolio / report to prove what you've done.

You should work hygienically and safely when cooking, or you'll lose marks (or a finger).

6) There are lots of ways you can structure this part of your portfolio, but remember to talk about why you chose each dish, the skills you're using for each dish, and a list of ingredients — don't forget to pop in those photographs you took too.

Non-Exam Assessment Advice

Part 3 — Planning and Making the Final Dishes

You could make three main courses, or you could make a starter, main and dessert.

1) Next, you'll have to <u>plan</u> and <u>justify</u> your choices for the <u>final three dishes</u>.

2) Give a <u>written explanation</u> for each dish you plan to make. Say how they fit the <u>task</u>, any <u>technical skills</u> you'll use, plus any further reasoning (e.g. how your <u>trial dishes</u> influenced your choices or if the results of any <u>sensory tests</u> have led to new ideas).

3) On the day, you'll have <u>three hours</u> to <u>prepare</u>, <u>cook</u> and <u>present</u> all three dishes, so you'll need a time plan to keep you on track.

4) Make a time plan that's easy to understand, and include timings, what you need to do at each stage, as well as any <u>food safety</u> notes.

Time	What I need to do	Notes / Health & Safety
9:00	Weigh out my flour, salt, cheese, spinach (etc) for my **ravioli dish**.	Wipe surfaces with antibacterial cleaner beforehand (and after handling any raw ingredients).
9:15	Start preparing the shortcrust pastry for my **apple pie** by rubbing the butter and the flour together.	Make sure to wash my hands after weighing out the ravioli ingredients.

5) You'll need to "<u>dovetail</u>" your three dishes to get them finished in the three hours you have — this means that rather than making each dish in order from start to finish, you'll have to keep working on <u>all three dishes</u> across the three hour period.

6) Be sure to take <u>photos</u> of your dishes, both <u>during the process</u> and as <u>finished dishes</u>.

You'll Need to Show...

- Your use of <u>technical skills</u> and <u>equipment</u>.
- Your ability to follow <u>food safety</u> rules.
- Your use and understanding of a wide range of <u>ingredients</u>.
- Your awareness of <u>food provenance</u>, e.g. <u>seasonality</u>.
- Your use of <u>cooking times</u> and different <u>cooking methods</u>.
- Your ability to <u>test for readiness</u>.
- Your ability to <u>judge</u> and <u>adjust</u> the <u>sensory properties</u> of your <u>dishes</u> during cooking.
- Your use of a good <u>time plan</u> and <u>dovetailing</u>.
- Your use of good <u>portion control</u>.
- Your <u>presentation</u> and any <u>finishing touches</u> you added to your dishes.
- The <u>complexity</u> of your dishes.

Part 4 — Analysis and Evaluation of your Final Dishes

1) This is the last bit — hooray! You'll need to write up a <u>detailed analysis</u> of your final dishes.

2) Your analysis should be tailored to your chosen brief, but don't forget to include stuff life:

- A <u>sensory test</u> of the finished dishes.
  Make sure you use the correct <u>sensory descriptors</u> here.
- A <u>review</u> of the <u>technical skills</u> used.
- Any <u>modifications</u> you made during the task.
- Any <u>improvements</u> that could be made.
  <u>Comparing</u> your dishes with other students' can be helpful here.

3) Here's a (<u>very brief</u>) example of how you could structure your analysis. Yours should include much more detail though — the more detail, explanation and description you add the better:

Analysis: Vegan ravioli with a spicy tomato sauce
I presented my ravioli with a spicy tomato sauce and sprigs of parsley. The technical skills I used were pasta making and making a sauce... (etc.)

Sensory Test:
Aroma scored most highly (33/40). This is likely due to the herbs and onions I added to my tomato sauce... (etc.)

Characteristic	Taster A	B	C	D	Total
Flavour	8	8	7	9	32
Texture	6	7	8	8	29
Appearance	5	6	6	6	23
Aroma	9	8	9	7	33

However, appearance scored the lowest (23/40), so I should work on making the sauce look more attractive. For example, I could work on making it less lumpy... (etc.)

Review of technical skills:
I weighed out my ingredients using precise electric scales, and then used an electric food mixer to combine them and make a dough. I kneaded and folded the dough until it was elastic and smooth... (etc.)

Presentation:
The sauce and parsley garnish (which I finely chopped) adds two different, bold colours to the dish, making it look more appealing... (etc.)

Nutritional value:
The dish was nutritionally well-balanced. It was low in saturated fats (only 6 g per portion) as it did not contain any butter. It also contained lots of fibre (3.4 g per portion). However, it could be improved by adding more protein... (etc.)

You could include a nutritional info table here (see p.24).

If relevant, you should also include costings for your recipes (see p.26).

You can have your own section for modifications and improvements, but you can also incorporate them into your analysis like this.

4) That just leaves the <u>exam</u> to do. Phew...

Exam Advice

Here's What to **Expect** in the **Exam**

1) At the end of your GCSE Food Preparation and Nutrition course you'll have to sit <u>one</u> exam — it will make up <u>50%</u> of your <u>total mark</u>.

2) The questions in the exam will test you on <u>all areas</u> of the <u>course</u> that we've covered in this book.

3) The way your exam is <u>structured</u> will depend on the <u>exam board</u> you're with:

AQA

- The paper is worth <u>100 marks</u> and will last <u>1 hour and 45 minutes</u>.
- The paper will be split into <u>two sections</u> — <u>Section A</u> and <u>Section B</u>.
- <u>Section A</u> consists of <u>20 multiple choice questions</u> worth one mark each — each question has one correct answer and three incorrect answers, so <u>only pick one answer</u> for each question.
- <u>Section B</u> consists of <u>5 questions</u> — they may have <u>multiple parts</u> and be <u>different styles</u> and <u>lengths</u> — <u>extended response</u> questions (see next page) are worth the <u>most marks</u>.

Eduqas

- The paper is worth <u>100 marks</u> and will last <u>1 hour and 45 minutes</u>.
- The paper will be split into <u>two sections</u> — <u>Section A</u> and <u>Section B</u>.
- In <u>Section A</u>, you'll be given <u>questions</u> related to some '<u>visual stimuli</u>'. The visual stimuli could be a set of <u>images</u> showing a <u>cooking method</u> or the stages of <u>making a dish</u> etc.
- <u>Section B</u> questions will have <u>different styles</u> and <u>lengths</u> — <u>extended response</u> questions (see next page) are worth the <u>most marks</u>.

OCR

- The paper is worth <u>100 marks</u> and will last <u>1 hour and 30 minutes</u>.
- The entire paper is made up of <u>10 compulsory</u> questions.
- Questions will have <u>different styles</u> and <u>lengths</u> — <u>extended response</u> questions (see next page) are worth the <u>most marks</u>.

Remember These **Tips**

1) <u>Always</u> read every question <u>carefully</u> — don't write an essay about vitamin C if it's asking about vitamin D.

2) Write your answers <u>clearly</u>, using <u>good grammar</u>, <u>spelling</u> and <u>punctuation</u>.

3) <u>Underline</u> any <u>key words</u> in the question — this helps you focus on the important parts that you want to write about.

4) Use the correct <u>terminology</u> — know your foody terms, you can't talk about them if you don't know what they mean.

5) <u>Don't panic</u> — if you really can't do a question, just leave it and move on to the next one. You can come back to it at the end.

Understand the **Command Words**

Questions will often use <u>command words</u> — they are words that tell you <u>how</u> to answer the question. If you <u>don't know</u> what they mean, you might not answer the question <u>properly</u>.

State / Identify — You should give a <u>short answer</u> or <u>select an item</u> from a <u>table</u>, a <u>list</u> or similar — you don't need to explain why.

Define — You should give a <u>clear</u>, <u>precise</u> meaning of the word or phrase.

Outline — You should give a <u>brief summary</u> of a process.

Describe — You should give a <u>detailed description</u> of something.

Explain — You should <u>give reasons</u> to show <u>why</u>.

Discuss — You should make a <u>balanced argument</u> covering a range of opinions.

Assess / Evaluate — You should use <u>evidence</u> and your <u>own knowledge</u> to come to a <u>conclusion</u>.

Exam Advice

Plan Out Your Answer to Extended Response Questions

Extended response questions are longer questions worth 6 or more marks and with a scary number of dotted lines underneath... They often use command words like discuss, evaluate or assess (see previous page).

- Your answer must be well-written (good spelling, grammar and punctuation) and well-structured.
- Before you start an extended response question, jot down the points you want to make and plan your answer to help structure it well and avoid repeating things.
- You might have to weigh up the advantages and disadvantages of something, or cover both sides of an argument then form your own opinion.
- Make absolutely sure you're answering the question and not just waffling on.

Here's an example:

> Underline key words in the question — your answer should discuss both of these groups.

7   Evaluate the value of packaging for manufacturers and consumers and discuss ways to limit the impact packaging has on the environment.

[8 marks]

> You'll need a well-structured answer showing detailed knowledge to get all 8 marks.

Packaging helps protect and preserve a food product whilst it is being transported and stored, preventing it from being damaged or contaminated, and extending its shelf life. Metal cans, for example, are strong, and are sealed and heated to kill off microorganisms. Correct packaging helps reduce food waste and also helps the manufacturer save money. Packaging is useful for consumers too, as food labels have to include certain information by law (such as allergens and 'use by' dates).

> Shows good knowledge of current food labelling practices.

This information is particularly valuable for consumers with dietary requirements. For example, coeliacs can check for gluten in the ingredients list and people with religious beliefs can check foods have been prepared in the correct way (e.g. kosher food in Judaism). Manufacturing, transporting and throwing away packaging damages the environment (as this produces greenhouse gases), but there are ways manufacturers and consumers can limit this impact. Manufacturers could limit the use of 'excess' packaging and use recyclable materials, because recycling uses less energy than making new packaging from raw materials. All households in the UK have access to recycling services, so consumers should recycle paper, card, plastics and metal, and should also reuse plastic bags when they go shopping.

> The number of lines gives you a good guide to how long your answer should be.

> This answer has good grammar, spelling and punctuation.

> Shows good understanding of why this would limit the impact on the environment.

Value of packaging — Manufacturers — Preserves / protects products
Consumers — Food labels — Dietary requirements (medical, beliefs)

Reducing impact — Manufacturers — Use less ('excess') / Use recyclable materials
Consumers — Recycle - paper, plastics, metal, card / Reuse plastic bags

> This answer has been well planned out.

Practice Paper

Once you've been through all the questions in this book, you should be starting to feel prepared for the final exam. This practice paper will test you on Sections 1-5 of this book and contains a mixture of multiple-choice, short-answer and extended writing questions. Your exam might not look exactly like this paper, but it will give you some great practice with all of the topic areas.

Candidate Surname		Candidate Forename(s)

Centre Number	Candidate Number	Candidate Signature

GCSE
Food Preparation and Nutrition

Practice Paper
Time allowed: 1 hour 45 minutes

Instructions to candidates
- Use **black** ink to write your answers.
- Write your name and other details in the spaces provided above.
- Answer **all** questions in the spaces provided.

Information for candidates
- The marks available are given in brackets at the end of each question.
- There are 100 marks available for this paper.

Advice
- Carefully read each question before answering it.
- Try to answer every question.
- If you have time after finishing the paper, go back and check your answers.
- For multiple choice questions, you should shade in **one** box.
  For example: ●

Answer all questions.

1   A local cafe serves a full English breakfast. The chef fries the eggs in butter.

(a) Why is frying eggs in butter considered unhealthy?

....

[1 mark]

(b) Name the main type of heat transfer used when frying eggs.

....

[1 mark]

(c) Give **two** ways the chef could fry the eggs to make them healthier.

(i) ....

....

(ii) ....

....

[2 marks]

(d) Describe **two** other methods the chef could use to cook the eggs.

(i) ....

....

(ii) ....

....

[4 marks]

Eggs have many functions that can be used to create lots of different foods.

(e) Complete the table below by describing the function of eggs in each of the foods.
The first one has been done for you.

Food	Function of the egg	Description
Custard	Thickening	When the custard is heated slowly at a medium heat, the proteins in the egg yolk start to coagulate, causing the mixture to thicken.
Burgers	Binding	
Mayonnaise	Emulsification	
Sponge cake	Aeration	

[3 × 2 marks]

2 The photos below show two meals which are both good sources of carbohydrates and other nutrients.

Meal A
Tuna sandwich on wholemeal
bread, with tomatoes and cucumber.

Meal B
Wholemeal pasta with red peppers,
peas, sweetcorn and basil leaves.

(a) (i) Which food is the best source of complex carbohydrates in Meal A?

A   The tuna   ⬯
B   The wholemeal bread   ⬯
C   The tomatoes   ⬯
D   The cucumber   ⬯

[1 mark]

(ii) Which food is the best source of complex carbohydrates in Meal B?

A   The wholemeal pasta   ⬯
B   The red peppers   ⬯
C   The sweetcorn   ⬯
D   The basil leaves   ⬯

[1 mark]

(iii) Explain how the body digests complex carbohydrates for energy.

....

....

....

....

....

[4 marks]

Meal A provides fibre (in the wholemeal bread) and water (in the cucumber).

(b) Outline **one** function of fibre and water in the diet and **one** health problem caused by not getting enough in the diet.

(i) Fibre: ....

....

....

(ii) Water: ....

....

....

[2 × 2 marks]

(c) The peas in meal B are a source of folic acid. Why is folic acid important in our diet?

A	It helps protect the body from infection.	▭
B	It helps the body absorb calcium.	▭
C	It helps with growth and the production of red blood cells.	▭
D	It helps with the development of strong bones and teeth.	▭

[1 mark]

(d) For each of the following, identify **one** food from either meal A or meal B that is rich in the vitamin, and explain the role of the vitamin in the body.

(i) Vitamin A: ....

....

....

(ii) Vitamin C: ....

....

....

[2 × 2 marks]

3   Young people are at risk of developing rickets or anaemia if they are deficient in certain nutrients. Describe each of the conditions below and give dietary advice to help prevent them.

Condition	Description	Dietary advice
Rickets		
Iron deficiency anaemia		

[4 × 2 marks]

4 The menu for a wedding reception is shown below.

> <u>Menu</u>
>
> Spring Vegetable Soup with a Wholemeal Bread Roll
>
> Salmon en Croûte* served with Carrots, Asparagus and a Béchamel Sauce
>
> Selection of Cheeses
>
> Lemon Cheesecake with a Crunchy Biscuit Base
>
> *salmon wrapped in puff pastry

The bride and groom inform the caterer that some of their guests
have coeliac disease, while others have lactose intolerance.

(a) Suggest **two** ways the caterer could modify the menu for guests with coeliac disease.

....

....

....

....

[2 marks]

(b) Suggest **two** ways the caterer could modify the menu for guests with lactose intolerance.

....

....

....

....

[2 marks]

5   The 'danger zone' is a temperature range in which microorganisms, such as bacteria, grow quickly, spoiling high risk foods and making them unsafe to eat.

(a)   What is the temperature range of the 'danger zone'?

   A   5 °C to 37 °C   ⬭

   B   5 °C to 63 °C   ⬭

   C   37 °C to 63 °C   ⬭

   D   37 °C to 75 °C   ⬭

[1 mark]

(b)   Which **one** of the following pairs is most likely to contain the bacterium campylobacter?

   A   Unwashed vegetables and unwashed salad leaves.   ⬭

   B   Yoghurt and raw eggs.   ⬭

   C   Raw poultry and untreated milk.   ⬭

   D   Pâté and cooked shellfish.   ⬭

[1 mark]

(c)   Jenna cooks a chilli con carne that contains minced beef, beef stock and kidney beans.

   (i)   State why a cooked chilli con carne is a 'high risk' food.

   ....

   ....

[1 mark]

   (ii)   Describe how Jenna could safely store the cooked chilli con carne.

   ....

   ....

   ....

[2 marks]

Microorganisms can be transferred around the kitchen by cross-contamination.

(d) Discuss the sources of cross-contamination when making a chicken and bacon salad, and the methods of control that can be used to prevent it.

....

....

....

....

....

....

....

....

....

....

....

....

....

[6 marks]

(e) Not all microorganisms are harmful. Some of them are used in food production. Describe how **two** microorganisms are used in food production.

(i) ....

....

(ii) ....

....

[4 marks]

6 The pictures below show some of the steps that are used to make meringues.

(a) Sugar is essential when making meringues.
Give **two** ways that sugar affects the sensory properties of meringues.

(i) ....

....

(ii) ....

....

[2 marks]

(b) Meringues can collapse if the egg whites are whisked too much.
Explain why this happens.

....

....

....

[2 marks]

A manufacturer performed a profiling test on two different meringues. The results are shown below:

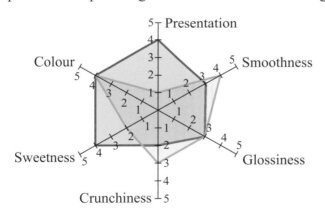

Key:
Meringue A
Meringue B

(c) Tick the box next to each statement to say whether it is True or False.

	True	False
(i) Meringue A is crunchier than meringue B.		
(ii) The presentation of meringue B should be improved.		
(iii) The colours of both meringues were equally appealing.		

[3 marks]

7　Food products go through stages of processing before they are packaged.

(a) Which **one** of the following is **not** an example of primary processing?

A　Milling wheat grains　　◻

B　Trussing a chicken　　◻

C　Adding moulds to blue cheese　　◻

D　Removing stones from fruit　　◻

[1 mark]

(b) Which **one** of the following is a **true** statement?

A　The 'best before' date is for products with a short shelf life.　　◻

B　The 'use by' date is for tinned and bottled foods.　　◻

C　The 'best before' date means foods eaten after this date might not be safe.　　◻

D　The 'use by' date is given as a safety warning.　　◻

[1 mark]

(c) Give **two** reasons why foods are packaged.

(i) ....

....

(ii) ....

....

[2 marks]

(d) List **three** pieces of compulsory information required on food packaging.

1. ....

2. ....

3. ....

[3 marks]

8   The Bello family go shopping once a week in a big supermarket.

Discuss how food manufacturers and the supermarket might influence what the Bello family buys.

....
....
....
....
....
....
....
....
....
....
....
....
....
....
....
....
....
....
....

[8 marks]

9 Adil and Barney are teenage boys.
   The nutritional information for their breakfasts are shown below.

Adil (Breakfast A)

Two poached eggs and tomatoes on toasted wholemeal bread, a banana and a 100 ml glass of orange juice.

Per portion	
Energy	516 kcal
Fat	14 g
(of which saturates)	4 g
Carbohydrate	72 g
(of which sugars)	35 g
Protein	25.5 g

Barney (Breakfast B)

Cornflakes with whole milk, two hot cross buns with salted butter and a 250 ml glass of orange juice.

Per portion	
Energy	817 kcal
Fat	19 g
(of which saturates)	10 g
Carbohydrate	145 g
(of which sugars)	76 g
Protein	16.5 g

The following information is for reference

	Recommended Daily Intake for a teenage boy (approximate)
Energy	2500 - 3000 kcal
Fat	85 g
(of which saturates)	30 g*
Carbohydrate	300 g
(of which sugars)	90 g*
Protein	50 g

*maximum intake

Use this information to answer the question on the next page.

Evaluate the suitability of Adil's and Barney's breakfasts, and suggest ways they could modify their breakfasts to better meet current guidelines for a healthy diet.

....

....

....

....

....

....

....

....

....

....

....

....

....

....

....

....

....

....

....

....

....

....

....

[10 marks]

10 Food insecurity is when people are unable to get enough nutritious food to stay healthy and active.

Assess the various factors that contribute to food insecurity and explain how people
and countries can help to improve the global food insecurity problem.

....

....

....

....

....

....

....

....

....

....

....

....

....

....

....

....

....

....

....

....

....

....

....

....

....

....

[12 marks]

END OF QUESTIONS

Section One — Food, Nutrition and Health

Page 7 (Warm-Up Questions)

1 Any **two** from:
   - Children
   - Teenagers
   - Pregnant women
   - Women who are breastfeeding (lactating)
   - People who are physically active

2 Any **two** alternative proteins from:
   - Soya beans
   - Tofu
   - Textured Vegetable Protein (TVP)
   - Mycoprotein

3 Saturated fat: E.g. Bacon and butter
   Unsaturated fat: E.g. Olive oil and peanuts

4 Any **three** problems from:
   - Fat-soluble vitamins (A, D, E and K) aren't absorbed by the body, leading to vitamin deficiencies and their associated health issues.
   - It may lead to weight loss (if there is also a lack of carbohydrate in the diet).
   - A person might be colder / find it difficult to stay warm because there is less insulation under the skin.
   - A person might bruise more easily because there is less fat to cushion them from knocks and bangs.

5 Any **one** reason, e.g.
   - Starchy foods provide energy (after being broken down into glucose).
   - Starchy foods contain lots of nutrients (e.g. B vitamins, iron and calcium).

6 They can use the glycaemic index to control and avoid surges in their blood sugar level, e.g. by eating low GI foods that cause a more gradual rise in blood sugar levels than high GI foods.

Page 8-9 (Exam Questions)

1 a) Amino acids *[1 mark]*

   b) Essential *[1 mark]* amino acids

   c) E.g. Excessive protein intake can put pressure on the liver and kidneys *[1 mark]* (as these organs help process proteins).

2 Vegetarians don't eat any meat or animal fat *[1 mark]* and lard comes from an animal source (it's made from pig fat) *[1 mark]*.

3 a) A low biological value protein is missing one or more of the essential amino acids we need *[1 mark]*.

   b) i) E.g. A vegan could use protein complementation *[1 mark]*, where a mixture of LBV proteins are combined *[1 mark]* to provide all the essential amino acids we need (the equivalent of HBV protein) *[1 mark]*.

   ii) E.g. Baked beans on toast / hummus on pitta bread / lentil soup with bread *[1 mark]*.
   Accept any combination of cereals and pulses or any other appropriate response.

4 a) Any **one** health issue from:
   - Obesity *[1 mark]* caused when the excess energy from sugars is stored as fat in the body *[1 mark]*.
   - Tooth decay (dental caries) *[1 mark]* caused when sugary foods (especially free sugars such as those found in fruit juices) erode teeth and create cavities (holes) *[1 mark]*.
   - Type 2 diabetes *[1 mark]* caused when excessive sugar in the diet leads to obesity *[1 mark]*.
   [2 marks available in total]

   b) E.g. Blood sugar levels drop *[1 mark]*, which can cause hunger, dizziness and tiredness because our bodies have less energy *[1 mark]*.

5 E.g. Wholegrain pasta is a complex carbohydrate *[1 mark]* which the body breaks down slowly *[1 mark]*, so the pasta will supply the marathon runner with a steady release of energy over a long race *[1 mark]*. Glucose is a simple sugar *[1 mark]* that is absorbed very quickly by the body *[1 mark]*, so the glucose tablet will provide the sprinter with a short burst of energy for their quick race *[1 mark]*.

6 Points you might include:
   Conditions John would be at risk of developing
   - Excess fat can lead to weight gain and obesity (which is a risk factor for many health problems itself).
   - Obesity can lead to the development of type 2 diabetes.
   - Obesity increases the risk of having a stroke / various types of cancer.
   - Obesity puts strain on the skeleton, joints and muscles which could cause John to develop mobility issues.
   - John's blood cholesterol level could increase, which would also increase his risk of having a heart attack / developing coronary heart disease.
   - John may experience psychological conditions (such as body image issues) if he gains weight and becomes unhappy with his appearance.

   Changes John could make to reduce his fat intake
   - He could eat less fast food (as these are often high in fat, especially saturated fats).
   - He could eat less treats that are high in fat, e.g. ice cream / cake / chocolate (lots of treats contain hidden fats, which means you can't see the fat inside the food).
   - He could 'graze' (snack on the go) less, because many snacks (e.g. crisps, biscuits and chocolate) are high in saturated fat.
   - He could cut down on fried foods (e.g. chips / a traditional English breakfast) as they are very high in fat.
   - He could choose cooking methods that require the least amount of fat, e.g. grill foods because no fat is added.
   - He could cook meals from scratch so that he has more control over every ingredient that goes into his meals.
   - He could cook using low-fat alternatives, e.g. using skimmed milk instead of whole milk / using leaner mince.
   - He could use smaller quantities of fatty foods when cooking, e.g. putting less cheese on the top of nachos.
   - He could use vegetables to 'bulk up' meals after the quantity of fatty food in the meal has been reduced.
   - He could trim excess fat off foods such as bacon / chicken.
   - He could drain off any excess fat that has melted out of food during cooking (e.g. minced beef).

   How to mark your answer:
   - One health risk with little to no explanation and only brief reference to a change John could make to his diet *[1-3 marks]*.
   - Two health risks with some explanation and at least two changes John could make to his diet *[4-7 marks]*.
   - Three health risks with detailed explanation and at least three changes John could make to his diet *[8-10 marks]*.

Page 14 (Warm-Up Questions)

1 Vitamin A is needed for good eyesight, growth, a healthy immune system and healthy skin. Vitamin K helps clot blood, heal wounds and maintain our immune system and bones.

2 E.g. citrus fruit (e.g. oranges)
   Scurvy is caused by a deficiency of vitamin C — citrus fruit, green veg and potatoes are rich in it, so will all do the job.

3 It's unlikely that we'll build up an excess because water-soluble vitamins are excreted in our urine.

4 Any **two** from:
- Cook fruit and vegetables for the shortest amount of time possible (because B vitamins and vitamin C are destroyed by heat).
- Cook fruit and vegetables in as little water as possible (e.g. by steaming) and don't leave them to stand (B vitamins and vitamin C will dissolve into the water).
- Eat fruit and vegetables as soon as they have been cooked (keeping them warm will cause vitamins to be lost over time due to heat).

5 Any **two** from:
- It helps to keep the digestive system working.
- It prevents constipation.
- It helps prevent cancer of the colon / bowel.
- It helps lower cholesterol.
- It helps prevent heart disease.
- It helps prevent high blood pressure.
- It helps you feel fuller for longer.

6 E.g. From sweating and passing urine.

7 E.g. When a person is hot or exercising.

Page 15 (Exam Questions)

1 a) Vitamin B1 (thiamin) *[1 mark]*

   b) Vitamin B12 (cobalamin) *[1 mark]* and vitamin B9 (folic acid) *[1 mark]*

2

Deficiency	Health risks associated with this deficiency
Vitamin D	Bone diseases *[1 mark]*, e.g. rickets / osteoporosis (where bones become brittle) *[1 mark]* / osteomalacia (where bones become softer) *[1 mark]*. *[2 marks available in total]*
Vitamin E	E.g. weak muscles *[1 mark]* and sight problems *[1 mark]*.

[4 marks available in total — as above]

3 a) No *[1 mark]*

   b) E.g. It's recommended that children take in lower proportions of fibre than adults because the 'fullness' fibre gives them can stop them from eating foods that contain important nutrients *[1 mark]*.

4 Any **four** reasons why hydration is important for health, e.g.
- Water is needed for the process of digestion *[1 mark]*.
- Water is needed to get rid of waste from the body (excretion) *[1 mark]*.
- Water helps us to sweat and maintain our body temperature efficiently *[1 mark]*.
- Water keeps the skin in good condition *[1 mark]*.
- Water helps keep our blood at the right viscosity (thickness) *[1 mark]*.
- If our blood is too thick, it puts more pressure on the heart because it has to work harder to pump the thicker blood around *[1 mark]*.
- If we can't maintain our body temperature, we could suffer from exhaustion and fainting *[1 mark]*.
- Water is needed to keep the brain functioning properly (keeping our decision-making and reactions quick) *[1 mark]*.

[4 marks available in total]

Page 21 (Warm-Up Questions)

1 All of the following:
- Starchy carbohydrates
- Fruit and vegetables
- Dairy products and alternatives
- Beans, pulses, fish, meat and other protein.
- Oils and spreads.

2 E.g. Reference Intakes are guidelines for the amount of nutrients / energy that an average adult requires each day.

3 a) E.g. Toddlers need calcium for healthy teeth and bone development.

   b) E.g. Teenagers need protein to help tissue growth and repair, which is especially important for rapid growth spurts.

   c) E.g. Pregnant women need folic acid because it reduces the chance of birth defects in babies.

   d) E.g. Elderly adults need vitamin B12 to help keep the brain healthy / prevent memory loss.

4 Body mass index

5 a) The risk of developing anaemia can be reduced by eating foods high in iron, e.g. red meat.

   b) The risk of developing diabetes can be reduced by maintaining a healthy weight (not being obese / overweight).

Page 22 (Exam Questions)

1 a) Coronary heart disease *[1 mark]*

   b) Any other **two** risk factors, e.g.
   - High blood pressure *[1 mark]*
   - Lack of exercise *[1 mark]*
   - Smoking *[1 mark]*
   - Eating lots of saturated fats *[1 mark]*
   [2 marks available in total]

   c) E.g. Blood vessels become restricted due to fatty deposits *[1 mark]* and blood isn't able to reach the heart as efficiently *[1 mark]*. This can lead to problems such as angina and heart attacks (where blood clots stop oxygen from reaching the heart muscle) *[1 mark]*.

2 a) Iron is needed to form red blood cells in the blood — it's particularly important for teenage girls because they lose iron when they have their period *[1 mark]*. Vitamin C helps the body absorb iron *[1 mark]*.

   b) Teenagers need calcium for healthy bones and teeth / to help the skeleton reach peak size and bone density *[1 mark]*. Vitamin D helps the body absorb calcium *[1 mark]*.

3 Points you might include:

Starchy carbohydrates
- Food item: wrap / rice / pasta / couscous / sweet potato.
- Starchy carbohydrates are an important source of energy for teenagers.
- Low GI foods (e.g. wholemeal pasta) provide slow-release energy, which is filling.

Fruit and vegetables
- Food item: apple / banana / carrot sticks / evidence of a fruit or vegetable included in a dish, e.g. pasta salad with tomato or couscous with red pepper.
- They provide fibre for a healthy digestive system.
- They are good sources of vitamins, e.g. red peppers are high in vitamin C. Vitamin C is important for healthy skin and to help absorb iron (which is particularly important for teenage girls).

Beans, pulses, fish, meat and other protein
- Food item: tuna / ham / chicken / kidney beans / chickpeas.
- Protein is needed for growth and repair of body cells — important to cope with teenage growth spurts.
- Teenage boys need sufficient protein to support muscular tissue growth.
- Oily fish is high in vitamin A, which is important for growth and good eyesight.

Dairy and alternatives
- Food item: cheese / yoghurt / milk (cow's, soya or rice-based)
- Dairy products / fortified alternatives are high in calcium and vitamin D, which are needed for healthy bones and teeth — important for teenagers as their skeleton is still growing / not at peak size.

Oils and spreads
- Food item: butter or spread in a sandwich / olive oil in a salad dressing.
- They provide fat-soluble vitamins, e.g. vegetable oils are high in vitamin E (which is needed for a healthy immune system / skin) and vitamin K (which is needed to help clot blood and heal wounds).

How to mark your answer:
- One or two food items from different sections of the Eatwell Guide, with little to no explanation of their nutritional importance for a teenager *[1-3 marks]*.
- Three or four food items from different sections of the Eatwell Guide, with some explanation of their nutritional importance for a teenager *[4-7 marks]*.
- Five food items from different sections of the Eatwell Guide, with an explanation of their nutritional importance for a teenager *[8-10 marks]*.

You'll only get marks if you link food items to the correct nutrient that they are high in.

Page 29 (Warm-Up Questions)

1 E.g.
- Age
- Gender
- Weight / height
- Exercise
- Genetics

2 2000 × 1.5 = 3000 kcal

3 a) 50%

b) 35% (or less)

c) 15%

4 E.g. Manufacturers can use nutritional analysis software to see how different ingredients / amounts would affect the nutritional content of a recipe and to see how recipes could be modified to meet healthy eating guidelines.

5 a) E.g. Soya milk

b) E.g. Tapioca flour

Page 30 (Exam Questions)

1 a) PAL is your physical activity level *[1 mark]*. It is a measure of how active you are / how much exercise you get, expressed as a number *[1 mark]*.

b) E.g. If an athlete became injured, their PAL would decrease (because they would be less active) *[1 mark]*. This means their daily energy requirement would be lower *[1 mark]* and they would need to eat less food to maintain a healthy weight *[1 mark]*.

2

Ingredient	Amount	How could he modify this ingredient?
Full fat milk	1 litre	Any **one** from: • Use a low-fat milk (e.g. skimmed) or a milk substitute (e.g. soya milk) *[1 mark]*. • Dilute the milk by mixing it with some water *[1 mark]*. *[1 mark available in total]*
Garlic, crushed	Two cloves	
Dried pasta	500 g	Use a wholegrain pasta *[1 mark]*.
Butter	75 g	Any **one** from: • Remove the butter *[1 mark]*. • Use a low-fat spread / margarine *[1 mark]*. *[1 mark available in total]*
Plain flour	75 g	Use a wholemeal flour or a nutritious alternative, e.g. coconut flour.
Parsley	Small bunch	
Mustard powder	1 tbsp	
Cheese, grated (Cheddar or Gruyère)	200 g	Any **one** from: • Use a reduced-fat cheese *[1 mark]*. • Add herbs / spices to add flavour instead *[1 mark]*. *[1 mark available in total]*

[4 marks available in total — as above]

Section Two — Food Science

Page 38 (Warm-Up Questions)

1 Any **one** way, e.g.
   - Roasting meats and vegetables creates more intense flavours.
   - Fat can be added during cooking to increase flavour.
   - Caramelisation can happen, making food taste sweeter.
   - The flavours of different foods can combine during cooking.

2 Water is brought to the boil by conduction as particles in the pan vibrate and pass their heat energy on to the particles in the water, and by convection as convection currents in the water circulate warmer water around the pan until all the water in the pan is boiling.

3 Steaming
   This is because it's a gentler method, and as there's no direct contact between the carrots and the liquid, they keep more of their flavour / texture / colour / water-soluble vitamins.

4 E.g. Braising is a gentle cooking method which helps to tenderise meat, making it a good method for tougher pieces of meat.

5 Heat is transferred by radiation, convection and conduction.

6 Benefit: E.g. It's healthier than roasting because no fat is added and fat drips out of the food as it cooks.
   Drawback: E.g. The high heat can cause food to cook unevenly / makes it easy to burn the food.
   You could have said that grilled food can look cooked on the outside but still be raw on the inside, or that grilling on a barbecue can lead to cross-contamination if raw and cooked meats aren't separated.

Page 39 (Exam Questions)

1 a) Conduction *[1 mark]*

   b) Minced beef has a high fat content *[1 mark]*. When heated, the fat melts into the pan and cooks the mince *[1 mark]*.
   You could also get two marks by saying that the fat from the minced beef melts into the pan and prevents the beef from sticking to the pan.

2 a) Any harmful bacteria in the chicken (e.g. salmonella) will have been destroyed by the high temperature used during cooking *[1 mark]*.

   b) Any **three** reasons from:
   - It will taste better / have more flavour *[1 mark]*.
   - It will look more appealing (e.g. golden brown) *[1 mark]*.
   - It will smell more pleasant *[1 mark]*.
   - It will have a better texture (e.g. crispy outside) *[1 mark]*.
   - It will be easier to eat / chew / swallow *[1 mark]*.
   [3 marks available in total]

3 Any **four** from:
   - Smaller amounts of fat / oil are used *[1 mark]*.
   - Food is cooked quickly, so there is less time for the food to absorb fat during cooking *[1 mark]*.
   - There's usually a higher ratio of vegetables to meat / smaller amounts of meat used *[1 mark]*.
   - Little to no meat means little to no extra solid fats melting into the pan *[1 mark]*.
   - Foods are cooked quickly and retain their nutrients *[1 mark]*.
   - Vegetable oils (e.g. peanut oil) tend to be used, which are healthier than most solid fats *[1 mark]*.
   [4 marks available in total]

Page 45 (Warm-Up Questions)

1 Protein denaturation and coagulation.

2 E.g. When liquids containing proteins are agitated, the proteins denature, causing them to stretch, and incorporate air into the liquid. When the proteins coagulate, this air becomes trapped, creating a foam (e.g. chocolate mousse / cappuccino foam).

3 Sugars inside the onion are broken down by the heat and caramelise. This turns the sugars into a brown, sweet-tasting liquid, giving the onions a sweeter taste.

4 Shortening gives baked goods a firm and crumbly texture.

5 Hydrophilic means attracted to water, and hydrophobic means repulsed by water.

6 Bicarbonate of soda has an unpleasant alkaline taste that wouldn't be masked by the relatively plain taste of a sponge cake.

Page 46-47 (Exam Questions)

1 To aerate (trap air in) the mixture *[1 mark]*

2 a) E.g. Gluten allows bread to rise during baking *[1 mark]* because the coiled molecules of gluten give the bread dough elasticity (it is able to stretch and rise) *[1 mark]*.
   You could have also said that gluten holds the shape of the bread after baking (due to protein coagulation) or that gluten helps give bread a light, airy texture (due to the stretchiness of the dough).

   b) Shortening *[1 mark]*

   c) Rubbing fat into flour creates a waterproof covering over the flour particles *[1 mark]* which stops long strands of gluten forming when water is added to the mixture *[1 mark]*.

3 a) Any **two** from:
   - Warmth *[1 mark]*
   - Moisture / liquid *[1 mark]*
   - Food *[1 mark]*
   - Time *[1 mark]*
   - Neutral pH *[1 mark]*
   [2 marks available in total]

   b) i) Choux pastry dough contains a lot of liquid *[1 mark]*.
      ii) The high liquid content is needed to produce enough steam during baking to make the pastry rise properly *[1 mark]*.

   c) Bicarbonate of soda is suitable because gingerbread has a strong flavour *[1 mark]* that masks the unpleasant flavour that bicarbonate of soda leaves in food *[1 mark]*.

4 a) The plasticity of fats refers to the ability of fats to be spread and manipulated *[1 mark]*.

   b) Margarine has more plasticity than lard because margarine is made up of triglycerides *[1 mark]* that melt at lower temperatures than the triglycerides found in lard *[1 mark]*.
   This is why margarine is softer than lard at room temperature.

5 The egg yolks contain a natural emulsifier (lecithin) *[1 mark]* which holds the oily and watery parts of the hollandaise sauce together *[1 mark]* and prevents them from separating (so the emulsion sauce stays stable) *[1 mark]*.

6 When the mixture is heated, the bonds between the starch molecules start to break *[1 mark]* (the starch comes from the flour). This causes liquid to enter the starch granules, causing them to swell *[1 mark]*. Between 62 °C and 80 °C, the starch granules burst, releasing their starch into the liquid *[1 mark]* and causing the sauce to thicken *[1 mark]*.

7   Points you might include:

Creaming
- George could cream the butter and sugar together until the mixture is light and fluffy.
- Creaming traps air to form a foam and would help give the cake a spongy texture once cooked.

Beating
- Beating is a vigorous method of driving air into mixtures using a spoon / fork.
- George could beat the mixture when adding the eggs into the mixing bowl. Beating the eggs denatures the proteins, allowing additional air to be trapped in the mixture.

Whisking
- Whisking adds air in the same way as beating, but George would use a whisk instead.
- George could whisk while adding the eggs / sugar into the mixing bowl or while getting rid of any lumps.
- Whisking the eggs denatures the proteins, allowing additional air to be trapped in the mixture.

Sieving
- George could sieve the flour into the mixing bowl.
- When flour is sieved, air becomes trapped between the individual flour particles. This aerated flour is then normally combined with the rest of the mixture using another technique, e.g. folding.

Folding
- George could fold the cake mixture by pouring the cake mixture back over itself using a spoon or spatula.
- Each time the cake mixture is folded (poured) over itself, air becomes trapped in the mixture. This method would be most useful when incorporating the flour into the mixture.

How to mark your answer:
- One method George could use discussed with little to no explanation of how it aerates the mixture *[1-2 marks]*.
- Two or three methods George could use discussed, with some explanation of how they aerate the mixture *[3-6 marks]*.
- Four or more methods George could use discussed with detailed explanation of how they aerate the mixture *[7-8 marks]*.

Section Three — Food Safety

Page 56 (Warm-Up Questions)

1   A high risk food is moist and high in protein, which are ideal conditions for microorganisms to grow quickly in, e.g. cooked chicken.

2   E.g. There is mould growing on the tomato. *You can mention that the tomato smells off, that it looks different (cracked or wrinkly) or it tastes different / fermented.*

3   Refrigerating the beef will slow the growth of bacteria and extend the shelf life of the beef.

4   Modified atmospheric packaging is where packaging contains a specific proportion of gases to extend the food's shelf life.

5   a) Bacteria from raw meat or other high risk foods can contaminate other foods if they are prepared on the same chopping board that is not thoroughly washed.

    b) Pets can carry bacteria in their fur / bodies and can contaminate food by eating it, walking over it or laying droppings on work surfaces.

6   E.g. Yeasts are used to produce alcoholic drinks because they convert sugars in fruit into alcohol.

7   Probiotics: live bacteria which are said to give health benefits.
    Prebiotics: non-digestible fibres which help the growth of probiotics.

Page 57-58 (Exam Questions)

1   All **five** conditions:
- A warm temperature
- Plenty of moisture or water
- Plenty of food
- The right pH / not too acidic or alkaline
- Enough time
[2 marks for all 5 correct, otherwise 1 mark for at least 2 correct]

2   a) D — Enzymes are affected by high temperatures *[1 mark]*.

    b) i) Enzymic browning is where enzymes speed up the reaction with oxygen in the air and turn fruit and vegetables brown *[1 mark]*.

       ii) Any **one** method, e.g.
       - Adding an acid, e.g. lemon juice *[1 mark]*
       - Blanching vegetables *[1 mark]*
       - Cutting / peeling fruit and vegetables only when required *[1 mark]*
       [1 mark available in total]

3   a) The 'best before' date on the hazelnut chocolates is a measure of quality *[1 mark]* — the chocolates may not taste as good but should still be safe to eat after this date *[1 mark]*.

    b) The 'use by' date on the cream-filled doughnuts is a safety warning *[1 mark]* — the doughnuts may not be safe to eat after this date because the cream is a high risk food / could contain dangerous levels of pathogenic bacteria *[1 mark]*.

4

Type of bacteria	Onset time	**Two** food sources it might be found in
Campylobacter	2 to 5 days *[1 mark]*	Raw poultry Untreated milk
E.coli	1 to 3 days	Any **two** examples, e.g. Raw beef *[1 mark]* Unwashed salad leaves *[1 mark]* *[2 marks available in total]*
Staphylococcus aureus *[1 mark]*	1 to 6 hours	(High risk foods handled by a person carrying this type of bacteria)
Salmonella	6 to 72 hours	Any **two** examples, e.g. Raw poultry *[1 mark]* Eggs *[1 mark]* *[2 marks available in total]*

[6 marks available in total — as above]

5 a) They have been processed to create conditions that make it hard for microorganisms to grow (e.g. little moisture / too acidic) *[1 mark]*.

b) Jam is made by boiling fruit with sugar (and pectin) and sealing it in a glass jar *[1 mark]*. This preserves the food as the sugar prevents microorganism growth *[1 mark]*.
You could have said that the high temperatures would destroy microorganisms or that sealing it would stop oxygen getting in.

6 Non-pathogenic bacteria are used to thicken the milk / give the yoghurt a sour or tangy taste *[1 mark]*. They do this by fermenting the lactose in the milk *[1 mark]* and producing lactic acid (which acts on the proteins in the milk) *[1 mark]*.

7 Points you might include:
Preparing food
Staff should...
• wear a clean uniform, e.g. overalls, apron, hat or hairnet.
• be hygienic at all times — washing hands and equipment thoroughly with hot, soapy water and using sanitising sprays to keep work surfaces clean.
• use separate chopping boards for different food groups — e.g. red boards for raw meat, blue for fish, yellow for cooked meats, brown for vegetables, green for fruit and white for dairy.
• keep raw and cooked foods separate.

Cooking food
Staff should...
• cook foods to above 75 °C.
• avoid cross-contamination.
• use a temperature probe to check food has been cooked all the way through and to the correct temperature.

Serving food
Staff should...
• keep hot buffet food above 63 °C and for no longer than 2 hours.
• keep chilled buffet food below 5 °C.
• keep buffet food covered to avoid contamination from pests.
• make sure waste bins are not overfilled.

How to mark your answer:
• One or two procedures mentioned *[1-2 marks]*.
• Three or four procedures mentioned *[3-4 marks]*.
• Five or six procedures mentioned, with procedures covering preparing, cooking and serving food *[5-6 marks]*.
• Seven or more procedures mentioned, with procedures covering preparing, cooking and serving food *[7-8 marks]*.

Section Four — Food Choice

Page 67 (Warm-Up Questions)

1 E.g. People with low incomes will only be able to afford cheaper food options. This may lead to a poorer diet, as cheaper foods are often less healthy, e.g. highly processed, high in fat and sugar.

2 E.g. A person working long shifts may have less free time to exercise. Sedentary lifestyles burn far less calories than active lifestyles.

3 Any **five** factors, e.g.
• Physical activity level (PAL)
• Culinary skills
• Cost of food
• Seasonality
• Special occasions
• Availability

4 E.g. Muslims only eat meat that is halal (slaughtered in a specific way according to Islamic law) and do not eat any pork / pork products.
You could have mentioned Ramadan, where Muslims fast between sunrise and sunset, or that alcohol is forbidden.

5 E.g. Glamorgan sausage from Wales (Cheese and leeks coated with breadcrumbs). Cornish pasty from England (Pastry containing beef, potato, swede and onions). Haggis from Scotland (Lamb, suet, onion, oatmeal, spices and seasoning, traditionally encased in an animal's stomach).

6 a) E.g. Japanese:
Noodles, seafood (salmon, mackerel, squid), pickled vegetables, Wasabi paste.

b) E.g. Japanese:
Sushi — Sticky rice, often topped or rolled with raw fish and seaweed. Tempura — Seafoods, vegetables or meat coated with batter and deep-fried. Ramen — Noodles in a soup, topped with vegetables, meat, eggs etc.

Page 68 (Exam Questions)

1 Any **two** food choices, e.g.
Dana may choose...
• to eat a vegetarian or vegan diet / avoid meat products *[1 mark]*.
• to buy free-range products *[1 mark]*.
• to buy products which are part of food assurance schemes, e.g. RSPCA Assured *[1 mark]*.
[2 marks available in total]

2 a) Jhatka meat has been slaughtered in a quick and painless way / is allowed to be eaten by Hindus (and often eaten by Sikhs too) *[1 mark]*.

b) i) E.g. Jews eat food that is kosher (animals that have split hooves and chew cud / fish with fins and scales) *[1 mark]*. Jews do not eat dairy and meats that have been cooked together *[1 mark]*.
You could also get a mark for mentioning that kosher animals must be slaughtered painlessly / blood is drained away.

ii) E.g. Many Buddhists choose to be a vegetarian / vegan *[1 mark]* and do not drink alcohol because they believe it wrongly alters your view of the world *[1 mark]*.
You could also get a mark for mentioning that some Buddhists choose to fast from noon until sunrise the next day.

3   Points you might include:

Harriet's food choices
- Harriet is a professional cyclist so she has a high physical activity level (PAL) and will require a large amount of calories per day.
- Harriet may choose to base meals around protein for muscle repair and starchy carbohydrates for energy.
- Harriet lives on a farm, so may grow her own produce.
- Harriet lives in a remote area / may not have any supermarkets nearby, so the variety of foods available might be limited.
- Harriet enjoys cooking, so she may be willing to try new foods / ingredients / recipes.

John's food choices
- John is an office worker, so he likely has a low physical activity level (PAL) and will need fewer calories per day.
- John might buy 'low-fat' foods to help reduce his weight.
- John might replace sweet snacks with more fruit and vegetables / choose low GI foods that release energy more slowly to help reduce his weight.
- John dislikes cooking, so he might buy more ready-meals than individual ingredients.

How to mark your answer:
- One factor that affects either Harriet or John with little to no explanation as to how it affects their food choice *[1-2 marks]*.
- Two factors that affect Harriet and John with some explanation as to how they affect their food choices *[3-5 marks]*.
- Three or more factors that affect Harriet and John with detailed explanation of how they affect their food choices *[6-8 marks]*.

Page 74 (Warm-Up Questions)

1   E.g. All ingredients must be listed to comply with EU law and so people with certain dietary requirements can safely pick what to eat.

2   Any **two** examples, e.g.
- Traffic-light labelling to give guidance on the level of fat, salt and sugar
- Whether the product is suitable for a certain group (such as coeliacs).

3   E.g. The product could use certain words on its packaging such as 'fresh' or 'natural', and use the logo of an ethical scheme it is involved in, such as the FAIRTRADE Mark.

4   Any **five** sensory descriptors, e.g.
- Crispy
- Sour
- Tender
- Sweet
- Chewy

5   In a rating test, tasters score characteristics of a food using a scale, e.g. rating sweetness on a scale of 1-5.

Page 75 (Exam Questions)

1   Any **three** problems, e.g.
- The carbohydrate content isn't listed *[1 mark]*.
- The energy values use different units (kJ and kcal) *[1 mark]*.
- The nutritional information is given per 125 g instead of per 100 g *[1 mark]*.

[3 marks available in total]

2   a) No *[1 mark]*

    b) Any **two** reasons explained, e.g.
    - Mei has only chosen three tasters for her panel *[1 mark]* — this small sample size won't give an accurate result *[1 mark]*.
    - Tasters can discuss their opinions *[1 mark]*, which means they can influence the other tasters' decisions *[1 mark]*.
    - The sample sizes (500 ml) are too large *[1 mark]*, which means the tasters may 'be full' before drinking the second lemonade *[1 mark]*.
    - Water is not given in between samples to cleanse the palate *[1 mark]*.

    [4 marks available in total]

3   Points you might include:

How the manufacturer should carry out the test
- The test should be fair and unbiased.
- The test should use a large number of tasters.
- Tasters should be given clear instructions what to do.
- Tasters should try both fish pies and rate them (e.g. from 1-5) on certain characteristics.
- Characteristics might include: texture, smell, flavour, appearance.

How the manufacturer could analyse the results
- The average score from each characteristic should be calculated to create a profile of each pie.
- The profiles could be displayed visually on a star diagram.
- The profiles can be used to identify areas that could be improved.
- The recipe for the fish pies can then be adapted to improve the characteristics that didn't score very highly.

How to mark your answer:
- One detail discussed with little to no reference of how the manufacturer can analyse the results *[1-2 marks]*.
- Two details discussed with some reference to how the manufacturer can analyse the results *[3-4 marks]*.
- Three or more details discussed with detailed reference to how the manufacturer can analyse the results *[5-6 marks]*.

Section Five — Food Provenance

Page 82 (Warm-Up Questions)

1 Any **one** benefit of intensive farming, e.g.
   - It is efficient / produces high yields.
   - Products are often cheaper in shops.

2 Any **one** benefit of organic farming, e.g.
   - No chemical fertilisers / pesticides are used, so some people think organic products are safer to eat.
   - It causes less damage to the environment.

3 A GM crop is a genetically modified crop that has had its genes altered to give it useful characteristics.

4 A sustainable method is a method where limited resources aren't used up / the environment isn't damaged.

5 a) E.g. Beetroot / carrot / parsnip
   b) E.g. Onion / shallot / leek
   c) E.g. Lemon / lime / orange / grapefruit
   d) E.g. Plaice / halibut / sole

Page 83 (Exam Questions)

1 E.g. Factory-farmed animals are given little room / put in a cage / reared together with lots of other animals *[1 mark]*. Free-range animals are given more room / are free to roam *[1 mark]*.

2 E.g. The rice could be genetically modified to contain the vitamin that the children are deficient in *[1 mark]*.

3 Any **three** methods with explanation, e.g.
   - Fishing quotas *[1 mark]* set by the government limit the amount and species of fish you can catch *[1 mark]*.
   - Using larger mesh nets *[1 mark]* can allow smaller fish that are accidentally caught to escape *[1 mark]*.
   - Longline fishing *[1 mark]* uses a fishing line with baited hooks — it catches fewer fish and has a smaller chance of catching unwanted fish *[1 mark]*.
   [6 marks available in total]

Page 89 (Warm-Up Questions)

1 E.g. Plastic is lightweight, so requires a small amount of energy to transport.

2 E.g. 'Pick your own' strawberries might be fresher / tastier / more nutritious and cheaper than those from a supermarket. Strawberries picked at a local farm will be better for the environment as they'll have fewer food miles.

3 E.g. banana milkshake — bananas have to be imported from tropical countries and lots of energy is used to pasteurise and refrigerate milk.
   Obviously, there are many possible answers here — make sure you explain why your product has a high carbon footprint.

4 The greenhouse effect is the process where heat becomes trapped by greenhouse gases in the atmosphere and redirected back to Earth.

5 E.g. Higher sea levels could flood low-lying farmland.

6 E.g. People in food poverty may rely on cheaper, ready-made foods that are often higher in fat / sugar than nutritious fruit and vegetables. An incorrect balance of fats and sugars can increase the risk of diet-related health problems such as obesity / diabetes.
   You may have discussed other health problems here, e.g. those caused by a vitamin or protein deficiency.

7 a) Availability is where countries are able to produce sufficient food to feed their populations, with excess food being exported to countries that need it.

   b) Access is where food is affordable to all, or that there is sufficient land and resources available for people to grow their own food.

   c) Utilisation is where people are educated on food and nutrition, so that a greater variety of foods are used, food waste is reduced, the nutritional value of foods is retained and illness from cross-contamination is prevented.

8 The FAIRTRADE Mark is for products where the farmers / producers have been guaranteed a fair wage for their produce.

Pages 90-91 (Exam Questions)

1 a) E.g. Packaging protects and preserves food and reduces food waste, which saves the manufacturer money *[1 mark]*.
      You could have said that manufacturers can include non-compulsory information on packaging to make their product more appealing.

   b) E.g. Manufacturing packaging uses lots of energy, which may require natural resources / fossil fuels *[1 mark]*. Litter can also hurt animals if they get trapped or entangled in it *[1 mark]*.
      There are other ways you could have mentioned — e.g. plastics take a long time to biodegrade in landfill sites and heavy packaging requires extra energy to transport.

2 Benefit: E.g. Producers are able to grow food in areas that were too cold before *[1 mark]*.

   Drawback: E.g. Pests and microorganisms can invade new regions that were too cold for them before *[1 mark]*.

3 a) Any two reasons, e.g.
      - Food is accidently overcooked or burnt *[1 mark]*.
      - Food is spoiled because it is not stored correctly, e.g. high risk foods in a domestic fridge *[1 mark]*.
      - Too much food is cooked and leftovers are not used or stored *[1 mark]*.
      - People don't use meal planning *[1 mark]*.
      - People use only part of a food, e.g. using lemon juice but not the peel *[1 mark]*.
      - People buy too much and don't use food before the use by date *[1 mark]*.
      - People don't understand best before dates and throw away food when it is perfectly safe to eat *[1 mark]*.
      [2 marks available in total]

   b) Any **two** ways, e.g.
      - Plan meals and only buy the ingredients that are needed *[1 mark]*.
      - Don't buy food just because it is on offer / a reduced price if it can't be used / stored *[1 mark]*.
      - Store food correctly — check labels to see whether it needs to be refrigerated, frozen or stored in a cool, dry place *[1 mark]*.
      - Freeze or refrigerate leftovers and use them in meals *[1 mark]*.
      - Use all parts of the food, e.g. bones for stocks *[1 mark]*.
      [2 marks available in total]

4 a) Any **one** reason, e.g.
- To give customers a greater variety of food products to choose from *[1 mark]*.
- To give customers food all year round and not just when it is in season in the UK *[1 mark]*.

[1 mark available in total]

You might have given a specific example here — e.g. we can't grow bananas in the UK, so they need to be imported.

b) Any **one** advantage with explanation, e.g.
- Transporting the food has less impact on the environment *[1 mark]* because local food has fewer food miles / less fossil fuel is needed to transport it than imported food *[1 mark]*.
- Local businesses are supported *[1 mark]*, meaning UK food producers earn more money and people's jobs are secured *[1 mark]*.

[2 marks available in total]

5 a) Food security is having access to enough nutritious food to stay healthy and active *[1 mark]*.

b) <u>Population growth</u>: There are more people to feed *[1 mark]*, so there will be less food available for each person *[1 mark]* (unless food production increases too).

<u>Wealth</u>: People on a low income may not be able to afford to buy nutritious food *[1 mark]*. Poor countries can't import food they need *[1 mark]*.

<u>Biofuels</u>: Land that could be used for food crops is being used for biofuels *[1 mark]*. If more biofuels are produced it reduces the amount of food crops that can be grown *[1 mark]*.

Page 97 (Warm-Up Questions)

1 E.g. Sorting into different sizes, crushing / pressing to make oil.

2 a) Cream is the milk fat that is 'skimmed' off the top of milk. (milk fat naturally rises to the top of milk).

You could have mentioned centrifugation which speeds up how quickly the milk fat rises (in the industrial production of cream).

b) Butter is made by churning cream. The cream is agitated and becomes thicker until it forms a solid mass of butter. Any excess liquid (buttermilk) is drained away.

3 Soya milk doesn't contain as much of some of the useful nutrients that are found in cow's milk. Soya milk is fortified (e.g. calcium is added) so the nutritional content is similar to cow's milk.

4 Colourings make the sweets more attractive and appealing for the consumer to eat.

Pages 98-99 (Exam Questions)

1 a) i) Any **two** from:
- Iron
- Calcium
- Vitamin B1 (thiamin)
- Vitamin B3 (niacin)

[1 mark available in total]

ii) Vitamin A and Vitamin D *[1 mark]*

b) Any **one** from:
- To improve the nutritional value / health benefits of the food *[1 mark]*.
- To replace nutrients lost during the processing of the food *[1 mark]*.
- To make the food more appealing to consumers *[1 mark]*.

[1 mark available in total]

c) Plant sterols can help reduce cholesterol for people with high cholesterol *[1 mark]*.

2

	Primary process	Why is this process carried out?
Vegetables	Any **one** process, e.g. • Washing *[1 mark]* • Sorting into sizes *[1 mark]* • Peeling *[1 mark]* *[1 mark available in total]*	Any **one** reason, e.g. • To remove dirt / insects / sprays *[1 mark]* • To ensure the consumer gets even-sized products *[1 mark]* • To save the consumer time *[1 mark]* *[1 mark available in total]*
Poultry	Any **one** process, e.g. • Removing feathers / organs *[1 mark]* • Tying legs / wings *[1 mark]* *[1 mark available in total]*	Any **one** reason, e.g. • To make the product more appealing to consumers *[1 mark]*. • To ensure that it cooks evenly in the oven *[1 mark]*. *[1 mark available in total]*
Fruit	Any **one** process, e.g. • Squeezing *[1 mark]* • Crushing *[1 mark]* *[1 mark available in total]*	Any **one** reason, e.g. • To make juices *[1 mark]*. • To extract oils *[1 mark]*. *[1 mark available in total]*

Or any other appropriate process, e.g. transporting.
[6 marks available in total — as above]

3 a) Any **one** heat treatment, e.g.
- Pasteurisation *[1 mark]* is where milk is heated to 72 °C for 15 seconds and then quickly cooled *[1 mark]*.
- UHT *[1 mark]* is where milk is heated quickly to 135 °C for 1-4 seconds and packed into a sterile container *[1 mark]*.

[2 marks available in total]

b) Any **one** correct product, e.g.
- Butter *[1 mark]*
- Cream *[1 mark]*
- Cheese *[1 mark]*
- Yoghurt *[1 mark]*

[1 mark available in total]

4 a) Any **two** suitable examples, e.g.
- Heating destroys B vitamins / vitamin C *[1 mark]*.
- Peeling the skin off a potato removes a source of fibre *[1 mark]*.
- Sieving crushed wheat grains removes fibre and vitamins *[1 mark]*.

[2 marks available in total]

b) Any **two** suitable examples, e.g.
- Salting / curing gives food a salty taste *[1 mark]*.
- Drying meat affects its flavour / how tender it is *[1 mark]*.

[2 marks available in total]

5 a) An E number is a code (e.g. E150a) that is given to an additive once it has passed a safety test and has been permitted to be used throughout the EU *[1 mark]*.
'E number' is often used to refer to the additives themselves too.

b) Points you might include:
Concerns over additives
- Some additives, e.g. sulphites, can cause allergy-like reactions or trigger intolerances.
- Some colourings, e.g. Sunset Yellow, have been linked to hyperactivity / poor behaviour in children.
- Flavourings and flavour enhancers can disguise poor quality ingredients, e.g. processed meat products, to make them taste better than they really are.
- Some additives may have long-term health effects we don't know yet as they build up in the body over a period of time.
- Colourings can trick consumers into thinking food contains certain ingredients — e.g. a pink colouring in yoghurts may make people think it contains strawberries.
- Salt and sugar are natural preservatives that are bad for our health (in large amounts) and increase the risk of diet-related health problems, e.g. diabetes or obesity.

How to mark your answer:
- One or two concerns of additives discussed with little to no explanation given *[1-3 marks]*.
- Two or three concerns of additives discussed with some explanation given *[4-6 marks]*.
- Four or more concerns of additives discussed with detailed explanation given *[7-8 marks]*.

Practice Paper

1 a) E.g. Because butter is high in saturated fat *[1 mark]*.

b) Conduction *[1 mark]*

c) Any **two** ways, e.g.
- Fry the eggs with an alternative to butter, e.g. vegetable oils (that contain more unsaturated fats) *[1 mark]*.
- Drain off as much of the butter as possible before serving the fried eggs *[1 mark]*.
- Use less butter to fry the eggs *[1 mark]*.
- Use an unsaturated fat cooking spray to fry the eggs *[1 mark]*.
[2 marks available in total]

d) Any **two** methods, e.g.
- Poaching *[1 mark]* — the eggs are broken and dropped into a pan of water just below boiling point *[1 mark]*.
- Boiling *[1 mark]* — the eggs (usually in their shell) are heated in a pan of boiling water until cooked *[1 mark]*.
- Scrambling eggs *[1 mark]* — the eggs are beaten together and moved around a pan until they are cooked *[1 mark]*.
[4 marks available in total]

e)

Food	Function of the egg	Description
Custard	Thickening	When the custard is heated slowly at a medium heat, the proteins in the egg yolk start to coagulate, causing the mixture to thicken.
Burgers	Binding	The proteins in the eggs (that have been mixed with the seasoned minced meat) coagulate when the burgers are cooked *[1 mark]*. This causes all the ingredients to bind and hold together *[1 mark]*.
Mayonnaise	Emulsification	Egg yolks contain an emulsifier (called lecithin) *[1 mark]* which keeps emulsions (e.g. mayonnaise) stable / stops the oil and water from separating *[1 mark]*.
Sponge cake	Aeration	When the egg is beaten, the proteins denature and stretch *[1 mark]*, allowing air to become trapped in the cake mixture *[1 mark]*.

2 a) i) B — The wholemeal bread *[1 mark]*

ii) A — The wholemeal pasta *[1 mark]*

iii) The complex carbohydrates we consume are mostly starch *[1 mark]*. During digestion, this starch is broken down into glucose *[1 mark]* (which is absorbed by the blood). Complex carbohydrates are broken down into glucose slowly *[1 mark]*, meaning they provide a slow, steady release of energy *[1 mark]*.

b) i) Fibre helps the digestive system work properly *[1 mark]*. A lack of fibre in the diet can lead to health problems such as constipation / bowel cancer / colon cancer / heart disease / high blood pressure *[1 mark]*.

ii) Water is needed for all the chemical reactions and processes that take place in our body (e.g. to control body temperature / to sweat / to keep our skin in good condition) *[1 mark]*. A lack of water (dehydration) can cause slower reaction times / poor decision-making / the blood to thicken (making it harder to pump blood around the body) / increases in body temperature / ineffective sweating *[1 mark]*.

c) C — It helps with growth and the production of red blood cells *[1 mark]*.

d) i) E.g. The tuna in the sandwich (meal A) is high in vitamin A *[1 mark]*, which is needed for good eyesight (especially seeing in the dark) *[1 mark]*.

ii) E.g. The red peppers / peas / sweetcorn / basil leaves in the pasta dish (meal B) are high in vitamin C *[1 mark]*, which is needed to help protect our body from infection / allergies *[1 mark]*.

3

Condition	Description	Dietary advice
Rickets	Rickets causes the bones of young people to become soft and weak *[1 mark]*, which can cause pain in the bones / deformities such as bowed legs / increase the chance of fracturing bones *[1 mark]*.	E.g. Eat more foods that are high in vitamin D *[1 mark]* such as oily fish / eggs / dairy products *[1 mark]*. *You could have also talked about increasing calcium intake / taking vitamin D supplements (especially in the autumn and winter).*
Iron deficiency anaemia	Iron deficiency anaemia is where you have a reduced amount of red blood cells *[1 mark]*, which can cause tiredness / a pale complexion / heart palpitations / headaches / abnormal fingernails *[1 mark]*.	E.g. Eat more foods that are high in iron *[1 mark]* such as dark green vegetables / red meat / eggs *[1 mark]*. *You could have also talked about increasing vitamin C intake (as this helps the body absorb iron) / taking multivitamin supplements.*

4 a) Any **two** modifications for coeliac disease, e.g.
- Use a gluten-free flour, e.g. rice flour, when making the bread roll *[1 mark]*.
- Replace the salmon en croûte with salmon fillets *[1 mark]*.
- Use a gluten-free sauce, e.g. lemon dill sauce, to replace the béchamel sauce *[1 mark]*.
- Use a gluten-free flour, e.g. rice flour, when making the pastry for the salmon en croûte *[1 mark]*.
- Use gluten-free biscuits for the cheesecake base (e.g. biscuits made with a blend of gluten-free flours) *[1 mark]*.
- Serve a different dessert course that is gluten-free, e.g. meringues *[1 mark]*.
[2 marks available in total]

b) Any **two** modifications for lactose intolerance, e.g.
- Use a milk alternative, e.g. soya milk, when making the béchamel sauce *[1 mark]*.
- Replace the cheese course with a lactose-free option, e.g. black tea / coffee *[1 mark]*.
- Use dairy alternatives, e.g. soya products, when making the cheesecake *[1 mark]*.
- Serve a different dessert course that is lactose-free, e.g. meringues *[1 mark]*.
[2 marks available in total]

5 a) B — 5 °C to 63 °C *[1 mark]*

b) C — Raw poultry and untreated milk *[1 mark]*

c) i) E.g. Cooked chilli con carne is ready-to-eat / moist and high in protein (which are ideal conditions for the growth of microorganisms) *[1 mark]*.

ii) Jenna could pour the chilli con carne into small containers and cover them *[1 mark]*. She could then let the chilli con carne cool before storing it in the fridge (below 5 °C and away from low risk foods) *[1 mark]*. *You could have said that to cool the cooked chilli more quickly, Jenna could cool the covered pan in a sink containing cold water.*

d) Points you might include:
Sources of cross-contamination
- Contaminated food, e.g. cross-contamination from the raw chicken / bacon to the salad ingredients.
- Contaminated work surfaces.
- Contaminated utensils, e.g. if the same knives are used to chop the raw chicken / bacon and the salad ingredients, or if spoons / forks have been used to taste the food and then put back in.
- Contaminated equipment (e.g. chopping boards / salad spinners / dirty tea towels).
- People, e.g. from unclean hands, hair, and wounds / by sneezing and coughing.

Methods of control to prevent cross-contamination
- Separate the raw and cooked ingredients.
- Wash the salad ingredients thoroughly.
- Use an antibacterial spray to sanitise the work surfaces.
- Use different utensils, e.g. different knives for the preparation of each ingredient, and not 'double-dipping' when tasting food.
- Use different equipment, e.g. coloured chopping boards for the appropriate foods / clean tea towels to dry the equipment.
- Cover all food when it's not being used to prevent pests from contaminating the food.
- Wash hands frequently, e.g. before starting to prepare the food and after handling the raw chicken / bacon.
- Don't touch the face / hair etc. and wear a hair net (and a beard net, if necessary) and gloves when preparing the food.
- Cover any cuts / sores or wear sterile gloves to handle food.

How to mark your answer:
- One or two sources of cross-contamination discussed but with little to no reference to how it can be prevented *[1-2 marks]*.
- Two or three sources of cross-contamination discussed with some reference to how it can be prevented *[3-4 marks]*.
- Three or more sources of cross-contamination discussed with detailed reference to how it can be prevented *[5-6 marks]*.

e) Any **two** examples, e.g.
- Moulds are used in the production of blue cheese *[1 mark]* to give the cheese a creamy texture, tangy taste *[1 mark]*.
- Non-pathogenic bacteria are used in the production of yoghurt *[1 mark]* to ferment lactose / produce lactic acid and thicken the milk / give the yoghurt a tangy taste *[1 mark]*.
- Probiotics (live bacteria) are supplements in some yoghurts *[1 mark]* which are said to give health benefits *[1 mark]*.
- Lactic-acid-producing bacteria are added to raw meats (e.g. pork / beef) *[1 mark]* to ferment sugar and create conditions that make it hard for pathogenic bacteria to grow (acidic and dry) *[1 mark]*.
- Yeast is used in the production of alcoholic drinks (e.g. wine) *[1 mark]* to ferment sugar / convert sugar into ethanol (alcohol) *[1 mark]*.
- Yeast is used in the production of bread *[1 mark]* as a raising agent to make bread dough rise *[1 mark]*.
[4 marks available in total]

6 a) Any **two** ways, e.g.
- The sugar makes the meringues taste sweeter *[1 mark]*.
- The sugar gives the meringues a brown colour when cooked (caused by the caramelisation of the sugar) *[1 mark]*.

[2 marks available in total]

b) If the egg whites are whisked too much, the set protein bonds can break *[1 mark]*, which allows all the trapped air to escape *[1 mark]*.

c)

		True	False
(i)	Meringue A is crunchier than meringue B.		✓
(ii)	The presentation of meringue B should be improved.	✓	
(iii)	The colours of both meringues were equally appealing.	✓	

[1 mark for each correct tick — 3 marks available in total]

7 a) C — Adding moulds to blue cheese *[1 mark]*

b) D — The 'use by' date is given as a safety warning *[1 mark]*.

c) Any **two** reasons, e.g.
- To preserve them (microorganisms and pests can't get into the food and spoil it) *[1 mark]*.
- To promote them (manufacturers can use marketing techniques to encourage customers to buy food products) *[1 mark]*.
- To protect them (stop the food from being damaged whilst being transported and displayed) *[1 mark]*.

[2 marks available in total]

d) Any **three** pieces of information, from:
- How to store the product *[1 mark]*
- What the product is (if it isn't obvious) *[1 mark]*
- The manufacturer's name and address *[1 mark]*
- A 'use by' date for high risk foods / 'best before' date for other food *[1 mark]*
- The country it comes from / origin (if it isn't obvious) *[1 mark]*
- The weight, volume or quantity *[1 mark]*
- The genetically modified ingredients used *[1 mark]*
- A list of ingredients *[1 mark]*
- The cooking instructions, if the product requires cooking *[1 mark]*

[3 marks available in total]

8 Points you might include:

Manufacturers
- Might put health claims (e.g. high in vitamin C) on packaging. This might influence the Bello family to buy their product as it suggests it has clear nutritional / health benefits.
- Might make healthier alternatives to existing products, e.g. with reduced sugar / salt. These may be more appealing to the Bello family as they suggest they are healthier options.
- Might promote moral values (e.g. Fairtrade / biodegradable) on their packaging. This makes the product look more ethical / environmentally friendly and so the Bello family might choose to buy it over a product that doesn't have these claims.
- Might include free extras with products, e.g. toys with children's cereal / vouchers for money off other products. The Bello family might choose these products because they appear to offer better value for money.
- Might use celebrities / characters / brands to endorse products. This might persuade the Bello family to choose one product over another, e.g. if a cereal has a favourite cartoon character on / a sauce is endorsed by a favourite chef.
- Might pay money to sponsor events / teams / people etc. E.g. Sponsoring a tennis tournament would allow the company to advertise their product across the event / put their logo on official merchandise. If the Bello family watch the event they might be more likely to buy the product because they will be more familiar with the logo.
- Might target adverts at certain customers, e.g. show a TV advert for a children's cereal during Saturday morning cartoons, or a new salad dressing during a cooking programme. The family might be more likely to buy a product they've seen advertised, especially if the adverts have been targeted to their interests.

The supermarket
- Might use special offers, e.g. buy one get one free / reduced prices this week only / buy three for the price of two / meal deals. The Bello family might buy these products if they feel they're getting better value for money.
- Might have a loyalty card scheme (where you get points for your shopping, which gives the Bello family offers based on their shopping preferences). This might persuade them to buy certain products if they have been specifically targeted towards them.
- Might use point of sale marketing (put products near the till). This might tempt the Bello family to buy them while they are queuing.
- Might place products targeted at children on lower shelves. This means they will be visible to the Bello children, who might ask their parents to buy it for them.
- Might have adverts (e.g. on TV, on billboards, in print media etc.) showing the products they have on offer. This might make the Bello family more likely to look for them in the shop.

How to mark your answer:
- One example of how manufacturers or the supermarket might influence the Bello family's choices with little to no explanation *[1-2 marks]*.
- Two or three examples of how manufacturers or the supermarket might influence the Bello family's choices with some explanation *[3-5 marks]*.
- Four or more examples of how manufacturers or the supermarket (at least one from each) might influence the Bello family's choices with detailed explanation *[6-8 marks]*.

9 Points you might include:

Energy content
- Adil's breakfast has fewer calories (516 kcal) than Barney's (817 kcal) — most of the energy in Barney's breakfast comes from the high carbohydrate and fat content.
- Teenage boys require around 2500 - 3000 calories a day.
- Barney has nearly a third of his recommended daily calorie intake in one meal. He could reduce the energy content in his breakfast by having either the cornflakes or the hot cross buns, or just one hot cross bun and / or less cornflakes.

Fat content
- Adil's breakfast has less fat (14 g) than Barney's (19 g) — most of the fat in Barney's breakfast comes from the butter, milk and hot cross buns, while Adil's comes from the eggs.
- Teenagers need fat in their diet as a source of fat-soluble vitamins, to make cholesterol and to provide a concentrated source of energy (especially useful if they are active).
- Neither breakfast has too much fat (85 g is the recommended daily intake), but Barney could reduce the amount of fat in his breakfast by using less butter / less milk or using semi-skimmed / skimmed / 1% fat milk instead.

Saturated fat content
- Adil's breakfast has less saturated fat (4 g) than Barney's (10 g) — most of Barney's saturated fat comes from the butter and whole milk, while Adil's comes from the eggs.
- It is recommended that teenage boys have a daily intake of no more than 30 g of saturated fat.
- Barney's breakfast contains a third of this daily amount. He could reduce the saturated fat in his breakfast by using less butter or a low-fat / vegetable fat spread.

Carbohydrate content
- Adil's breakfast has less carbohydrate (72 g) than Barney's (145 g) — most of Adil's carbohydrate comes from the wholemeal bread, which is a better source than Barney's hot cross bun and cornflakes because it's a complex carbohydrate with a low glycaemic index (GI).
- Teenage boys have a recommended daily intake of 300 g of carbohydrates each day.
- Barney's breakfast contains nearly half of this daily amount. He could improve this carbohydrate content by having a wholemeal hot cross bun (a source of complex carbohydrate). *Complex carbohydrates and low GI foods release their energy more slowly than simple ones and so would provide a steady release of energy throughout the morning.*

Sugar content
- Adil's breakfast has less sugar (35 g) than Barney's (76 g) — most of the sugar for both breakfasts comes from the juice.
- Guidelines recommended a daily intake of no more than 90 g of sugar and that no more than 5% of daily food energy comes from free sugars (orange juice contains a lot of these).
- Barney is already close to this daily limit, and could reduce his intake by drinking a smaller amount of juice or cutting down the amount of hot cross buns.

Protein content
- Adil's breakfast provides more protein (25.5 g) than Barney's (16.5 g) — most of the protein in Adil's breakfast comes from the poached eggs and wholemeal toast, while Barney's comes from the milk (all sources of HBV protein).
- Protein is particularly important for teenagers, who need it for the teenage growth spurt.
- Both breakfasts contain a good portion of the boys' recommended daily intake of 50 g. However, if Barney wanted to increase the protein content of his breakfast (if he won't take in enough protein later in the day) he could add some seeds to his cereal. If Adil wanted to reduce the protein content of his breakfast (if he takes in a lot of protein later in the day) he could have one egg on his toast rather than two.

How to mark your answer:
- One point about the suitability of the breakfasts but with little to no explanation or ways they could be modified *[1-3 marks]*.
- Two or three points about the suitability of the breakfasts with some explanation and ways they could be modified *[4-7 marks]*.
- Four or more points about the suitability of the breakfasts with detailed explanation and ways they could be modified *[8-10 marks]*.

10 Points you might include:

Factors that contribute to food insecurity
- Pests and microorganisms can damage crops / disease can infect reared animals, reducing the amount that's available / safe to eat.
- Countries may have climates unsuitable for farming, e.g. it's too hot / too cold / has too little rainfall, and so are unable to grow crops for themselves. This often means they have to import crops, which increases the cost of food for the consumer.
- Changes in climate affect the growth patterns of crops, which can result in reduced yields.
- Rising sea levels can cover low-lying areas of land, reducing the amount of land available for production.
- Floods can drown reared animals and damage / wash away crops and nutrients in the soil (making land less fertile for crop growth).
- Droughts can cause crops to fail and lakes / rivers to dry up, killing fish and other wildlife.
- Food production can be expensive, making it difficult for some people to start / maintain production. If fewer people are producing food, there is less food available.
- As biofuels (fuels from plant material) become more popular, more farmland is used to produce biofuels instead of food.
- The global population is increasing, but levels of food production struggle to increase at the same rate.
- Prices tend to increase when there is less food, making it harder for people on low incomes to afford a healthy, balanced diet.
- Wealthy people tend to have more disposable income and buy more food than they need, which results in more food waste.

How the global food insecurity problem can be improved
- Genetic modification can protect crops from disease / help them grow in harsh climates / increase their yields and nutritional value, e.g rice that has been modified to contain more beta-carotene (which provides vitamin A).
- Technology (e.g. the use of tractors and other mechanised equipment) can be used to make food production more efficient and increase the amount of food produced.
- The amount of food that's thrown away unnecessarily can be reduced. E.g. Supermarkets can sell misshapen fruit and vegetables at reduced prices, unwanted food can be donated to food banks and people can cook the right portion sizes.
- Less meat can be eaten, so more land can be used to grow crops instead of rearing animals. This would also make the crops used to feed the animals available for humans to eat.
- Sustainable farming techniques can be used, so limited resources aren't used up and food can be grown for future generations.
- Local food can be bought to reduce the carbon footprints of food and the effects of climate change (which would reduce the negative effects this has on food production).

How to mark your answer:
- One or two factors that contribute to fo‿ / ways the global food insecurity probl‿ with little to no explanation of any ‿
- Three or four factors that contrib‿ the global food insecurity probl‿ some explanation for most of ‿
- Five or more factors that c‿ ways the global food inse‿ with explanation for all‿

Glossary

Cuisine

Cross-contam‿

Glossary

5 a day	The Government recommends that everyone should eat at least five portions of different <u>fruits or vegetables</u> every day to promote good health.
additive	Something that's added to a food product to improve its properties.
aeration	When <u>air is added</u> to a mixture to help make it lighter, e.g. when making cakes.
allergy	An immune system response to a certain substance (an allergen), e.g. in fish, nuts and eggs.
alternative protein	A form of protein other than protein from meat which is suitable for vegetarians (e.g. tofu, TVP).
ambient food	A food that can be safely stored at room temperature.
amino acids	'Building blocks' of the body that make up <u>proteins</u>. Our bodies can make non-essential amino acids, but we have to get essential amino acids from foods.
anaemia	A condition where you have a reduced number of red blood cells, e.g. from <u>iron deficiency</u>.
antioxidant	A substance that protects our bodies from <u>free radicals</u> (chemicals that can cause cancer). Vitamins A, C and E are examples of antioxidants.
basal metabolic rate (BMR)	The <u>minimum</u> amount of <u>energy</u> needed to keep you alive each day.
basting	Putting the fat that has melted out of food back on top of the food while it's cooking.
'best before' date	A date mark on the packaging of lower-risk food (e.g. dried pasta) that tells you when the food is expected to deteriorate in quality.
biological value	A measure of the amount of <u>essential</u> amino acids a protein-based food contains.
blanching	A cooking process that involves plunging a food, e.g. fruit or vegetables, into boiling water before cooling them in cold / iced water (often used before freezing).
blended sauce	A sauce made from liquid and a paste of cornflour and water / milk.
braising	Slow-cooking food in a covered pot that also contains liquid, herbs and vegetables.
calorie	A measure of the amount of <u>energy</u> in food.
caramelisation	The browning of sugar and the change in its flavour when it's heated above a certain temperature.
carbon footprint	A measure of the impact something has on the environment, based on the harmful <u>greenhouse gases</u> produced.
cardiovascular disease	Any disease related to the <u>heart</u> or <u>blood vessels</u>, e.g. <u>coronary heart disease</u> (caused by a build-up of <u>fatty deposits</u> in arteries) and <u>strokes</u>.
cholesterol	A <u>fatty substance</u> that is essential for cell membranes. Too much cholesterol in the body can increase the risk of <u>cardiovascular disease</u>.
climate change	A gradual change in climate patterns, e.g. due to <u>global warming</u>.
coagulation	When denatured proteins join together, changing the appearance and texture of food, e.g. when egg white turns solid.
coeliac disease	Where the digestive system is sensitive to <u>gluten</u> and can't digest it.
conduction	The transfer of heat energy through <u>solids</u> by the vibration of particles.
convection	The transfer of heat energy through <u>gases</u> or <u>liquids</u> by circulating currents.
contamination	Transferring potentially harmful bacteria (or other microorganisms) from one thing to another, e.g. from raw food to ready-to-eat food via work surfaces, equipment or your hands.
	A style of cooking representative of a certain country or region.

Glossary

danger zone	The range of temperatures (5 °C to 63 °C) in which bacteria multiply very quickly.
denaturation	When the chemical bonds holding proteins together break down, causing the protein to unravel.
dextrinisation	When starch molecules break down into dextrins after being exposed to dry heat.
diabetes	A disorder where blood glucose levels stay too high because the pancreas either can't produce enough insulin or the body resists it.
dietary reference values	Estimates of the amounts of nutrients people need in their diet.
dry frying	Cooking food in a pan without added fat or oil, sometimes called dry roasting.
Eatwell Guide	Government healthy eating guidelines in the form of a pie chart that shows how much or how little of each food group your diet should contain.
emulsifier	Something that's added to food to hold together ingredients that don't usually stay mixed, e.g. oil and water.
emulsion	A mixture of oily and watery liquids, e.g. mayonnaise.
enzymes	Biological catalysts that speed up chemical reactions.
factory-farmed	Produced by an intensive farming technique where reared animals have little room to move.
Fairtrade Foundation	A charity that partners with food suppliers to try and improve their working conditions and income.
fat-soluble vitamins	Vitamins A, D, E and K found in fatty foods, that the body can store in fat tissue for future use.
fertiliser	Organic matter or chemicals that make soil fertile by supplying it with nutrients.
flavour enhancers	Additives, e.g. monosodium glutamate (MSG), that boost the existing flavour of a food.
food miles	The distance a food product travels from where it's produced or grown to where it's sold.
food poverty	Where a person is unable to afford or access sufficient nutritious food.
food security	Having access at all times to enough safe, nutritious food for an active and healthy life.
fortification	When extra nutrients are added to a food, e.g. in breakfast cereals.
free-range	Produced by a farming technique where reared animals have more space to move and live naturally.
garnish	A small addition to a dish that adds extra colour or flavour, e.g. a slice of lemon.
gelatinisation	When starch particles swell and burst, thickening a liquid.
gelation	The process where foods, e.g. custard, are set by chilling or freezing.
genetically modified (GM) food	Food that's had its genes altered to give it useful characteristics, e.g. GM tomatoes that have a longer shelf life than normal.
gluten	A protein found in wheat flours, that makes doughs elastic (stretchy).
glycaemic index	A number used to indicate the effect a food has on blood sugar levels.
halal	Slaughtered or prepared using a method that follows Islamic dietary laws.
heat transference	When heat energy moves from one place to another — by convection, conduction or radiation.
high risk food	A ready-to-eat food that, if not stored correctly, could grow harmful microorganisms.

Glossary

infused oil	An oil that has <u>absorbed</u> the <u>flavour</u> of herbs left to soak in it.
intensive farming	A farming method that produces <u>high yields</u> (production is often large-scale).
intolerance	An <u>inability</u> to eat a type of food without negative effects on the body.
julienne strips	Small, thin strips of vegetables.
jus	A thin sauce made from the juices from cooked meat.
kosher	Prepared food that follows the requirements of <u>Jewish dietary laws</u>.
lacto vegetarian	Someone who doesn't eat any meat, fish or eggs, but consumes milk and other dairy products.
lacto-ovo vegetarian	Someone who doesn't eat any meat or fish, but consumes milk, eggs and other animal products.
lactose intolerance	A digestive problem where the body <u>can't digest lactose</u> (milk sugars).
lecithin	A natural <u>emulsifier</u> found in egg yolks and soya beans.
macronutrient	A nutrient needed by our bodies in <u>large amounts</u>, e.g. fat, protein and carbohydrate.
marinate	To <u>soak</u> something in a mixture of things such as oil, wine, vinegar and herbs before cooking (to give it more flavour).
microfiltration	A process where milk passes through a fine membrane to separate the milk from souring bacteria.
micronutrient	A nutrient needed by our bodies in relatively <u>small amounts</u>, e.g. vitamins and minerals.
microorganism	A tiny living thing that includes <u>bacteria</u>, <u>moulds</u> and <u>yeasts</u>.
mineral	A <u>chemical element</u> that our bodies need in small amounts.
mould	A microorganism that can spoil food such as bread, cheese and fruit.
nutritional analysis	Working out the nutritional content of a food or recipe.
obesity	A condition where the body has accumulated <u>too much fat</u>.
omega-3 and omega-6	Groups of <u>essential fatty acids</u> that our bodies cannot make (they have to be eaten in our diet).
organic farming	A more natural method of farming, e.g. growing crops <u>without</u> artificial pesticides and fertilisers.
osteoporosis	A bone disease where bones weaken and become brittle.
pasteurisation	A process of heat treating food to destroy pathogenic bacteria. E.g. milk is pasteurised by heating it to around <u>72 °C for 15 seconds</u>.
pathogenic	Able to <u>produce disease</u>, e.g. some bacteria are pathogenic.
pesticide	A substance used to <u>kill pests</u> such as insects, weeds and fungi.
physical activity level (PAL)	A measure of how active you are / how much exercise you get.
plasticity	A property of fats that allows us to <u>spread</u> and manipulate them.
poaching	Cooking food in a pan of liquid below boiling point, e.g. poaching in a tasty sauce.
preservative	Something that's added to food to slow down the growth of bacteria and other microorganisms so that food lasts longer.
primary food processing	Changing <u>raw foods</u> to make them ready to eat or cook, or prepare them as ingredients for other food products.

Glossary

protein complementation	<u>Combining</u> low biological value proteins to give enough of all the <u>essential amino acids</u> we need.
radiation	The transfer of energy through waves of radiation (there's no direct contact).
raising agent	Something that releases bubbles of gas that expand when heated. Raising agents are used to make cake and dough mixtures <u>rise</u>.
Ramadan	A month in the Muslim year in which most Muslims are expected to <u>fast</u> from sunrise to sunset.
ready meal	A pre-cooked meal that's frozen or chilled — you just need to heat it up.
reduction	A process that <u>thickens</u> and makes <u>flavours</u> of liquids more intense by <u>evaporating</u> water.
Reference Intake	Guidelines for the amount of <u>energy</u> and <u>nutrients</u> an <u>average adult</u> requires per day. Often shown as a <u>percentage value</u> on food labels.
rickets	A condition in children where bones are soft and weak.
roux	A sauce base made from plain flour and melted butter.
saturated fats	A group of fats that come mainly from <u>animal</u> sources and are <u>solid</u> or <u>semi-solid</u> at room temperatures.
seasonal foods	Foods that are only available at <u>certain times</u> of the year, e.g. British-grown asparagus is only available in May and June.
secondary food processing	Changing <u>primary</u> processed foods into other food products, e.g. flour into bread.
shelf life	The length of time a food can last without <u>spoiling</u> or losing its <u>quality</u>.
shortening	The effect of adding fat to a floury mixture, giving it a crumbly texture. Also the name of a fat with 100% fat content.
stabiliser	Something that's added to food to stop mixed ingredients from <u>separating</u>.
sterilisation	A heat treatment where raw milk is passed through a steam chamber at <u>110 °C for 10-30 minutes</u>, killing all bacteria that are present.
sustainable	A sustainable process or material is one that can be used without causing permanent <u>damage</u> to the environment or using up <u>finite resources</u>.
temperature control	Controlling the temperature of food during preparation, cooking and storage, to <u>slow</u> the growth of microorganisms or <u>kill them off</u>.
temperature probe	A device used to measure the <u>internal temperature</u> of a food and check it is cooked all the way through.
trace element	A <u>mineral</u>, but one that is needed by the body in even smaller amounts.
ultra heat treatment (UHT)	A heat treatment where milk is heated to around <u>135 °C for 1-4 seconds</u> and packed into sterile containers. Also called ultra-high temperature processing.
unsaturated fats	A group of fats that come mainly from <u>vegetable</u> sources and are usually <u>liquid</u> at room temperature.
'use by' date	A date mark on the packaging of food that is a <u>safety warning</u> about when the food is likely to be unsafe to eat, e.g. high risk foods.
vegan	Someone who doesn't eat any products <u>derived</u> from <u>animals</u>, e.g. meat, eggs and cheese.
vegetarian	Someone who chooses to <u>not eat any meat</u>.
vitamins	<u>Organic compounds</u> that are needed by the body in small quantities to keep us alive and healthy.
water-soluble vitamins	Vitamins that <u>aren't stored</u> in the body and should be taken in <u>daily</u> (B vitamins and vitamin C).
yeast	A microorganism that can spoil food (e.g. berries). Also, used as a <u>raising agent</u> in bread making.

Index

Index

Index